WALL STREET WOMEN

WALL STREET WOMEN

Melissa S. Fisher

Duke University Press

Durham and London

2012

© 2012 Duke University Press
All rights reserved
Printed in the United States of America
on acid-free paper ∞
Designed by C. H. Westmoreland
Typeset in Arno Pro
by Keystone Typesetting, Inc.
Library of Congress Cataloging-in-
Publication Data appear on the
last printed page of this book.

For my Bubbe, Rebecca Saidikoff Oshiver, and

in the memory of my grandmother Esther Oshiver Fisher

and my grandfather Mitchell Salem Fisher

CONTENTS

ACKNOWLEDGMENTS

A commitment to gender equality first brought about this book's journey. My interest in understanding the transformations in women's experiences in male-dominated professions began when I was a child in the seventies, listening to my grandmother tell me stories about her own experiences as one of the only women at the University of Pennsylvania Law School in the twenties. I also remember hearing my mother, as I grew up, speaking about women's rights, as well as visiting my father and grandfather at their law office in midtown Manhattan: there, while still in elementary school, I spoke to the sole female lawyer in the firm about her career. My interests in women and gender studies only grew during my time as an undergraduate at Barnard College. Ultimately, when I entered graduate school, all of these experiences led me to decide to study the pioneering first generation of women on Wall Street for my dissertation research at Columbia University.

Powerful, elite women in finance during the nineties was not a conventional research topic to undertake within the discipline of anthropology. In graduate school I was fortunate to find the academic support of a number of pioneering female academics in their own right. The initial research for this book took shape under the guidance of Katherine Newman, who recognized an anthropological project in the study of women's professional mobility on Wall Street. Elaine Combs-Schilling, Jean Howard, Martha Howell, and Rosalind Morris guided me in thinking about gender and power; Saskia Sassen focused my attention on finance and global cities. In addition, Harrison White taught me a great deal about elite networks and the corporate arena. Their initial interest as well as enormous support from Wendy Mackenzie and Salvatore Pitruzzello provided the foundation of my research. I am also indebted to the Financial Women's Association of New York City (FWA), the Women's Campaign Fund (WCF), and the women and men on Wall Street and in politics who gave their time to this project, some of whom I have now known for over a decade and a half. I also want to thank my friends and colleagues from Columbia University who sustained me through graduate school: John Jackson, Greg Downey, and Paul Silverstein. The Alfred P. Sloan Foundation Research Program on the Workplace, Workforce, and Working Families; the Henry A. Murray Center at Radcliffe College Dissertation Award, the Department of Anthropology at Columbia University, and the (then-named) Center for Social Sciences at Columbia University provided the research funds that I needed to complete my initial fieldwork and archival research.

The writing of my dissertation took shape thanks to the intellectual guidance and inspiration of my advisor, Sherry Ortner, at Columbia University. She has always believed in me and my project. I am indebted to her sustained intellectual and professional support and owe her a special debt that cannot be repaid. Alice Kessler-Harris also provided invaluable scholarly inspiration and support during my time at Columbia. While I lived and taught in Washington, D.C., I transformed the dissertation into this book. I especially want to thank my developmental editor, Laura Helper-Ferris, for working with me and helping me find the joy in writing. Her wisdom and advice were invaluable. I also thank my uncle Franklin Fisher, Professor Emeritus in Economics at MIT, who provided intellectual, emotional, and financial support during the final write-up. In addition, I thank the faculty in and associated with the Department of Anthropology at Georgetown University for their interest in my work: Fida Adely, Denise Brennan, Rodney Collins, Rochelle Davis, Laurie King, Gwen Mikell, Joanne Rappaport, and Susan Terrio. I have been fortunate at Georgetown to have received a number of grants that allowed me to conduct follow-up research with the first generation of Wall Street women throughout the 2000s. My research assistant, Elizabeth Keenan, was invaluable in helping me prepare this book for publication. Notably, portions of my 2004 article "Wall Street Women's Herstories" informed parts of chapters 1 and 3 of this book.

I have also benefited from the generosity of Christina Garsten of the University of Stockholm, who has provided scholarly inspiration and warm collegial friendship. I especially want to thank Christina and the

Department of Anthropology and Centre for Organizational Research at Stockholm University, Sweden, for providing me a home to begin writing my book. I also benefited from my time spent as a Visiting Fellow at the Lancaster Institute for Advanced Studies Program on the Knowledge-Based Economy. I am grateful for feedback from and conversations with Angel Kwolek-Folland, Pamela Laird, Gregory Downey, Kenneth Lipartito, Mary Yeager, Adrienne Sörbom, Linda Basch, Brian Hoey, Joyce Goggin, Marieke de Goede, Caitlin Zaloom, Karen Ho, Bill Maurer, Hiro Miyazaki, Douglas Holmes, Tim Maletfyt, Eric Lassiter, Annette Nyqvist, Linda Smircich, Marta Calás, Daniel Walkowitz, Jocelyn Willis, Helena Wulff, Marietta Baba, Tracy Lovatt, John Tutino, and Beverly Sauer. I was also fortunate to develop and share my work most recently at the Isenberg School of Management at the University of Massachusetts, Amherst; the Center for the Education of Women at the University of Michigan, Ann Arbor; as well as the Conference on Critical Finance at the University of Amsterdam.

I owe my family an enormous debt of gratitude. My mother, Joanne Hamburger; my father, Robert Wang; my sisters Deborah and Tova Wang; my aunt and uncle Franklin Fisher and Ellen Fisher; and my aunt and uncle Wesley Fisher and Regine Fisher have provided strength, nurturing, and love. I would also like to acknowledge my family members Joe Oshiver, Michael Oshiver, Jackie Oshiver, Roberto Hamburger, Francine Shapiro, and all my cousins and their children. Important friends and colleagues have supported me throughout the research and writing process. I am especially grateful for the warmth, understanding, and encouragement of my very close friend and colleague Laurel George and a very special group of long-time and loyal friends: Rachel Esner, Lisa Hajjar, Tara Susman-Peña, Melissa Cefkin, Debby Everett-Lane, Anna Maslakovic, Ashwini Tambe, Elie Cossa, and Sarah Lawrie.

I am also deeply indebted to Courtney Berger, my editor at Duke University Press. Courtney has provided invaluable guidance and support. I am enormously grateful to her as well as to Ken Wissoker, Editorial Director at Duke University Press; to Courtney's assistant, Christine Choi; to the copyeditor Christine Dahlin; and to their colleagues at the press, for their confidence in my work. Courtney's enthusiasm and inspiration have helped make this book a reality.

Finally, I am fortunate to stand on the shoulders of many other female pioneers, including my own Bubbe, Rebecca Oshiver. Bubbe came to the United States at age fourteen to pursue a different kind of life for herself and for other women. She did not go to school herself, but she sent my grandmother Esther Oshiver to college and to law school at a time when few women attended such institutions. Every graduation for a woman in my family is a graduation for Bubbe. I dedicate this book to her.

WALL STREET WOMEN

Patricia Riley and I sat in her small office in one of the major Wall Street firms in midtown Manhattan. It was March 1994, the first day of my fieldwork on the pioneering generation of women on Wall Street.[1] Patricia was one of the most senior women in global finance, a veteran with more than twenty years in the area of research. When she first entered the world of finance in the seventies, researchers were considered to be support staff for investment bankers and traders, helping them make deals. But by the time of our conversation, which occurred within a bull market, research strategists such as Patricia were part of the "front office" and were among the most valued employees because they were understood to be generating revenue for the firm. Soon Patricia and I were deep into conversation about her life, career, and why she and other women had been so successful in finance. Her account drew on the differences between men and women and risk taking:

> I think that when women look at stocks, they have a lot more respect for the concept of risk. This serves them well. Men are classics. I constantly get this—they are at a cocktail party, and they get a hot tip. If you suggest electronics, they want to buy it. But women will sit there and say "like my family's IRA account" or whatever. The women want something conservative, something long term, something they can hold on to for a couple of years. Meanwhile the men always want something that is going to double the next week. I don't know whether it is good or bad. But, in terms of outcome, I think that women's attitudes are better for investing.

Patricia's version of gender difference was characteristic of the nineties, when Wall Street women invoked and reframed the figure of the "consumer" as feminine in order to highlight their own ability to forecast, sell, and buy stocks. They used gendered assumptions about their roles as mothers making family purchases in order to sell themselves as economic experts who were careful, risk aware, and, in the end, better investors than their male counterparts. Her narrative revealed a key dynamic in which women gained entrée to the male precincts of Wall Street by playing on (and not explicitly challenging) traditional connections between femininity, motherhood, and work. Wall Street women, like Patricia Riley, were not radical feminists. They tended to view the financial world as a site of meritocracy. Influenced by tenets of liberal feminism, they believed they would become equal with men by working from within rather than against the world of finance. Their beliefs in the gendering of risk allowed them to make it within the hegemonic gendered system of Wall Street.

And the gendered discourse of risk that Patricia offered also helped people make sense of the financial debacle of 2007–9, when a series of collapses in bank and insurance companies triggered the biggest financial crisis since the Great Depression. Shortly thereafter, which is to say fifteen years after my talk with Patricia about gender and risk, Debora Spar, the president of Barnard College, published an op-ed in the *Washington Post* entitled "One Gender's Crash":

> As the financial debacle unfolds, I can't help noticing that all the perpetrators of the greatest economic mess in eight decades, are, well men. Specifically they are rich, white middle-age guys. . . .
>
> Although the Y-chromosome is undeniably overrepresented along all tiers of finance, it is particularly overrepresented at the highest levels and in those sectors most deeply implicated in the current crisis. . . . Clearly, some greater force is at work here, something more than the traditional clubbiness of Wall Street or the obstacles that still confront women juggling work and family. It may be that women perceive and act on risk in subtly different ways: that they don't, as a general rule, embrace the kind of massively aggressive behavior that brought us a Dow of 14,000 and then, seemingly overnight, a crash of epic proportions. Whether it be from a protectiveness born of biology or a reticence imposed by social norms, women may be less inclined than men to place the kind of bets that can get them in real trouble.[2]

In the wake of the economic meltdown, academic, journalist, and Wall Street women's voices appeared to be in some agreement in identify-

ing women's feminine qualities as uniquely suited to lead—even re-
pair—the financial debacle. Far more than any of its predecessors,
including the Great Depression, the crisis of 2007–9 was being depicted in strikingly gendered terms. Nicholas Kristof echoed Spar in
his own op-ed piece, recounting a query overheard at the World Economic Forum in Davos, Switzerland, wondering if "we would be in the
same mess today if Lehman Brothers had been Lehman Sisters. The
consensus (and this is among the dead white men who parade annually at Davos) is that the optimal bank would have been Lehman
Brothers and Sisters." The story circulated through the media, the halls
of Wall Street, and within on- and offline communities of businesswomen.[3] Like the other accounts, it articulated a divide between
masculine, greedy, risk-taking actors and financial practices, leading to
the crisis, and a more feminine, conservative, long-term approach,
possibly helping the economy to avoid crisis or to fix it (de Goede
2009; Cameron et al. 2011; McDowell 2011).[4] For a moment, it appeared that women could and would be the saviors of the world's
global economy: this idea of women's place in finance stood in stark
relief to the gendered ideology that favored elite men's leadership
during the sixties and seventies, but it relied on some of the same
conservative definitions of femininity that had once prevented women
from being viewed as traditionally successful market leaders.

This ethnography follows the first generation of women as they
entered Wall Street in the sixties and made their way up the male-
dominated corporate structures within investment banks. I focus on a
small, very successful cohort within that generation, who initially met
one another while working full-time, often as each was the single
professional woman in one of the major investment banks or brokerage houses, and who developed lifelong relationships with one another through their involvement in the Financial Women's Association of New York City (FWA)—a network of women dedicated to
advancing women in finance—during the seventies. I begin with an
exploration of the women's relationships to feminism and finance as
young adults; I then track changes in those relationships as they built
careers and networked with other women on Wall Street during the
eighties and nineties. I move on to explore how the women incorporated tenets of feminism and the market into their political networks
as they became more successful professionally. I conclude by examining the women's contemporary political and philanthropic work,
which, in the wake of the crisis, increasingly supported the economic

and political advancement of women and a corresponding feminization of the market.

The Making of Market Feminism

The central discourses and practices of key members of the first generation of Wall Street women allow us to see precisely how they arranged the formerly opposed domains of feminism and the market into new constellations. In this book, I explore the shifting relationship between feminism and financial markets through an ethnographic exploration of the women's lives over time. And I map multiple ways to understand this relationship. Sometimes the women, as they moved up the career ladder in finance, had fully mainstreamed liberal feminist tenets into the marketplace, making feminism more market-friendly and thereby creating a form of market feminism (Eisenstein 2009; McRobbie 2009; Kantola and Squires forthcoming). On the other hand, one can also see these formations in struggle and negotiation, particularly as the women, through their contemporary, socially responsible investment projects, sought to make feminist interventions into the marketplace. Ethnographically exploring how the women themselves reflect on, critique, and sometimes re-work the changing relationship between markets and feminism, thus allows us to problematize the idea that market capitalism always and inevitably subsumes feminism (Gibson-Graham 1996, 2006; Rosenblum 2009).[5] This book will also provide insight into the engendering of finance from the sixties to the 2007–9 economic crisis.

Inspired by feminist practice theory, I start with the insight that various structures of power constrain but do not determine people's everyday practices, and that, in turn, people's everyday practices reproduce and sometimes change those very same structures (Ortner 1996: 1; Ortner 2006).[6] Thus, the culture and structure of finance, namely on Wall Street, shape and constrain the thoughts and practices of research analysts, brokers, investment bankers, and traders about the market, market making, and the production of market subjects (Miyazaki 2006; Maurer forthcoming: 10).[7] Wall Street, as such, is an ethos and set of practices embedded in an intricate network of institutions, investments, and people (Ho 2009); it is a kind of "social imaginary" of the relationships between institutions, structures of meaning and power, and practices in global finance (Cameron et al. 2010). This imaginary becomes embedded in financiers' habitus, a deeply buried structure that shapes Wall Street men's and women's dispositions to act in such a way that they end up accepting and most often reproducing the dominant gendered, classed, and raced system of the marketplace—ways of performing gender and whiteness, making deals, and pursuing profit—without being made to do so entirely explicitly (Bourdieu 1984; Ho 2009: 11).[8] The specific social construction of members of the first generation of Wall Street women is worked out in the give and take of everyday human interactions from the sixties to the present. Wall Street women's career experiences and discourses are local and historically specific instances of global capitalism (Sahlins 1988; Ho 2009).

The history of finance itself has been made possible through the contested historical articulations and political struggles among financial actors, including the first generation of financial women and others, about the gendered meanings of money, capital, and risk, and more recently of microfinance and corporate social responsibility (Kwolek-Folland 1994; de Goede 2005b; Griffin 2009; Maurer forthcoming).[9] The "organization of global finance has a gendered structure" (Assassi 2009: 2). Neoliberal discourses—which support the idea of the free market—are inherently gendered and are embedded in financial institutions, including financial-service firms and the World Bank (Griffin 2009). Neoliberalism is most often understood to be an economic doctrine, a "theory of political economic practices that proposes that human well being can best be advanced by liberating individual entrepreneurial freedoms and skills within an institutional framework characterized by strong private property rights, free markets, and free trade" (Harvey 2005: 3). Human beings are thus understood to be rational and gender-neutral subjects. But neoliberalism can also be conceptualized as the various means by which traditional governing activities, including the pursuit of gender equity, are recast as nonpolitical and nonideological problems that need technological solutions (Ong 2006: 3). There is thus nothing purely economic about neoliberalism. Neoliberalism is inherently a political, gendered project with a market agenda (Griffin 2009: xiv).[10]

Neoliberalism and other gendered discourses shape the cultures of global markets, Wall Street firms, and financiers. And financiers reproduce and sometimes change the gendered culture of finance through their everyday practices (McDowell 1997; Fisher 2004; de Goede 2005b, 2009; Ho 2009). Wall Street women and men are thus structurally embedded agents; their individual and collective agency is culturally shaped and organized (Ortner 1997: 10; Fisher 2004; Langley 2008). Finance is ultimately a performative practice (Callon 1998; Mackenzie 2006; Holmes 2009). Wall Street women's gendered performances in finance "do not exist in addition to, or are of secondary importance to real material finance structures, but are precisely the way in which finance," including crises, is materialized and gendered (de Goede 2005b: 7–8, 39–45; 2009).[11]

But another kind of historical and cultural process is essential to understanding the formation of Wall Street and financial actors and their agency, particularly the first generation of women and their success: the feminist movement that sought and continues to seek the advancement and equity of women.[12] The world of financial capital and markets helped shape Wall Street women's habitus and agency, but the liberal feminist movement of the late sixties and early seventies—including the idea of women's equality—created the very possibility for women to enter into finance in the first place (Ortner 2003: 206; Laird 2006). And feminism changed during the eighties and nineties as the women moved up the corporate ladder. Some academic and activist feminists continued to think of feminism as a singular movement expressing a coherent understanding of a shared, arguably "romantic sisterhood" (Ong 2006: 32). But African Americans and other actors marginalized by such a unified notion began to critique the movement's lack of attention to other structures of inequality including race, class, colonialism, and sexuality, thereby increasingly drawing attention to issues of diversity, difference, and power (Dirks et al. 1994; Ortner 1996). In this context, the women's movement appears to have been "eclipsed by an expansive, polycentric, heterogeneous discursive field of action" composed of sometimes aligned though often fragmented national and transnational feminist networks that drive forward gender equality demands (Kantola and Squires forthcoming: 8). At the same time, "gender and diversity management" has emerged as a key human resources strategy in the United States (Dobbin 2009; Squires n.d.: 3). Human resources personnel and executives, including some members of the first generation of Wall Street women, increasingly mainstreamed tenets of liberal feminism and the idea of diversity into global corporations and financial firms. The once clear disconnection between feminism and the corporate arena, in which feminism as a social movement was understood to be separate and opposed to the world of business, has become increasingly less clear and more complicated (Laird 2006; Dobbin 2009; Squires n.d.).[13]

It is difficult to completely remember the extent of sexual discrimination in the United States, as well as how thoroughly ideas of masculinity structured Wall Street in particular during the sixties and seventies. Wall Street changed in part because governmental agencies successfully broke down some of the discrimination through a variety of efforts. The Equal Employment Opportunity Commission (EEOC) and other entities had brought several major lawsuits against Wall Street firms on behalf of women beginning in the seventies (and in fact lawsuits are still being pursued today). Wall Street also changed because the first generation of women had changed it. They did not participate in the full-blown feminist movement of the day, but their mere presence on the Street began to change the rules of the gender game. The women helped incorporate aspects of liberal and other forms of feminism first into financial institutions and later in the American political system, bringing together market, feminist, and eventually political sensibilities (Eisenstein 2009; McRobbie 2009; Kantola and Squires forthcoming). Throughout the last three decades of the twentieth century and the beginning of the new millennium, the women created the grounds for bringing feminism into conversation with the market. And as the recent economic crisis exposed the need for new leadership on Wall Street and in the global economy, gendered understandings of women as being more conservative and risk aware resurfaced, clearing the ground for the possible feminizing of markets (Rosenblum 2009: 56).

The women's individual and collective biographies—before they came to Wall Street, in the world of finance, and in their professional networks—shaped their initial understandings of the relationships between the marketplace and feminism as well as those relationships with the workplace, gender, and class. And through their everyday practices, they worked on, debated, and attempted to figure out both their identity as professional women, and the extent to which, and even the ways in which, they could begin to change the gendered culture of finance and politics. They became market-feminist subjects as young adults participating in the bear market of the seventies while also being influenced by the women's movement. Through their college years and early education on Wall Street, they developed dispositions that helped them survive: they learned how to carry themselves and how to embody a professional-managerial classed feminine identity in the workplace and within their networks. When they felt out of place as women in the highly masculine environments of trading floors and boardrooms, they coached one another on the best ways to display professional, confident, female selves. And they honed these bodily techniques over time until they felt and appeared to be completely natural not only to themselves and each other but to everyone around them. Thus, the women's appearance and performances of caring and risk aversion were not simply attributes they were born with. They learned these ways of acting, and being thought of as successful in finance, through their experiences in the financial world. More largely, they initially embraced feminist ideologies covertly or quietly in the FWA of New York City. But, increasingly, they acknowledged and acted on their feminist disposition more publicly in the Women's Campaign Fund (WCF), which was a bipartisan group of women (and some men) founded in 1974 that was committed to electing pro-choice women into governmental office. This group developed a market-feminist habitus that allowed them to embrace some ideologies of the Wall Street workplace (such as meritocracy, the bottom line, and purported gender neutrality) while also advocating for specific tenets of liberal and cultural feminism, such as gender equality and the celebration of gender differences, including women's supposed innate risk-averse qualities. By the time of the 2007–9 financial crisis, some of these gendered performances of finance were so naturalized that the next generation of women could and did argue that women's unique caring, risk-wary abilities made them uniquely positioned to save the global economy from the verge of catastrophe. As a result, some members of the first generation have served as transitional figures between different constellations of gender, financial markets, and feminism. Their stories help to illuminate how the balance of power shifts back and forth between their making of market feminism and its opposite pole: the feminizing of markets. That is, feminist ideas and practices have never been completely co-opted by capitalism, nor has feminism entirely transformed financial firms, actors, and practices. Nor am I arguing that the women progressed from being dupes to being total feminist change agents. Rather at different moments, women deployed varying notions of meritocracy, equality, and gender difference in relation to the corporation and marketplace to try to advance themselves and other women on Wall Street.[14]

The playing field was not an even one. Financial networks and organizations are key sites that produce and constrain financial agents;

financial actors' subjectivities arise from particular workplace and economic models, corporate culture, and organizational values and practices of Wall Street financial institutions (Riles 2006; Zaloom 2006;
Ho 2009: 11, 214). The institutions and buildings of finance—Wall
Street investment firms, the Chicago Board of Trade, and merchant
banks in the City of London—were and continue to be gendered
spaces in which (mainly) men perform hypercompetitive masculine
performances, part of the male drama of capital that constructed
women as inferior, "other," or "invisible" (McDowell 1997: 28; de
Goede 2005b, Zaloom 2006: 113; Ho 2009). Women's entry onto Wall
Street as professionals has made that gendering much more visible.

Moreover, we can see that finance capital was (and is) not only
performed within the "strict" world of finance. It is also situated and
performed in a range of everyday spaces and organizations, including,
for example, state agencies (Martin 2002; Langley 2008: 11). Gendered performances of finance take place within a variety of urban
spaces and networks beyond the traditional boundaries of Wall Street,
including financial women's organizations and their political networks. Wall Street women's networks, like other female work-related
networks, play an important role in constructing women's identities
and politics in and out of the workplace (Brodkin-Sacks 1988; Lamphere et al. 1997). So the subjectivity of financiers does not entirely
arise from their experiences directly within the confines of the workplace; the culture of Wall Street firms itself is less bounded, more
porous, contextual, and continually shifting (Ho 2009: 214). Financiers—both men and women—and their professional networks inhabit and use the urban landscape more broadly, in places beyond the
workplace, in places that increasingly blur domains long understood
to be separate: work and leisure, work and community service, politics and the market, and feminism and the market. Wall Street wom-
en's networks used actual material spaces—part of but separate from
daily work life on the Street—in which they produced new discourses
and images of gender relations, finance, feminism, the working self,
and subjectivity. Moreover, women's networking practices show us
how to read New York City as a global financial city built out of
heterogeneous networks, spaces, and practices (Farías and Bender
2009).

My ethnographic approach to the women within this first generation thus adds texture, nuance, and specificity to work in the social
sciences on finance (specifically the gendering of finance); anthropo-

logical and historical studies of elites, gender, and social movements (Ortner 2003; Laird 2006); and critical feminist studies of recent shifts on feminism in the context of neoliberalism.[15] Notably, much of the small but growing scholarship on market feminism is theorized by feminist political theorists and socialist feminist sociologists (Eisenstein 2009; Kantola and Squires forthcoming). These works provide powerful overarching narratives on shifts in feminism and neoliberalism in a single society or range of societies across a variety of cultural contexts and times. I bring this narrative into conversation with ethnographic theorizing, effectively substituting the in-depth study of a single cohort of social actors (the first generation) and their networks over the past five decades for the broadly comparative approach often used by feminist theorists. My work brings together domains—the worlds of elite finance and elite feminism—that have, up until now, remained undertheorized and underexplored ethnographically. Moreover, rather than agreeing with market-feminist scholars that market ideologies always absorb and co-op feminism, my work also ethnographically explores how Wall Street women increasingly engage the other or opposite pole: they also feminize markets, especially in their postretirement projects. We can see glimmers of change among some firms—some populated by members of the first generation—that are beginning to feminize markets by developing alternative, socially responsible investing approaches that focus, for example, on advocating gender equality on corporate boards.

The first generation of women to successfully advance on Wall Street, their making of market feminism, and their feminizing of markets have thus been overlooked by anthropologists, sociologists, and historians. Moreover, much of the scholarship on women in male-dominated industries in finance and business in the United States has tended to refrain from addressing the phenomenon of powerful women (Brondo and Baba 2006).[16] This book seeks to illuminate these women's history, to chart their careers up the corporate ladder, and to capture the cultural and political dimensions of their experiences. In doing so, I challenge four widespread myths about pioneering female executives and finance: the nonfeminist female financier; the lone female pioneer; the upper-class female financier; and the separation of the financial market and neoliberalism from gender and feminism.

The Myth of the Nonfeminist Female Financier

The traditional perception of women on Wall Street, particularly of members of the pioneering generation, holds that the women accepted and wholly adopted the masculine culture of finance in order to succeed professionally, and that they did not identify as feminists or with the feminist movement that in part was responsible for opening the doors for them into the business world. But some of the women had attended all-women's colleges where they read Betty Friedan's *The Feminine Mystique* (1963) and *Ms.* magazine, and they were aware of female consciousness-raising groups. By the time they entered Wall Street they began to question and even push against the gendered rules of their firms. Some of the women used the FWA to meditate on the meaning of being a successful female on Wall Street and on their own relationships to finance, femininity, masculinity, and the feminist movement.

Most of the women did not speak out against the male establishment in general, or of Wall Street in particular. Nor did the FWA as an organization publicly take a stance. Instead the FWA presented its group as a business organization focused on advancing women in finance. They left "politics" outside. But to accept this as evidence that the women and their networks had internalized and thus merely reproduced the male-dominated culture of finance and America in general is to ignore the strength of the feminist movement of the sixties and seventies. It is also to misinterpret women's silence as acquiescence, and to construe feminism and the acting out of feminism in relatively narrow terms as the organization of formal feminist activist groups, radical feminist theorizing, and direct action. Indeed, the history of the first generation of women's resistance to the male-dominated world of Wall Street actually began before the women were even hired into their first jobs. Even in their early twenties, fresh out of college, some of the women came to New York with their own ongoing sense of feminism and feminist politics. However, the ideology in finance that supported men as leaders and deal makers—the male power structure—constrained the women (and their networks). More often than not, at least in the early years (the seventies and even eighties), they refrained from tactics that directly challenged the male hegemony. Nonetheless, in the midst of building careers on Wall Street, they not only survived but broke through gendered barriers. To do so required the women to work toward redefining gender roles while maintaining a conservative ability to fit in and not make waves by challenging the whole gendered system.

The Myth of the Lone Female Pioneer

It has become a common understanding that women in the corporate world, particularly during the seventies, were lone pioneers, token women (Kanter 1977). There were, in fact, very few professional women in each firm at that time: there were only a few hundred on all of Wall Street at the very most. But their isolation actually forced them to seek out other women (like themselves) by attending FWA meetings and in some cases becoming active members of the FWA board. One striking strength of the FWA was its ability to provide its members with not only some of the resources necessary to learn to maneuver on Wall Street, but also to provide a female space for the women to meet one another and build important ties and friendships with one another. This domain was attached to but separate from Wall Street firms. Regularly attending meetings, and forging ties of mutual understanding, they fostered deep friendships that provided emotional support as they dealt with difficult male bosses, for example. This does not mean that the women did not at times compete with one another or even like one another. But to ignore the role of female networks and friendships in the history of Wall Street women's advancement is to obscure the meaning and impact of all female ties on women's careers in finance.

Some from the first generation participated in the FWA only fleetingly; those with ambitions to become investment bankers, in particular, came to rely far more on senior male mentors than on their female counterparts. Others, primarily in what became the more feminized area of research, relied far more and far longer on their female FWA friends for support and help with finding jobs. But in either case, the FWA played a major role in all of these women's lives.

By the late eighties and early nineties, some of the women decided to become more overtly political outside their firms. One by one they joined and brought one another into the Women's Campaign Fund (WCF), a bipartisan organization that helped advance pro-choice women into elected office. Their decision to become publicly active in women's politics—to professionally and financially support women's leadership in government, and specifically pro-choice women's leadership—proved to be remarkable in a decade of backlash against feminism. Politics and popular culture were filled with conservative, anti-women sentiment under the auspices of Ronald Reagan's and George Bush's presidencies (Faludi 1991). As active members of the WCF board, the women fought to incorporate feminist ideas into the political system—ideas that were far more radical than anything they had been able to espouse in the FWA. They were the first female market actors to collectively push the agenda of women's politics.

The Myth of the Upper-Class Female Financier

Most people assume that the women pioneers on the Street were, by and large, from the upper middle class, specifically that the women were graduates of one of the elite women's colleges that made up the "Seven Sisters" and were thus well positioned to follow in the elite footsteps of their fathers and brothers into finance, law, medicine, and government. Moreover, people have projected the glamour of eighties Wall Street back into earlier times, imagining seventies versions of Gordon Gekko spouting "greed is good" mantras and jobs offering the promise of huge salaries and a life of limousine rides and champagne. In reality, most of the women and much of the culture of Wall Street were different. And the specific small group of women that I follow in this book was exceptional: they came out of more solid middle-class urban and suburban backgrounds (e.g., from Brooklyn, New Jersey, and Connecticut) and had attended smaller, less elite women's colleges and state universities, including Manhattan College, Wilson College, and SUNY Albany. (Ivy League universities were not open to women during the sixties. Columbia College, for example, did not go co-ed until 1983.) Their fathers tended to be salesmen in insurance and business. Their mothers were stay-at-home moms. While a handful of the women had earned business degrees from elite universities by the time they came onto Wall Street, most worked full-time while going to New York University's business school at night and had met one another through their participation in the FWA. Moreover, they made their way into Manhattan's financial district amid the seventies during one of the worst recessions in the history of the city, nation, and, indeed, world. They lived in cramped studio apartments and walked or took the bus to work. Often, particularly at the beginning years of their careers, the women were uncertain as to what kind of dress to wear to a business dinner party, what kind of wine to order at such an event, or even what fork to use for the salad. They hired speakers to talk to the group not only about finance, but also how to succeed and be viewed as successful women on Wall Street and beyond.

Only over time, as the women were promoted up the career ladder, and the world of finance grew in what became an age of globalization, deregulation, and shareholder value did their salaries increase. Only then did they move to spacious Upper East Side apartments and buy summer homes on the water in Connecticut. They attended wcf fund-raising parties at the headquarters of Pfizer and other major corporations. The women thus became members of America's professional elite, and in some cases they joined the new superclass global elite (Rothkopf 2008). The women thus did not just use the fwa and later on the wcf as gendered spaces to figure out their relationship to gender, finance, and feminism. They also used these spaces to learn how to act like professional managerial women.

The Myth of the Separation of Finance from Feminism

Classic economists consider the financial market to be an abstract system (de Goede 2005b: 3–4; Langley 2008; Ho 2009). Markets are either sites of continual, rapid flows of capital (Zaloom 2006) or zones of rational action populated by self-interested subjects whose sole goal is the pursuit of profit (Zaloom 2006; Assassi 2009; Griffin 2009). In either case, the market is portrayed as separate and apart from the effects of society, culture, and gender (McDowell 1997; de Goede 2005b: xxv; Ho 2009). Historical and contemporary accounts of finance typically write out debates over the proper meaning of being a female or male investment banker (Kwolek-Folland 1994; de Goede 2005b: 21–46; Fraser 2005; Maurer forthcoming). As a result, finance and economics are understood as depoliticized domains of activity (de Goede 2005b; Langley 2008; Holmes 2009). In turn, political struggles and social movements, including feminism, are thought to be outside the sphere of the marketplace. Social movement actors are understood to critique capitalism, not partake in it.

During the sixties, Manhattan's downtown financial district was only a few miles away from Greenwich Village, one of the major hubs of the women's movement. But the differences in the culture of each of these two neighborhoods could not have been more different. When the first generation of women made their way onto Wall Street, the world of New York City finance was a male-dominated space in lower and midtown Manhattan. Women, for the most part, worked as secretaries, stenographers, bookkeepers, receptionists, or, in a few relatively rare cases, researchers (Gonzalez and Gonzalez 1958; Fisher 2010). In 1967, Abbie Hoffman and his fellow "Yippies" burned dollar bills, danced in the streets surrounding the New York Stock Exchange, and "announced to the press that they were emissaries from a 'new generation' that laughed at money and lived free" (Fraser 2005: 525). On August 26, 1970 (Women's Rights Day), a tiny group of women demonstrated in front of the New York Stock Exchange on behalf of their rights on Wall Street.[17] Unlike the Yippies, they believed in the institution and wanted to belong to it and create change from within it.

None of the women that I write about participated in or even remember this women's protest. For most of their lives, those in the first generation were forced to keep their sense of themselves as professional women in finance separate and apart from their identification with and identity as feminists. This was particularly true during the early decades of their careers during the seventies, eighties, and even nineties. Indeed, most of the women, even when they experienced sex discrimination—even when they were not promoted as quickly as their male counterparts—tended to view the financial world as a site of meritocracy and hence gender neutrality. Early on, the women believed that they could make it on Wall Street based on their own merit. Influenced by tenets of liberal feminism, they also believed that they would become gender equals by working from within and not against the world of finance. As one of the most perceptive members of the first generation of Wall Street women put it, "When I walked into the door of my firm, I left my feminist concerns and ideas, my work in the FWA and WCF, behind me." When they became managing directors, thereby becoming members of the senior-most echelons in finance, the women were often reluctant to have their firms incorporate gender and diversity efforts; they believed that such efforts, in helping women advance, would single them out as "minorities," a category that they found undesirable. In many circumstances, they were reluctant to publicly align themselves with the idea that women and men were different, for difference was the grounds on which men denied them success and advancement. Yet they celebrated, even drew on, other notions of differences from men in order to enter and move up the corporate hierarchy: they believed, for example, that women were better investors (and hence better researchers and brokers) because they were conservative, risk-averse, careful actors.

Although they brought the market and feminism together in their own lives, most members of the first generation of women were able to be successful in part by separating the world of Wall Street and the market from the world of feminism, and to some degree from the FWA and the WCF, for a very long time. But the financial crisis (and the subsequent firing of vast numbers of women from Wall Street) along with the 2008 presidential election—which included Hillary Clinton's defeat for the Democratic presidential ticket, and Sarah Palin's failed run on the Republican vice presidential ticket—forced them to question that separation. Witnessing women losing out in both domains— politics and finance—members of the first generation began to question the efficacy of the women's movement. When they reached their fifties and sixties, near the end of their professional careers on Wall Street, their earlier and ongoing history with feminism came to the fore of their psyches.

In the final chapters of this book, I address the ways in which the first generation—along with other professional elite women (and men)—changed their relationships to both the market and feminism. At the end of the first decade of the 2000s, some of the women chose to retire and continue to be active in women's politics and to join various for-profit and non-for-profit boards, in many respects mirroring the traditional retirement practices of elite businessmen (Ostrower 1992). But some of the women chose a strikingly different path. Eschewing the world of formal politics, they began to engage in and often lead organizations that allowed them to draw on their skills in finance and markets and apply that expertise to helping solve problems of women's equity from the boardroom to the factory floor. They fused the ideologies of the marketplace and feminism, thereby setting the grounds for feminist interventions in the marketplace.

Under neoliberalism during the eighties and nineties, market-driven calculations and rationality as forms of governance were introduced into the management of a variety of subjects and spaces in economic and political spheres (Ong 2006; Lewis et al. 2008: 43). Some members of the first generation, for example, remade forms of feminism into diversity management and gender-mainstreaming programs and policies within global corporate institutions, including Wall Street. In the new millennium, a more inclusive neoliberalism purportedly seeks more socially interventionist and ameliorative projects (Peck and Tickell 2002; Garsten 2008; Lewis et al. 2008). Contemporary feminist philanthropists, including members of the first generation of Wall Street women, now advocate introducing market mechanisms into the social lives and cultural practices of poor women, drawing these women into the market (Elyachar 2005: 5). They promote, for example, implementing business measures and social technologies into spaces traditionally considered to be separate from the free market. They work hard to show donors that market mechanisms can empower and enrich less-developed countries. They are also responsible for introducing feminism in understandable and palpable ways into the marketplace so that (predominantly) male corporate CEOs and executives can view the marketplace as a space in which they can simultaneously pursue gender equality and profit. In this more social interventionist, ameliorative moment, we can see that women are beginning to bring feminist change directly into market practices and the marketplace. But the outcome of such practices still remains to be seen.

A Cultural Genealogy of Wall Street Women and Market Feminism

The history of the first generation shows that, while bringing the marketplace and feminism together in various institutions and projects may seem odd and even paradoxical, the contemporary convergence did not come out of nowhere. It is possible to see the slow growth of the seeds of market feminism on Wall Street from the sixties to the present. The past decade has seen the rise of feminist, primarily socialist feminist, arguments to the effect that "feminism" has been "seduced" by "global elites using women's labor and ideas to exploit the world" (see, e.g., Eisenstein 2009). It is clear that the domains of the marketplace and feminism, of finance and morality, are blurring together in this postmodern, late financial capitalist, neoliberal world. It is equally clear that these changes were not brought about by abstract systems such as the marketplace or finance. Rather they are the product of the first generation's actions, that is, of the interplay among the women's lives, the formations (namely the marketplace and feminism as well as gender and class) that made them, and the formations that they, through their everyday and collective networked practices, played a role in reproducing and sometimes changing.

While the feminist movement and the desire for profit accumulation were not new, what is clearly unique in the recent history of Wall Street is the linkage between feminist ideologies (traditionally seen as alternative or opposed to the market) and financial capitalism. Less than two decades ago, women's attitudes toward conservative, risk-aware thinking provided them with a way to insert themselves within particular areas of Wall Street—namely research and sales—as opposed to the more masculinized areas of investment banking and trading (Zaloom 2006; Ho 2009). Paradoxically, combining gender with the market, which early feminists would have found unthinkably conservative, took these women to causes and engagements that were far more radical than anything they had done before. Today, in contrast—and notably in the wake of globalization, deregulation, privatization, the shareholder revolution, the rise of diversity policies, and the recent crisis in the financial world—women's feminine qualities seem to provide the grounds to establish them as equal to (if not better leaders than) men. Ironically, notions of the differences between women and men serve as the ground—in market feminism—to establish women's equality, if not superiority, to men. Furthermore, the act of mainstreaming feminism into the marketplace enables (some) women and their organizations to see themselves as activists, agents of change, political actors. We have reached the point where some Wall Street women are attempting to make real feminist interventions into the marketplace, a phenomenon that pushes us to rethink the meaning of feminist politics today. Along with constructing market feminism, the women are also attempting to feminize the market.

The members of the first generation—their careers, professional and political networks, and eventual full engagement with market feminism—are thus a rich ethnographic resource for understanding the mainstreaming of feminism. They reacted to the engendering of finance through their everyday practices over the last four decades, and they actively contributed to that gendering. They have negotiated and defined the often uneasy relationship between feminism and the world of finance. The women did not always maintain strict boundaries between the market and outside space, and they did not always (or easily) bracket corporate life from their personal experiences, feelings, and lives as women.[18] The structures of meaning and power on Wall Street shaped and constrained the women's senses of self, success, and action, as it did for men's. Nonetheless, women played the game of upward mobility in high finance with skill, knowledge, and intelligence (Ortner 1996: 12–13). They did not entirely transform the financial culture of work, but their presence and their actions began to loosen up the gendered hegemonic order on Wall Street.[19]

Fieldwork on Wall Street

My study of women in finance has been a long time in the making. I spent the mid- to late nineties, while I was in graduate school, conducting fieldwork among the first cohort of Wall Street women. I spoke to them at their firms, discussed and met others in their professional networks, and attended meetings of political organizations in Manhattan.[20] Between the spring of 2006 and summer of 2008, I returned to conduct follow-up fieldwork with the women, who at that point in time were in the midst of retiring. Given some dramatic events that followed 2008—the financial crisis, Hillary Clinton's campaign for president, and the ongoing economic recession—I decided to return to the field one last time during the summer and fall of 2010.

In earlier years in anthropology it was common practice to begin ethnographies with a tale of one's entry into the field (Clifford and Marcus 1986). However, given my own long-term involvement with the first generation over three major stints of fieldwork, questions about what "entering" and "leaving" the field mean are more complex. Indeed, as anthropologists increasingly study institutions of power and elites, they engage in multisited "yo-yo" fieldwork in which they move between and around various sites as well as attend conferences and write papers between field stints (Marcus 1995; Gusterson 1997: 116; Wulff 2009: 142). In my Wall Street project I have shifted back and forth between more sustained fieldwork in the women's firms and networks and more intermittent visits and attendances at their networked events.

Part 1: The Nineties

The challenges associated with social scientists gaining access to powerful institutions and people has been discussed by sociologists for some time (Jackall 1988) and more recently by anthropologists (Ortner 2003; Downey and Fisher 2006; Ong and Collier 2006; Garsten 2009; Wedel 2009; Hannerz 2010). My own entry into the world of the first generation of Wall Street women—their networks, their firms, and, in some cases, their homes—went surprisingly smoothly. As a Ph.D. student at Columbia University, a powerful New York City institution itself, I was positioned well to make a case to Wall Street women for working with me. That is, my own social and cultural capital (education, family background, and class) opened doors.[21]

My actual "entry" could not, however, have transpired without the enormous interest, help, and insight of a then middle-aged woman returning to school for a masters in liberal arts at Columbia University with a focus on anthropology. I met Madeline Winters in one of my courses on American culture. She came from the higher tiers of New York and American "society"—what some might call "old money." She was (and continues to be) a major activist and fund-raiser for women's issues in the city and the nation. I think it was our mutual passion for women's rights that initially brought us together. It was also Madeline who noticed what was happening in the lives of women on Wall Street and in politics in the early nineties. Women were "breaking glass ceilings"—and increasing numbers of them were making their own money, and large sums of it. When Madeline started fund-raising for women in politics, she found (much to her initial surprise) that it was Wall Street women who were passionate about supporting women running for office—particularly pro-choice women. Upper-class women were far less interested; they did not consider raising funds for female politicians to be part of their philanthropic obligations. Madeline and I talked a lot about the importance of documenting the moment at hand ethnographically, and she encouraged me to take this on as my own project.

So Madeline brought me to events sponsored by the Women's Leadership Circle of the WCF in New York City. Madeline was a board member. A significant number of first-generation women were, it turns out, active in the organization in the nineties. During the first meeting I attended I heard the women talking about "swat teams"—teams of women who were recruiting and networking with other women to join the WCF and to give money to the organization in order to train, launch, and support women politicians.

Several months into my fieldwork I discovered that some of the Wall Street women in the WCF had known one another originally, in the seventies, through their participation in the FWA of New York City. Thus, by the time I "arrived" on the scene, I was already in the middle of the women's history of networking and career making. To learn more about that history I needed to talk individually to the women.

Madeline, her investment-banking friend Mindy Plane, and I sat down for a 7:00 A.M. breakfast at Le Brasserie on East 53rd Street. They collaboratively came up with a list of about twenty first-generation Wall Street women whom I could contact at their recommendation. An astonishing number of the women—nearly all of them—agreed to participate in my study.

This is how I initially came to know, interview, and travel through a relatively tightly clustered network of senior-level women on Wall Street from 1993 to 1996. During each interview I asked each woman to tell me about her career, mentoring, and networking experiences. Also, if she told me a story about a mentor, colleague, and occasional mentee who had been important to her in some capacity during her professional life, I did my best to follow up, with the woman's approval, to interview that particular person or set of persons as the case might be. As a result, I interviewed several male CEOs on Wall Street who had mentored some women and were interested in advancing women in finance in general. Once or twice I interviewed a woman's partner or spouse. And because a number of the women spoke of the important role the FWA had played in their careers, especially in the seventies and eighties, I started attending FWA events and, in time, exploring the association's archives.

Moving between the tight circuit of senior women and their friends, colleagues, and organizational networks, I was at least partially retracing the steps the women had taken to form ties—in and out of firms—over time. My ethnographic path provided me with important insights into the underlying architecture of the women's networks and mentor making, and the roles such ties had played in their lives and careers. I began to understand that the preexisting structures and conditions of the first generation's networks—in the seventies and eighties—had given rise in part, to the career and political networking that I then observed in the nineties.[22]

Part 2: The Mid-2000s

In the spring of 2006, I attended the fiftieth anniversary celebration of the FWA. Only a few of the women I had spent time with a decade earlier were there. I wondered where the rest of them were: Were they still working on Wall Street? Had some begun to retire? What kinds of organizational networks and projects were they now involved in? And, given my interest in returning to the "field," would I be able to find the women—and how? My fieldwork in the nineties, had, as I discussed above, been relatively local and bounded in part because most of the women I followed were living in as well as working in New York City and the tristate area.[23]

By now, the women had achieved significant upward mobility on Wall Street and within American society. They were all bona fide members of the corporate financial elite within the United States. In some cases, they were also part of a growing female national elite composed primarily of women in finance and politics. Some had also participated in feminist-oriented, elite, activist-oriented, transnational networks, often engaged in making market practices feminist. And a few were even members of what David Rothkopf (2008) calls the "superclass"—the new male-dominated, global power elite. The women were thus all elites, but they occupied different positions within the structure of elites. Their particular positions depended upon their career and networking histories as well as their contemporary engagement in various types of networks and projects. They were operating in a newly globalized financial and political world in what Sherry Ortner (1997) refers to as the "postcommunity."

It turned out that I was able to find most of the first cohort of Wall Street women from my original fieldwork. I accomplished this by contacting a few of the women via email, who, in turn, gave me the names and emails for other women. Given that the women were now spread throughout the globe in places as distant as China, I decided to seek out twenty women to interview and spend time with in, as it turned out, the northeast corridor. Meeting up in New York City and Washington, D.C., did not necessarily mean that the women now lived and worked in either city full-time. Some did live in these cities and continued to work within the world of finance: some were in the public sector; others in the area of corporate socially responsible investing; and still others were active on not-for-profit boards of organizations engaged in microfinance. However, many, I discovered, were moving about a great deal. Some spent part of their time "in retirement" (for example, living in Florida during the winter months) and the rest of the year in Manhattan and taking numerous trips in between for board or charitable work in places such as in the East and in South Africa.

Fortunately, since the women all spent part of their time in New York City—often for board meetings—I was able to meet up with all but one of the women I was interested in following up with. This time my fieldwork no longer took place, for the most part, in firms on Wall Street—or in the women's apartments. Instead, during the spring and summer of 2008, I often met up with the women in the various clubs around Manhattan: the Women's National Republican Club, the University Club, and the newly minted Core Club in midtown. I also occasionally got together with some of the women in the office rooms of foundations in which they served on boards. I followed them to political events and fund-raisers. By the end of the summer of 2008 I had, I thought, completed my final round of research on Wall Street women. I was, it would turn out, mistaken.

Part 3: The Crisis of 2007–2009 and Beyond

In September 2008, the crisis had effectively halted global credit markets and had required unprecedented government intervention. I was curious about the effects of these events on the first generation. By that point in time, I was already planning to attend a conference at Columbia University's Institute for Research on Women and Gender. I decided to take advantage of my upcoming trip to Manhattan to see some of the Wall Street women. On the morning of September 14, I invited Mindy—via email—to join me at the conference. That night Lehman Brothers declared bankruptcy after failing to find a buyer. Mindy emailed me on September 15: "With meltdown on Wall Street —I am very busy and do not have time to attend this. As a director of [a major asset firm] you can understand. I am about to email them after I respond to you. While I disagree with Palin (she is really in demand—I have never seen this in politics—good for her) on social issues, I am 100% behind her." Mindy explained her reasons for supporting Palin, her feelings that Palin was being mistreated more than Hillary, and she then ended with an abrupt note: "Off to my Wall Street stuff—enjoy the conference." Of course, her tension was palpable; I was surprised that she had even taken the time to write to me. But I found it interesting that she assumed that my conference would focus on the current election—on the formal national domain of women and politics—the implication perhaps being that the McCain/Palin ticket would deal with the financial crisis better than Obama would. Palin at that point in time had proclaimed that she was a feminist for life. She and other Republican women were claiming to speak for "women," cultivating women's votes and the support of some "women's" or "feminist" organizations. Given her conservatism, Palin pushed the boundaries of feminism—however contested they already were—in the twenty-first century.

Given the sudden onset of the financial crisis, less than one month after the formal end of my follow-up fieldwork, I wondered what the women's reactions might tell us about their shifting relationship to financial capitalism over time. Would the women react by continuing to engage in their various feminist-oriented political and philanthropic projects? Would those projects change shape? Or would the women choose other paths? What about the younger generation of women on Wall Street, and their careers and politics? I could already see from Mindy's brief email that the financial crisis was directly affecting her board work. I could also see that Sarah Palin's recent entry into the public sphere was shaping Mindy's views about women and politics; did she and her more democratic pro-Hillary, pro-Obama friends even share a common "feminist" agenda? These then were the empirical and theoretically oriented questions that motivated my third and final return to the field, which ultimately took place during the summer and fall of 2010. I followed up with the smaller group of women I had, by that point in time, known for over a decade and a half.

Most members of the first generation were already actively engaged in postretirement practices by the time the financial crisis initially hit. However, Constance Burk, whom I had met initially in the nineties while I was in the midst of my first stint of Wall Street fieldwork, was not doing so. In 2008, I had attempted to meet with Constance a number of times but Constance had just taken on a new senior-level position in a major global investment bank and was helping to grow the bank's business internationally. It was nearly impossible for us to meet in person then, given Constance's work and travel schedule, so we emailed back and forth occasionally. At the time, I thought that Constance was one of the last standouts of the first generation—one of the very few who was still working full-time in the world of finance, and had, in fact, survived the downsizing on Wall Street, particularly among women, in the aftermath of the 2007–9 financial crisis.

In the summer of 2010, however, I began to receive emails from Constance expressing an interest in meeting with me. During one of her visits back to the city, she and I met for a lengthy talk in her pied-à-terre in Brooklyn Heights overlooking the Manhattan skyline. Constance was distressed because she, like many other high-ranking women, had been recently let go from her firm. She was depressed because the first generation, her generation, was leaving finance "without leaving a legacy." In spite of their success during the past three decades, they had not, in the end, brought real change to the gendered dimensions of Wall Street. Constance wondered where she and members of her generation "were going from here." Then she lit up, telling me, "Maybe we need to get everybody together and sort of figure out next steps." Thus, on a cool, crisp, bright Friday morning in mid-November, about a dozen members of the first generation of women on Wall Street, Madeline Winters, and I came together in New York City to discuss the past, present, and future of women on Wall Street. This book is their story.

In the next chapter, I discuss briefly a history of Wall Street and then explore the entry of the women into Wall Street during the sixties and seventies. In the following chapters, I discuss the ways they became market-feminist subjects in the seventies and eighties as well as how their experiences in finance affected them during the nineties. Chapter 2 examines their advancement within the male-dominated corporate hierarchy, as well as the ways they used female spaces such as the FWA to mediate their relationship to finance and feminism, setting the grounds for their making of market feminism beyond their personal lives. Chapter 3 unravels the ways Wall Street women drew on gendered discourses of finance to insert themselves within the more feminized areas of research and more masculinized domains of investment banking. It highlights the paradoxes between feminism and market ideologies during the nineties. Chapter 4 focuses on the women's eventual participation in the WCF and the ways the women incorporated elements of liberal feminism into their political networks and practices. Chapter 5 centers on the women's post–Wall Street careers during the 2000s and their contemporary market-feminist projects, including their participation on the boards of organizations that use market mechanisms to help poor women enter into the global marketplace. I conclude by examining the first generation's experiences in the aftermath of the 2007–9 crisis and the ways in which in the contemporary moment the upcoming generation of women is making their own versions of market feminism by adding in new layers, finding ways to package tenets of feminism and neoliberalism of the free market for surprising new subjects, and creating the grounds for making markets feminist.

CHAPTER 1

BEGINNINGS

Muriel Siebert went to the New York Stock Exchange for the first time in 1953, as a twenty-year-old tourist.[1] She got to see a new public reception and exhibition room at the exchange, recently opened as part of an expanded public relations campaign on Wall Street aimed at the burgeoning middle class after the Second World War (Traflet 2003: 6–7). She loved it: "After absorbing all that fierce energy, I turned to my friends and said, 'Now, *this* is exciting. Maybe I'll come back here and look for a job.' At the time tourists were given a piece of ticker tape printed with their name as a souvenir. I still have the few inches of worn and faded tape that said, 'Welcome to the NYSE Muriel Siebert'" (Siebert 2007: 1).

In 1954 she did indeed return to Manhattan, a few months shy of graduating from a small women's college in Florida; having grown up in Cleveland in the worst of the Depression, she had five hundred dollars in her pocket and drove an old Studebaker. But when she arrived in New York, she found few job prospects. "Turns out I wasn't so welcome after all," she noted wryly in her autobiography. Merrill Lynch turned her down because she did not have a college degree. She then lied to Bache & Co. about having a degree and was offered her choice of two positions: one in the accounting department that paid $75 a week and the other in research that paid $65 a week. She chose research because "it sounded more interesting" (Siebert 2007: 5–6). Thirteen years later, in 1967, Siebert became the first woman to buy a seat on the New York Stock Exchange; two years after that she founded her own brokerage firm. She was a pioneering woman on Wall Street, and a singular figure. But right as she was opening up her own business, other women were following in her footsteps, albeit a small group of roughly sixty individuals—the first generation of women in finance.

Born just after the end of the Second World War in the Northeast (see Mayo et al. 2006: chap. 2), these women were the children of the members of a vastly expanding postwar American middle class. Their childhood and adolescence occurred during periods of enormous economic growth in the United States.[2] Economic prosperity enabled most of their parents to send them to college, albeit often smaller women's colleges rather than the Seven Sisters or other top schools. All of this went a long way toward producing a particular gender and class profile of this generation as they worked their way into the professional-managerial class. Fresh out of college, the cohort made their initial entry onto Wall Street circa 1969. They read Betty Friedan's *The Feminine Mystique* (1963) and, like Siebert, were drawn to the excitement, energy, and possibilities of Manhattan. The possibilities of huge salaries and power did not entice them; rather, they were inspired by the onset of the feminist movement and the idea that they could make a different kind of life and independent living for themselves in New York City (Ortner 2003; Coontz 2011). Some found jobs in brokerage firms through ads in the *New York Times*; others came to work in finance at the suggestion of a family member or college friend.

Their individual and collective career biographies intersected with a particular moment in the history of financial capitalism, the engendering of Wall Street institutions, and the feminist movement to shape the women as gendered market subjects. From the start of their career paths, the women encountered a disconcerting combination of new opportunities and constraints. The economy was beginning to crater and the city was about to sink into the depths of the recession of the seventies. Working in a bank was not a glamorous career path. An MBA was only just starting to be a useful credential, but prospects of being wined, dined, and lured onto working on Wall Street by major firms, making lots of money, and climbing the class ladder were not yet fantasies in the career dreams of men or women. Most graduates of elite East Coast colleges were pursuing careers in business, rather than on Wall Street.[3] Such students, predominantly men from old-moneyed wealthy families, found their jobs through family ties. It would be another decade until Michael Douglas's Gordon Gekko in *Wall Street* captured the American imagination and Melanie Griffith's *Working Girl* made her triumphant climb on Wall Street (Traube 1992).

But change was beginning to stir in the worlds of education, business, and finance. Deregulation and increased competition among firms were opening the class system in finance to a new cadre of workers recruited mainly out of the top elite university's "families," rather than individual families (Ho 2009: 60). Admission to this new kind of club depended less on social factors such as family background and more on educational credentials, particularly pedigreed business-degree credentials (Mayo et al. 2006: 149). More and more firms offered training programs within their firms, but training programs on Wall Street did not open up to women until the mid-seventies.

Most members of the first generation were thus double outsiders: first because of their gender and second because of their educational backgrounds and class. Instead of attending business school and training programs, they worked to gain occupational experience in low-level, white-collar work (see Buhlmann 2009). Like Siebert, they tended to land jobs in what was becoming a more feminized area of finance—research—and, unlike her, they attained educational credentials later on by going to business school at night while working full-time in research, a "back-office" support function on Wall Street. But the women were also uniquely positioned to push through emerging cracks in the gender system in finance in the context of the deregulation and globalization of finance. Beginning in the mid-seventies, the area of research became increasingly important to firms, and analysts became valued employees: they eventually joined investment bankers and traders in the "front office."

And the first generation worked together to lift themselves up. At the beginning of their careers, each woman felt isolated as one of the only professional women working within her respective firm. But gradually many were able to form ties with one another, at night classes in business school and at meetings of the Financial Women's Association (FWA) of New York City. They fostered their own female financial networks early on that were connected to Wall Street but were outside the walls of their specific firms. This network became an alternate training ground for the women. The professional and personal relationships they formed within the FWA became central to their working lives, some far outlasting their initial involvement. The women were never entirely defined only in relation to elite men on Wall Street, as important as some of these relationships became in terms of mentorship.

We can see the importance of the biographical and institutional in constructing financial subjects: pioneering Wall Street women emerge out of a specific set of early entry routes into finance, career positions, experiences, and trajectories within a particular economic period and, in a majority of their cases, a tough bear market. We can also read the importance of feminism to their career pathways, aspirations, and networks, and to the cultural values they formed about gender and finance along the way (Ortner 2003; Laird 2006).

The Male-Dominated Landscape
of Finance through the Fifties

Wall Street is the general name given to New York City's downtown financial district, a physical place composed of small colonial streets, the New York Stock Exchange, and the towers of major investment banks. "Wall Street" also signifies an ethos and set of practices embedded in an intricate network of institutions, investments, and people (Ho 2009: 6). Even its landscape is steeped in the history of American politics, culture, and finance. After the American Revolution, New York was the nation's first capital. The site of the city's first City Hall was 26 Wall Street. The First Congress of the United States met in Federal Hall in the district to write the Bill of Rights. George Washington was inaugurated in Federal Hall on April 30, 1789. In 1792, a group of male traders allegedly met under a buttonwood tree—on the location of what is now 68 Wall Street—to establish a formal stock exchange. While the buttonwood story appears to be largely legend, there was, according to the historian Steven Fraser, a concerted effort at self-regulation during the late eighteenth century on the part of the embryonic Wall Street community (2005: 17). For most of the two centuries to follow, aristocrats, confidence men, and financial tycoons understood Wall Street to be a male space where elite men participated in the market, making money for themselves and their families. Despite this segregation, a few women defied gendered conventions and made a name for themselves early on in finance. For example, the late nineteenth-century female speculator Hetty Green was nicknamed the "Witch on Wall Street" because of her supposed magical abilities to predict the future of the stock market with success. But she was a rarity.

With the passing of the Nineteenth Amendment in 1920, women appeared to have finally attained the political equity they had long been fighting for. New social and legal ideas about gender, along with the ascent of corporations and professionalism, began to open certain business arenas for women (Kwolek-Folland 1998: 87). For the most part, women could not enter the male-dominated fields of management, law, or medicine, but they did enter the workforce in increasingly higher numbers in clerical and secretarial positions (101).

During the twenties, Wall Street, along with flappers, jazz, and the radio, symbolized an era in the United States that was marked by enormous optimism. For most of the decade, the majority of Americans dreamed they could become part of the burgeoning middle class by investing in the stock market (Fraser 2005: 366–67). In the meantime, urbanization, in places like New York City, reached a climax with the onset of the erection of several major skyscrapers (Willis 2001: 8). New cathedrals of capitalism, like Irving Trust's headquarters, transformed the financial district and the lower Manhattan skyline (Abramson 2001: 3).

The Great Crash of 1929 abruptly shut down the American dream of becoming rich through investing. Americans suddenly viewed Wall Street as the principal villain in the nation's financial and social downfall, and they stopped trusting it with their money or their hopes (Fraser 2005: 414). The industry shrank. Bankers, nicknamed "banksters," were considered manipulative at best and corrupt at worst (Hayes and Hubbard 1990: 25). The enormous grip Wall Street had had on the social imagination of the United States evaporated, not to be experienced in such a way again until the Reagan revolution in the eighties (Fraser 2005: 396). The allure of making lots of money and being part of the professional-managerial elite by working on Wall Street practically vanished.

Wall Street became a state-regulated, closed, domestic financial space (Hayes and Hubbard 1990: 25). The Crash, the Depression, and the Second World War had significant effects on the regulation and structure of investment banking in particular. Financial-market stabilization was finally achieved by a series of governmental acts under New Deal reforms, notably the Glass-Steagall Act in 1933 and the Securities and Exchange Act in 1934 (Fraser 2005: 459). Glass-Steagall separated commercial banking (the deposit and lending of loans) from investment banking (the mediation between sellers and buyers or various assets) (Eccles and Crane 1988). Unbeknownst to the majority of Americans, banks during the twenties had gambled with and lost their depositors' money in bad investment deals. To avert future massive losses, Glass-Steagall forced banks, such as J. P. Morgan, to choose one of two institutional paths. In the Morgan case, the firm decided to maintain its commercial practice and private banking clients. Several partners, however, remained in investment banking and then created Morgan Stanley.

The "Chinese wall" separating Wall Street firms from commercial banking in the securities business created a cartel-like industry. Other new governmental measures targeted the gambling practices that risked producing another crash. The Securities and Exchange Act of 1934, which set up the Securities and Exchange Commission (SEC), was designed to ensure that the American public was provided with adequate information regarding securities and training practices in order so that they could make wise investment decisions (Sobel 1980: 167; Fraser 2005).

New Deal reforms helped the domestic situation, but the Second World War had a devastating effect on international financial practices. It destroyed confidence in bond issuers and credit institutions (Hayes and Hubbard 1990). Out of this situation emerged the development of strategies intended to ensure the growth and stability of national capitalist economies and agendas. The postwar years witnessed the organization of a new international regulated space composed of nation-states managed by a set of international institutions. Under the Bretton Woods system, constructed in 1944, governments of leading economies practiced collective management based on a set of agreed-upon rules, including fixed exchange rates and national controls over employment, savings, and interest rates (Corbridge and Thrift 1994).

Postwar Wall Street was a ghostly place (Fraser 2005: 474). The new regulatory shifts had transformed the Wall Street of the forties into a small wholesale industry that dealt primarily with corporations and wealthy investors, who were mainly well-to-do businessmen and their families (Welles 1975: 145). Investment banks were caught up in an impoverished war environment for underwriting and trading. In contrast with the large institutional structures of commercial banks and their high volume of business, Wall Street firms experienced a relative dearth of activity (Hayes and Hubbard 1990: 103–4).

A handful of firms—Morgan Stanley; First Boston; Dillon, Read; and Kuhn, Loeb Co.—emerged in the reorganized industry as the strongest and most prestigious investment banks (Hayes and Hubbard 1990: 105). The Street hired only small numbers of new personnel, and those who were hired reflected the visible religious-ethnic characteristics of different investment banks that went back to their nineteenth-century origins. Morgan Stanley's roster of clients was composed of blue-chip corporations. The firm's partners matched their clients' WASP, Ivy League, "white-shoe" pedigree (Hoffman 1984: 36). First Boston, a spin-off of Chase Bank, also boasted blue-chip clientele (49). Kuhn, Loeb Co., the archetype of a German-Jewish "Our Crowd" investment house, specialized in rails, steel, and utilities (51). These financial institutions did not compete for their clients. In theory, a "gentleman's agreement" prevented firms from raiding each other's client lists. Bankers engaged in ongoing professional and social relationships with industrial capitalists and affluent individuals. The three-martini lunch symbolized the masculine style of long-term "relationship banking" practices.

Partnerships, in both WASP and Jewish firms, were the predominant organizational form, though these partnerships were often closer to the model of the "family firm" of nineteenth-century businesses (Kwolek-Folland 1994: 129). The banks were deeply hierarchical. At the upper tiers, male partners ("fatherly executives") exercised total control over decision making. A small supporting cast of clerical workers, predominantly male, operated in the lower tiers. Entry and advancement into the higher echelons depended on family, religious, and school connections. Fathers prepared their sons (and nephews and sons-in-law) to take over their positions as partners of their firms (Laird 2006).

The men occupying the power structure worked in an elite homosocial world. Although the white, upper-class male dominant order was never completely dominant or static, gendered boundaries remained fairly rigid until bankers and office workers were drafted into the armed forces during the Second World War. In the men's absence, Wall Street firms recruited white women with experience in education, hospital administration, and welfare work to fill clerical and professional positions (Kwolek-Folland 1998: 149). Firms generally prohibited black women from taking advantage of these opportunities (Gregory 1998: 54).

In spite of white women's entry into the financial world, the dominant gendered imaginary, in social policies and everyday practices, still linked women's proper role to the home. Indeed, as the feminist historian Alice Kessler-Harris points out, "In the 1940s, through the 1950s, and into the 1960s, the idea of gender difference remained embedded in marriage patterns and family lives, social traditions and economic possibilities" (2001: 204).

During and beyond the Eisenhower bull market (1954–69), the power structure and elite family structures of Wall Street slowly began to unravel (Fraser 2005: 476, 516). These shifts in class, ethnicity, and, as we shall see, generation were reflected in changes in relationships between financial firms and their corporate clients. New corporate forms and subjects transformed the established male leadership of the Street. The period of the extended postwar economic expansion witnessed the emergence of new firms, managerial practices, executive entry routes, and ways of training men. The dearth of men during the Depression and the war contributed to a generational gap between the partners of firms (who were mostly in their sixties) and the majority of younger men working their way up the corporate ladder (Fraser 2005: 478). While some sons went into their fathers' firms, firms that were not family-owned now recruited others.

The family-firm structure of commercial banks (as opposed to investment banks or brokerage houses) also began to break down during the fifties. This period witnessed a series of merges among New York City banks. Historically, J. P. Morgan had operated as a loosely organized, closed class-bound partnership, recruiting partners predominantly from among family, friends, and well-known business associates (Rogers 1993: 199–200). In 1959, the bank merged with Guaranty Trust, resulting in the nation's biggest trust (201). Over the next several decades, Morgan transformed itself into a larger bureaucratic organization (202). However, even as it grew in the sixties, it remained largely composed of professionals from the white upper-class. Under Glass-Steagall, the bank also continued as a commercial bank rather than as an investment bank or brokerage house.

In the meantime, a combination of men who were old-timers and new transformed American business and financial practices on Wall Street. Two tycoons plus newly welcomed Eastern European Jews shook up the relatively staid world of postwar Wall Street. Thomas Mellon Evans, along with a handful of others, pioneered the first corporate raids. Nicknamed the "white shark," he built the first conglomerates by merging disparate industries such as canned goods, textiles, and clothing producers into single, massive corporations (Henriques 2000: 16–17; Fraser 2005: 487–88). He reshaped the ways these companies conducted business with their workers, executives, and shareholders. Long before the advent of "investor capitalism" of the eighties and nineties, Evans insisted that firms operate for the benefit of their stockowners. He wielded a ruthless corporate machismo that focused on downsizing companies to achieve the maximum profits (Henriques 2000: 14–17). Charles Merrill built a brokerage firm designed to draw middle-class investors back into the market (Perkins 1999; Traflet 2003: 14; Fraser 2005: 493–94). He transformed brokerage by advertising aggressively and making the selling of stocks to individuals into a salesman's art. He modernized the brokerage business by creating a new kind of organizational form on Wall Street: the large retail house with complex administrative and operations structures, expanded research departments, hundreds of branch offices, thousands of enterprising salesmen, and a new training program for brokers (Welles 1975: 146). Merging had enabled companies to capitalize on their current stock values (Brooks 1973: 156). The new retail firms began to disrupt the classed hierarchy in finance. In the public imagination, established firms such as Morgan Stanley were replaced by Merrill Lynch and other "wire houses" (firms that did most of their business by telephone) (Welles 1975: 146–47). Wall Street embraced the new conglomerate "glamour stocks" in electronics, plastics, and other Cold War–inspired technologies (Geisst 1997: 284). Amid speculative stock fever, self-made men arose, a "new crowd" of Eastern Jewish descent. This group made its way into burgeoning areas of money, management, trading, and brokerage (Erlich and Rehfeld 1989: 34). From the perspective of elite, more established men, these new men were contributing their own brash machismo (13). The journalist John Brooks suggested that they exhibited "a style more inclined to dash and daring as opposed to respectability, less concerned about preservations of values and appearances and more sympathetic toward speculation and outright gambling" (1973: 118). It was during this period that trading rooms became dens of incivility known for their locker-room crudity, while the upper-class accents of an earlier era began to dissipate (Fraser 2005: 509; Zaloom 2006: 11).

Women were not entirely invisible. As a 1958 article in the *New York Times* pointed out, "Physically, [women] play a part in the sense that each weekday the Street's stone and concrete canyons echo to the click-click of approximately 60,000 high-heels as secretaries, stenos, bookkeepers, receptionists, ticker operators, file clerks, messengers and pages pour out of subways and into offices."[4] But in those offices, most women were made less visible and had to work well behind the scenes in subordinate positions. One Wall Street woman remembered in a 1994 interview, "The secretaries all had to come in and wear hats and gloves. In the bathrooms, they had light bulbs, with the partner's name. The partner would ring you up on his desk. If you were in the bathroom, you had to run out immediately."

And men did not consider women to be players in the market; as the 1958 *Times* story put it, "Exclusivity exists in spite of the fact that women play a tremendous role in the life of Wall Street.... This ... infiltration of Wall Street has not, however, done much to open the way for promotion and pay to the women in question or to women in general. It is extremely unlikely that any of the faithful privates in the Wall Street army mentioned above—the clerical help and receptionists—will attain any notable financial positions unless she is able to marry the boss, outlive him and inherit his share of business."[5] The *New York Times* reporters accurately portrayed the male-dominated hegemony of postwar finance. But their understanding that women only worked as support staff, and their prediction that these women were unlikely to advance up the corporate hierarchy were not entirely on the mark. Indeed, by the time the article was published, there were actually a small number of women working their way into the professional area of research (Fisher 2004). In 1969, the Wall Street journalist Martin Mayer noted the presence of exactly one Asian American; one African American; and one woman, Muriel Siebert. Siebert's first job, notably, was in research.[6] She was part of a small but growing group of (mostly white) middle- and upper-middle-class women who took advantage of the growing labor opportunities during the early Cold War economy (Kessler-Harris 2001: 26).

Women were gaining visibility as investors and clients. Merrill Lynch offered a four-week investment course for women clients to encourage greater numbers of female investors. Several brokerages targeted women in advertising campaigns, offering "services" such as free courses in investments (Welles 1975: 146–47), playing on their presumed maternal instincts of care (Fraser 2005: 494). The courses taught women to take only the most conservative approaches to dealing with money, savings, and stocks (Fraser 2005: 494–95). These initiatives opened doors to women as investors. Wall Street firms recognized that hiring some women into their public relations departments might bring in even more female customers. By the late fifties, Merrill hired women to write for the firm's business news publication, *Investor's Reader*. Margaret Beer Platt became the *Reader*'s senior editor during the sixties (FWA Newsletter 1996).

A decade later, Wall Street began hiring women to assist on converting the stock exchange's use of punch cards to computers. Computer

Femininity in a Wall St. Equation

Girl With Slide Rule Studies Computers on Trinity Place

By VARTANIG G. VARTAN

While a large part of Wall Street's working population spent yesterday puzzling over the stock market decline, an attractive girl with hazel eyes and ash-blonde hair calmly was discussing automation.

She is Janet Norman a mathematician in her mid-twenties on the staff of the American Stock Exchange.

Her latest project involves possible steps for changing the exchange's clearing corporation, which processes buy and sell orders of subscribing members, from a punch-card to a computer operation.

Is it distracting to have such a pretty girl—a trim 5 feet 3 inches tall in a size 7 dress—wielding a slide rule around the nation's second largest stock exchange?

"I haven't heard a single complaint," responds Donald R. Meng. As vice president in charge of the data systems division, he is Janet's boss. "She is a very competent employe," he adds.

As for Janet, who joined the exchange in May of last year, she observes: "I like the

Continued on Page 47, Column 1

The New York Times (by Ernest Sisto)
Janet Norman at work at the American Stock Exchange

1. Janet Norman at work at the American Stock Exchange.
(From "Femininity in a Wall Street Equation,"
New York Times, June 22, 1965)

programming was, at the time, viewed as a female occupation. Women's "natural" feminine traits—being patient, detail-minded—were understood to make them ideal computer programmers.[7] In a June 1965 article entitled "Femininity in a Wall Street Equation: Girl with Slide Rule Studies Computers on Trinity Place," the *New York Times* depicted Janet Norman wearing a sleeveless tailored dress, with her hair coiffed in a bouffant, and carefully studying a slide rule (see figure 1). Norman explained why computer programming was a perfect fit for women: "Women are endowed from birth with certain information retrieval talents." The article briefly described her job as a senior system analyst at the American Stock Exchange. But it quickly reassured readers that she was still very much a "vivacious girl who leads an active social life away from the electronic computers. 'I'm not too mathematician-like after 5 P.M.'"

During the sixties, stockbrokers rose to heights previously unknown on Wall Street. Although they were outcasts generations earlier, stockbrokers crept into the highest status group of the professional-managerial class with doctors, executives, and judges (Geisst 1997: 281). And the shifting position of male stockbrokers would have implications for the status of professional women in finance. In the "go-go" and "boom-boom" years of the sixties in American finance, the new male hero— the stockbroker—made sense.

The appearance of these men went further to dislodge the hegemony of an earlier gentlemanly banker masculinity, already shaken by the "new crowd" of Jewish men. New forms of masculinity elevated qualities excluded from the earlier ideal. Aptly named "gunslingers," brokers embodied a youthful "Marlboro Man" salesman masculinity (Fisher 2004). Their success, like that of the "new crowd," depended less on their family and class connections, and more on the "performance"—the new buzzword in finance—of themselves and their stocks (Mayer 1969; Erlich and Rehfeld 1989: 16). The revolution in the stock market brought the cultural revolution of the sixties to Wall Street. Martin Mayer documented what he called the brand-new "performance oriented world" of late sixties Wall Street. His opening chapter was entitled "Performance: New Money Calls Forth New Market." The second part of the book was called: "Performers: And New Markets Call Forth New Men."[8]

Brokers, Research Analysts, and Cracks in the Gender System on Wall Street

To be a successful man on Wall Street has always depended upon a man's ability to make deals and money. Classed and gendered definitions of the kinds of skills, forms of training, and types of occupation have, however, shifted over time. During the fifties and sixties, building a career in the brokerage business entailed becoming admired for one's technical and intuitive ability to quickly pick and sell hot stocks (Sobel 1977: 71). The rules of the brokerage game included acquiring, maintaining, and growing an established client base of investors. Selling stocks required brokers to spend time outside of the firm traveling, visiting, and calling on clients. A large, highly active client base allowed brokers to make huge sums of money, to become celebrities on the Street, and, at times, to move up into senior positions. Brokers made it appear as if they were earning all this money, and achieving all this power and fame, on their own. However, their stock-picking game relied upon the work and written reports about industries produced by analysts, mainly men, working in the undervalued area of research.

In contrast to brokers, analysts were less well paid and less visible on the Street and in American culture in general. Brokers were picked for their charm, "frat-boy" outgoing personalities, "risk-taking" natures, and ability to make friends and sell to the public (Sobel 1977: 116–39). Analysts were regarded, for the most part, as introverted, quiet, detail-oriented college men who spent the bulk of their time squirreled away in cubbyholes writing their reports (Mayer 1955; Sobel 1977).

Brokers were on the front line of finance. Analysts remained at home in the back office. Male analysts were thus lower ranking and, arguably, symbolically feminized men. "Domesticated men" or not, they were structurally disadvantaged players in the games of finance. They held less prestigious jobs and lived in less exclusive areas than their broker counterparts. However, the hidden and feminized nature of the work helped crack open the door to women's entry into research. Louise Harris—a first-generation Wall Street woman born in Manhattan, raised in a rural area outside the city by bohemian parents —found her first job in finance in the area of research. She remembered, "Women were mainly bank tellers. But the real glory was in research. I didn't have to be 'white-shoe.' I was with the geeks—they were a different breed who worked in wrinkled shirts."

Women and the Early Quest for Gender Equality on Wall Street: The Early Sixties to the Early Seventies

Wall Street women were not the only group of women making headway into traditionally male-dominated professions during the sixties and seventies. By the early sixties the place of women in the workplace in the United States had shifted, and this shift took on increased momentum in the seventies. Legal changes were among several sources of women's advancement in business after 1963 (Kwolek-Folland 1998: 174). The passage of the Federal Equal Pay Act in 1963 was followed closely by the inclusion of sex and race as a protected category in the 1964 Civil Rights Act.[9] The alliance of race and sex, though not always a comfortable one, became particularly visible in the formation of the Equal Employment Opportunity Commission (EEOC) in 1965 and the EEOC's subsequent actions against discriminatory practices in the workplace (Kessler-Harris 2001: 246). Frustrated by the EEOC's initial lack of focus on sex as well as on racial discrimination, a group of middle-class women formed the National Organization for Women (NOW) in 1965 to battle for women in cultural, legal, political, and business arenas (Laird 2006: 226). The formation of NOW marked the official beginning of the second wave of the mainstream liberation women's movement in the United States (the first wave having been the movement for the right to vote during the early twentieth century). NOW, for example, added abortion rights to its agenda in 1967 (McBride-Stetson 2001: 251).

By 1966 there were about sixty professional women on Wall Street, and the majority of them worked in research (Brooks 1973: 108). The other women continued to occupy "nonprofessional" clerical and secretarial positions. The most significant landmark in finance—marking a shift in the gender system on Wall Street—took place on December 28, 1967, when Muriel Siebert became the first woman to buy a seat on the New York Stock Exchange (for $445,000). All of the other 1,365 members were men.[10] Dealing with discriminatory practices and pushing for the advancement of women and African Americans remained an arduous process. The Civil Rights Act and institutionalization of the EEOC did not immediately make much of a legal dent on Wall Street. In the mid-sixties, "professionally, prejudice against women in the financial business," according to John Brooks, "was wide, deep, and largely unquestioned" (1973: 108). Nevertheless, in spite of such rampant unfairness, ideas of gender equality and ending sexual discrimination began to inflect the gendered habits of some working women and men—on Wall Street and in the larger American public imagination—by the mid- to late sixties (Kessler-Harris 2001).

On August 26, 1970, Women's Rights Day, a group of Wall Street women demonstrated in front of the New York Stock Exchange on behalf of their rights. According to a *New York Times* reporter, rather than burn bras they handed out Equal Rights Amendment literature.[11] That same year, the radical feminist poet and editor Robin Morgan published *Sisterhood Is Powerful: An Anthology of Writings from the Women's Liberation Movement*. A 1970 *New York Times* article, entitled "Women's Lib Bearish in Wall Street," noted that "in the long run," Morgan declared, "we should bring it all down—with industrial sabotage and secretarial sabotage—because Wall Street is the essence of white male power gone mad."[12] Morgan also pointed out that "in the short run the women of Wall Street should organize for their rights as women."[13] Indeed, radical ideas, for the most part, did not even percolate on Wall Street, even among those small numbers of women participating in the new "consciousness-raising sessions" that "women on Wall Street" held in the cocktail lounge of the Coachman overlooking Trinity Churchyard.[14] As Alice Kessler-Harris points out, "Only the most far-sighted feminists in the early 1970s dared to talk about transforming language, or the family, or the early education programs" (2001: 268).[15] So when women on Wall Street focused on change making, as they did when handing out literature about equal rights, they pushed for rights for women. Equal rights meant raising their jobs and salary levels to equal those of men.[16] Like the majority of mainstream feminists of the era, they did not address providing ways for poorer women to have the same kind of education that gave them (and other largely white middle- and upper-middle-class women) an advantage in moving onto and up the professional ladder (Kessler-Harris 2001: 268). None of the women whom I have come to know had protested in 1970 or perceived of themselves as active members of the movement. Muriel Siebert herself did not march on Wall Street in August 1970.[17] According to an article in the *New York Times* about the presence of eleven young female pages on the floor of the New York Stock Exchange, when Siebert was asked about her feelings toward the feminist movement, she crisply replied that she did not regard her presence on the floor as women's liberation. Instead, she insisted that "she [was] motivated by business necessity, and so was the personnel department of the New York Stock Exchange."[18]

Class, that is, shaped the women's politics. The *New York Times* article entitled "Women's Lib Bearish in Wall Street" pointed out that the stakes for Wall Street women were different from the stakes of other protestors: "The Robin Morgans and the Betty Friedans do not punch 9-to-5 clocks in banks and brokerage houses. The sisters who do cannot afford inflammatory rhetoric. Compared with Greenwich Village and the Upper West Side, Wall Street women's liberation is appreciably more subdued and nervously anonymous." Moreover, class split women within Wall Street: "In the financial community, women's liberation is an amoebic and poorly organized movement that ranges from militant-minded clerical workers pursuing the old dream of unionizing their female colleagues who occupy the mass position at the bottom of the Wall Street power pyramid, to a chapter of Older Women's Liberation (35 and up) that favors actions geared to coaxing women shareholders to do business only with women brokers."[19]

Of course, class, education, and position within the labor market produced splits among women living in New York City, in the nation, as well as in the feminist movement; the Wall Street women were mostly white, so the split produced by race was largely invisible to them. However, the women's protest in front of the Stock Exchange signaled the nascent call for equal rights brought on by the civil rights and feminist movements, along with legislative change. The *New York Times* had taken note of some of these changes at play in a 1969 article entitled "Woman, 36, at Top in Brokerage House" (see figure 2). The article declared, "Peggy Schulder is a member of a growing breed that does not fit the Wall Street stereotype. For one thing she does not come from one of those moneyed families whose names have been identified with the brokerage business for decades."

Schulder had grown up in Queens as the daughter of a postman. She attended parochial schools and eventually went to Fordham University at night where she majored in mathematics, and she started her Wall Street career in the research department of Merrill Lynch.[20] This lower-middle-class background was a rarity for someone on Wall Street, but she was not a complete anomaly. Indeed, when the first generation of Wall Street women arrived circa 1970, they were a mixed lot in terms of class origins. A few came from traditional elite backgrounds, that is, WASP and Jewish Manhattan-based families. Having attended one of the Seven Sisters, which included Barnard, Smith, and Wellesley, these women followed in the power elite career tracks of their fathers and grandfathers in business and government and on Wall Street. They were part of the first group of elite women to break into the male-dominated business schools of Harvard and Columbia in the late sixties and seventies. Most of the women, however, came out of more solid middle-class, suburban (e.g., Westchester County, New York; New Jersey; and Connecticut) backgrounds and attended smaller, less elite women's colleges and state universities, including Manhattan College, Wilson College, and SUNY Albany. Their fathers tended to be salesmen in insurance and business. Their mothers were stay-at-home moms. Moreover, unlike their more elite peers who had business degrees by the time they came onto Wall Street, these women

Woman, 36, at Top in Brokerage House

Peggy Schulder is a member of a growing breed that does not fit the Wall Street stereotype. For one thing, she does not come from one of those moneyed families whose names have been identified with the brokerage business for decades.

For another thing, she was educated as a mathematician, not as a securities salesman. But perhaps most significantly, she is a woman who has risen to the top in what traditionally has been a man's industry. She is the president of a fast-growing brokerage house with a long roster of institutional clients.

A few weeks ago, at the age of 36, Miss Schulder took the helm at Auerbach, Pollak & Richardson, Inc., from Richard E. Jennison, her longtime associate, who departed to establish his own money-management organization.

Miss Schulder, who is married to Daniel Blitz, a scientist and inventor, thus became one of the few women in Wall Street history to become the top officer of a brokerage concern. What is more, it took her less than eight years to climb from the bottom to the top of the ladder at her company, helping to reshape it drastically along the way.

Auerbach, Pollak & Richardson is one of a small number of rapidly expanding securities houses that have chosen to concentrate on institutional business by providing high quality investment research. Others in the group include Donaldson, Lufkin & Jenrette and Faulkner, Dawkins & Sullivan.

Before Miss Schulder and Mr. Jennison joined Auerbach in 1961, it was an old-line brokerage house functioning primarily in the role of a specialist on the floor of the New York Stock Exchange. The house did not even have a research department and lacked a single institutional client.

Auerbach's institutional brokerage business has increased at an average rate more than 50 per cent year for the last five years. How it changed so dramatically and became what it is today is in no small sense the story of Miss Schulder. She was always one of those bright students who made the boys in her class jealous and angry. The daughter of a post office clerk, she grew up in Queens,

The New York Times

Peggy Schulder, new president of Auerbach, Pollak & Richardson, Inc., a fast-moving brokerage house.

attended parochial schools there and went to Seton Hill College in Pennsylvania on a scholarship.

She abandoned the scholarship and returned to New York, where she worked by day to put herself through Fordham University by night. She graduated magna cum laude in mathematics from Fordham in 1953 at the age of 20. Ironically, she had already decided that working at jobs related to mathematics did not interest her.

"They were all too isolated from the total picture," she recalled recently. "They were too segmented. I decided mathematics wasn't for me." The securities industry was recommended to her by a placement officer at Fordham.

"I thought about it," she said, "and decided that would be just fine, because it obviously embraced entire concepts. They said Merrill

Lynch was looking for people and so I went to see them, but they weren't really interested in girls in their registered representative training course. They suggested I go into research."

During her eight years at Merrill Lynch, Pierce, Fenner & Smith, Inc., Miss Schulder covered a number of industries, became involved in portfolio management, was the concern's money-market specialist for a while and was head of its office equipment research group when she left to join Auerbach in 1961.

"Dick Jennison went there to start their institutional business and I joined him a few months later," she said. "For a while, we were the entire research department. But as we developed the business, we hired analysts. Their research at first was concentrated in the office-equipment and electronics industries and Auerbach was

among the first to do exhaustive comprehensive reports on such performers as Xerox and Control Data.

Both she and Mr. Jennison became partners in 1964. Later the same year, when the firm was incorporated, Mr. Jennison became its president and Miss Schulder became vice president, a director and a voting stockholder. In 1966 she was named chairman of the executive committee.

Auerbach is an unusual concern today. It has a number of stockholders, but none of the stockholders whose names it bears is alive. "Nobody in our firm is on commission," Miss Schulder said. "Our philosophy is to compensate our people fairly, but to orient them to our clients' welfare."

Institutional investors discuss ideas with Auerbach's analysts, but the analysts do not take the orders. Clients call the concern's order room directly. "We want to make sure our clients are as close to the market as possible," Miss Schulder said.

Auerbach's growth has been so rapid that its office is overflowing the 20th floor at 30 Broad Street. Miss Schulder's own former office is being broken up into three smaller ones and the entire operation will move to new facilities at 1 New York Plaza.

Does being a female in her profession cause any special problems for Miss Schulder? "I don't really even think about it," she said.

Outside the office, her consuming hobby is travel. She and her husband, who is an executive with Sanders Associates, have covered a good portion of the world in their wanderings. Their plans often are made on the spur of the moment.

Occasionally, they will fly to a foreign country, rent a car and drive through the countryside for days at a time, living out of a lone suitcase, eating strictly at nontourist restaurants and staying wherever they can find accommodations at sunset.

They rarely map out a complicated itinerary in advance. On a recent trip to India, they decided three days before they left that the weather in Japan would be better than in the Middle East during the early part of their voyage. So they went around the world in the opposite direction from the one they had

TERRY ROBARDS

2. Peggy Schulder, the new president of Auerbach, Pollak & Richardson Inc., a fast-moving brokerage house. (From "Woman, 36, at Top in Brokerage House," *New York Times*, March 23, 1969)

—like Peggy Schulder—worked full-time while going to business school at night.

All of the first generation of women—regardless of their class or educational background—forged career paths on Wall Street during a decade that underwent enormous social and economic change. Indeed, feminists in the seventies did not just focus their energies on supporting women entering the workplace. They also began to address women's reproductive rights. Notably, in 1971, just at the moment in which many first-generation women were entering finance, two young feminist attorneys brought a constitutional challenge to the Texas criminal abortion law in the case of *Roe v. Wade* (McBride Stetson 2001b: 251). In the wake of the case, various abortion reform groups and women's movement organizations, such as NOW, came together to form what would become the pro-choice movement (253). And the defenders of the law to keep abortion a crime, including Americans United for Life, created what would become the pro-life movement.

On January 22, 1973, the Supreme Court overturned the Texas law and established guidelines for the state's regulation of abortion. The debate about the federal funding of abortion did not, however, wane. Instead it grew and began to dominate the public agenda. Interestingly enough, during the early seventies, the abortion issue crossed party lines, which is a stark contrast to the volatile, bipartisan nature of the debate today. There was no clear-cut pattern of support from or opposition from either the Democratic or Republican parties. In the context of this short-lived bipartisan moment, many of the first organizations of the second wave of the women's movement were themselves bipartisan, eschewing affiliation or support for either political party. For example, the first woman's PAC, the Washington-based Women's Campaign Fund (the WCF), was established in this bipartisan context in 1974. It supported pro-choice female candidates running for office.[21]

During the seventies the WCF was composed of female activists and was supported by a number of key political women and men. None of the first generation of women on Wall Street became publicly active in the organization or the debate over abortion. The women could not risk being viewed as radical feminist activists in the masculine environment of Wall Street—regardless of their personal experiences or feelings about abortion. Moreover, they were too busy and focused on making their way into the male-dominated world of finance, a world that was being rapidly transformed. However, the women's interest in participating in the abortion rights movement would change over time.

In addition to dramatic social change, the seventies saw the inauguration of the radical restructuring of the United States and world economy; the deindustrialization of the United States and the rise of the service sector; and the ideological shift to neoliberalism (Eisenstein 2009: 23).[22] The seventies were a crucial decade, when some of the calls for national as well as international deregulation, in the making since the sixties, took hold. By the early seventies, conditions supporting the 1945 Bretton Woods agreement—the international set of institutions and rules for global trade—were falling apart. The United States led the trend toward deregulation when President Nixon suspended convertibility of the dollar into gold (Fraser 2005: 532). The fracturing of the link between currencies and gold, the basis of the international monetary system, led to the disintegration of the fixed exchange system in 1973. The structure of Wall Street at large and work practices in finance were also in flux. By the early seventies, the New York Stock Exchange (NYSE) was losing business to the other exchanges because of its high charges for executing orders. Commission rates were high and fixed. During this period, New York City's position as a major center for financial intermediation was weakened. The United States was in the beginning of a recession. The "go-go" years were over (Fraser 2005: 535).

On May 1, 1975, the SEC finally abolished the rules fixing the commissions charged by stockbrokers to allow institutions to compete more intensely with one another. The effects were dramatic and far-reaching. Commission rates soon dropped to between 40 percent and 50 percent of their earlier fixed-rate levels. The new business environment placed considerable strain on firms, especially the research boutiques that traditionally provided analysis freely to banks in return for commissions on their business. Some were liquidated, while larger institutions acquired others. At the same time, however, research, the area that most women occupied (a cheap source of labor in a bear market), became increasingly important to business operations in the organizations that survived. In a competitive atmosphere, firm-research capacities grew as banks diversified into national and international business areas. The arts of financial forecasting were also on the rise.

Although men still held the highest positions on Wall Street, women nevertheless were the unexpected beneficiaries of the fallout from increased deregulation and the ensuing globalization of the economy.

Feminism in the Sixties and Seventies and Social Objectives: Two Biographies

Deirdre Parliament became one of the first women to break several glass ceilings in the area of research. An only child, she was born in October 1947 in a suburb in Westchester County, New York. Her father worked as a manufacturing salesman. Her mother worked as a clerk in a doctor's office, until she left the workforce in order to take care of Deirdre full-time. Both parents raised Deirdre to have high aspirations. Deirdre attended one of the Seven Sisters. She graduated in 1968—the year of student riots on college campuses, civil rights protests in the south, and protests against the exploitation of women by the Miss America Pageant led by feminist activists. But Deirdre did not actively participate in any of the movements: "At college women's issues were in the air, civil rights issues, antiwar issues. I mean that was the period of time that I was in college. I thought the women's movement was a big deal. But I was not terribly active in any real organizations. I did not go to consciousness-raising sessions. But I had a real sense of women working. I thought it was an important thing—that women should be able to work, and should not just be hired hands" (2008).

In the fall of 1968 Deirdre became one of a handful of women to attend an Ivy League business school in the northeast. She had read an article in a magazine that said that 90 percent of women held clerical jobs. Deirdre had no intentions of becoming a secretary in an office: "I concluded that one way to avoid a secretarial job was to go to business school so that when I graduated I could get a good job. And this was the end of the sixties. I had this philosophy that business was at the heart of social change, and that somehow if more people with the right liberal ideas would be part of corporate structures that the world would somehow become a better place. I figured that I would be a force for social change—by going into business" (1994).

"Fascinated by NYC," she moved to Manhattan after graduation from business school in 1970. But landing a good job on the executive track in the corporate world as a woman was not so easy. Male managers at consulting firms were simply not interested in hiring women.

They believed it was inappropriate for women to travel with men on business trips. Moreover, very few firms were hiring at all, as the city was in the midst of a deep financial recession. After six months of trying to find employment in the private sector, Deirdre had not received a single offer: "In the meantime a female friend of mine at business school and I had done our master's thesis together on low-cost housing. I still had these social objectives in mind. One of our professors had said that we should look into mobile homes. So we decided to start a mobile home park. We spent six months looking at properties, trying to get zoning changes. Nothing came of our hard work. I finally decided that I probably should get a job—that starting a mobile home park was not a great career path." It was the fall of 1971. Again Deirdre turned to her classmates from business school for advice on finding a professional position. A female classmate, who by that time was working at a brokerage firm on Wall Street, introduced Deirdre to one of her male colleagues. Deirdre was instantly hired as a security analyst in the area of research. She remained in research, working her way up during her entire career, until leaving Wall Street some thirty-plus years later.

Patricia Riley, another pioneer in the area of research and a good friend of Deirdre Parliament in the seventies, was born in New Haven, Connecticut, in 1951. She was the eighth child of Irish American parents. Her father and stay-at-home mother believed in sending their six sons off to Ivy League colleges to prepare them for big careers. They sent their two daughters to a local, all-girls Catholic college to get teaching certificates, in case, as Patricia explains, they needed to support themselves: "If some tragedy occurred—like your husband dying —and, God forbid, you might have to go to work. You could always fall back on your teaching certificate" (1994).

Patricia was one of four women in a class of three hundred to major in economics. She loved the subject. By the time she graduated college in 1971, Patricia knew she wanted to work. Her career aspirations were, however, vague:

> I knew so little about the working world. My father worked in an insurance company as everybody did in the area. After I graduated, he arranged some interviews for me. I kept thinking about those horrible, boring insurance companies. I thought I would shoot myself if I had to get up every day and do that. It was then that I quickly

decided I would come to Manhattan, the day after I graduated—at least there would be something more exciting in the city. But my aspirations were so ill-defined. I think they were probably limited to old Bette Davis movies—where Bette Davis has a job as an editor of a magazine. (1994)

Like Deirdre, Patricia did not actively participate in the women's movement. But she was very much aware of its existence:

I was heavily influenced by the women's movement. It was in its birthing stage at the point in which we were in college. I was aware of the movement. We were watching it with interest. *Ms.* magazine started around 1970 or 1971. We were all reading the magazine. It was very inspirational. I also read *The Feminine Mystique* when I was in college. That book had a huge influence on me. I read it and I thought, yes, Friedan's right—those women are throwing their lives away. I am never going to live in a suburb, have babies and do nothing! (1994)

Patricia found her first job on Wall Street through an ad in the *New York Times,* and she was hired as a research associate securities analyst at a brokerage firm in midtown Manhattan. The director of research bragged that he was the only one in the company who hired women because he could "get the talent cheaper." He paid Patricia less than a secretary was compensated, but Patricia was grateful for the professional opportunity.

Patricia entered the business with only a college degree, and no training program would admit a woman. So she acquired analytic skills on the job: "I worked with a senior analyst. I got stuck working with the utilities analyst, a consumer product man. It was the pre-computer age. Before they even had calculators you were using adding machines. You had to do all these spreadsheets by hand. It was really boring. But what you did learn was the relationship among numbers, value, and what made for a good stock" (1994). Patricia stayed at the firm—learning how to read spreadsheets by hand and how to handle visits with clients—for the next five years. At her boss's suggestion, she also attended NYU's business school at night. There she met several women who would become lifelong friends. One of them, Mindy Plane, was working in the investment department of a commercial bank. Also in her early twenties, Mindy encouraged Patricia to join the Financial Women's Association (FWA) of New York City, where she was already a member. The association was originally created by a group of eight female security analysts barred from joining men's professional groups in finance in 1956 (Fisher 2004). By the mid-seventies, it was composed of more than a hundred women on Wall Street: bankers, stockbrokers, traders, economists, and financial analysts (Fisher 2010). The primary goal of the FWA, from its inception, was occupational mobility, ensuring that women move up the corporate ranks on Wall Street. FWA women viewed the network as an elite, female, financially focused entity defined by business principles, rather than as a pro-feminist organization oriented toward fighting gendered discrimination and sexual harassment in the workplace (Fisher 2006: 211). They wanted to find success in the corporate workplace based on their merit, and only their merit. Lenore Diamond, another member of the FWA during the seventies, characterized the organization as "cautious" in its pursuit of its goals.

Patricia, Deirdre, Mindy, and their female peers on Wall Street came of age as young adults at the same time the feminist movement began to gather significant force in the late sixties and seventies. Like most of the other members of the first generation, they did not get directly involved in the women's movement. They were, as Sherry Ortner suggests in writing about her female high school classmate graduates of 1958, part of the "Friedanesque vanguard—discontented, restless, pushing on doors without knowing what was on the other side" (2003: 259).[23] While the women themselves did not practice feminism, the ideas of feminism—that women deserved to work—resonated with their own ambitions.

The association at that point in time was composed primarily of middle-class women who had graduated from smaller women's colleges and had attended NYU's business school at night while working full-time during the day. However, some of its members, like Deirdre, who joined the organization in 1972, were from more upper-middle-class backgrounds. Some of the women who attended NYU at night walked home together—to the Upper East Side—during the good weather. They talked about their dreams of becoming vice presidents in their firms in ten years' time or less, on their own merit.

Like Muriel Siebert, the women did not for the most part perceive themselves as feminists but rather as professional women pursuing careers in finance—a perception further solidified by their participation in the FWA. While the women and the FWA did not outwardly support the fight for equality, they benefited by the Friedanesque feminist activists' fight for the elimination of gender discrimination in the workplace. Indeed, the push by both feminist and civil rights leaders to create laws ensuring gender and racial equality in the workplace would help further open the doors of Wall Street to women like Patricia, Deirdre, and Mindy (Laird 2006).

Feminism, the FWA, and the 1973 Suit against Merrill Lynch

At the same time that Patricia, Deirdre, and other first-generation women were trying to build rungs on the lower ends of corporate ladders in finance, the EEOC's affirmative action programs and suits on behalf of women against corporate America and Wall Street came to a head. Notably, although the EEOC had brought numerous claims of racial bias to court in the sixties, the Justice Department did not prosecute a single case of discrimination against women until 1970 (Kessler-Harris 2001: 277). By 1970, the EEOC had received more discrimination complaints against AT&T, then the nation's largest private employer, than against any other firm. In December 1970, the EEOC, along with the Federal Communications Commission (FCC), charged AT&T with a host of violations, including violations of the Equal Pay Act of 1963, the Civil Rights Act of 1964, various executive orders, state laws and city ordinances, and even the U.S. Constitution (Laird 2006: 253). A few years later, organizations including NOW and the American Civil Liberties Union filed statements in support of charges concerning discrimination on Wall Street. Among the most egregious charges were that, "as of May 1973, nearly 97 percent of Merrill Lynch's 5,197 account executives were white males while 125 were females, 31 were Spanish-surnamed Americans, and 11 were blacks. Moreover, as of March 1974, 85% of all blacks, 85% of all women, and 78% percent of all Spanish-surnamed employees were assigned to office clerical jobs."[24] Merrill Lynch vehemently denounced all of the charges, maintaining that its employment practices were "fair." It went even further in calling itself "an innovator among securities companies in seeking minority group members and women for career opportunities."[25] Nevertheless, the firm finally settled for a modest amount and agreed to do what the commission required: improve its diversity (Benn 2000: 170).

In addition, the EEOC intervened on behalf of Helen O'Bannon, an unsuccessful applicant for a position with Merrill Lynch as an account executive. O'Bannon sued the brokerage firm on the ground that it had discriminated against her on the basis of her sex.[26] Specifically, she sued the company over the entrance exam for its broker-trainee program in 1972. Merrill's entrance exams asked questions like, "When you meet a woman, what interests you most about her?" Not only did such a question assume that the candidate was a heterosexual man, the answers added insult to injury: here the correct answer was her beauty; the fewest points were given to those who answered her intelligence (Roth 2006: 3).

Wall Street firms were now on notice. Soon after the suit, men on Wall Street—some well-intentioned, others deathly scared of being sued—began to actively recruit women and minorities. Finding minorities and women, however, proved to be a challenge, because of other levels of institutional discrimination. In the nineties, John Whitehead from Goldman Sachs recalled the initial situation facing firms: "We recruited professionals largely out of graduate schools, and there were very, very few women who went to graduate business schools. That was a handicap for us. My class at Harvard Business School, class of 1947—a hundred people in the class— . . . there weren't any women" (cited in Benn 2000: 171–72).

Instead of going to business school, most women coming right out of college tended to choose other industries over Wall Street. Anne Prescott, for example, graduated from Smith College in 1968. She came from a well-known banking family in Manhattan. Her father was the chief economist from the fifties through the eighties at a major blue-blood commercial bank. Anne loved to visit him at work once a year. He would take her to lunch in the fancy executive dining room, which Anne always found very exciting. But, when it came down to choosing her own career path she had no interest in tackling Wall Street. "I went into the glamour thing which was publishing. Time Inc. was hearing the footsteps of the law and decided to allow women to have trials as writers. This was all happening very slowly, but I loved the reporter / research job. That was a fabulous job! For my good work I was awarded a trip with my boss to watch one of the Apollo liftoffs!" Even after women starting going for MBAs, said Whitehead, "We tried to hire them but we were handicapped by the fact that women who graduated from business schools tended . . . they went to work for Macy's, they went to work for consumer product companies, not Wall Street because Wall Street had a reputation of being prejudiced against women." Men on Wall Street thus encountered some difficulty in finding women to hire in the early seventies. They could not easily find them in Ivy business schools. They could not necessarily start drawing them in from other "more glamorous" female industries. Compelled then to find professional women on Wall Street, the men (and a few women) turned their attention to the one space in which they could find more than one or two women in finance in New York City—the FWA.

Inclusion and the Ebb of Discrimination: The End of the Seventies

In 1976, Patricia was informed by a woman in the human resources department of her firm that she was vastly underpaid. Determined to change the situation, Patricia confronted the director of research. The director refused to give her a raise because, as he explained to Patricia, her MBA was from New York University. She did not have an Ivy League MBA. Fortunately this was around the same time an executive in the research department of a major brokerage firm in the wake of the 1973 suit had been given a mandate to hire a woman. According to Patricia, "A woman working at this brokerage firm, a woman I knew through the Financial Women's Association, gave the executive my name. I went down and interviewed with him. He asked to see my reports. He offered me the job—and doubled my salary! . . . I went to work at the brokerage firm. It was the first time I had ever worked in a place in which I felt a man respected me. I finally did not feel I was being discriminated against" (1994). Patricia remained working happily at the firm for several years. She felt included—a member of the team. She was finally being appropriately financially rewarded for her hard work. She was even the first professional woman at the firm to have a baby.

Then, as Patricia explains, she made a mistake. A small managing firm offered to make her a partner, so she took a position with them. But the promise never materialized. Patricia did not like any of her colleagues. By 1980 she was desperate to get out of an increasingly difficult work situation. And, in the meantime, she found herself pregnant with her second child. In her search for a way out, she called Deirdre: "I called Deirdre Parliament, who was working in the research department of another firm. Now Deirdre was one of the women on Wall Street who had been very successful. I had just met her through the Financial Women's Association. It wasn't that she was a great buddy, but I felt that I could call her up." Deirdre asked Patricia to meet for lunch. The two women got along famously. Deirdre herself had had a young child while working at her firm. She explained to Patricia how she had managed to limit her own travel for the job until her son turned five and went to kindergarten. Within a month Patricia accepted a job at Deirdre's firm, where Deirdre helped make sure that Patricia was given maternity leave. Patricia took a few weeks off and was soon back working full-time. She was thrilled that she had found a way to successfully combine career and family. Only later on in her career would she wonder what would have been had she had the "freedom" to travel and take on international positions. In the meantime, she concentrated on moving up the corporate ladder while hiring a live-in nanny to take care of her two children.

Patricia and Deirdre, with other members of the first cohort of women to enter Wall Street in the early seventies, were the first professional women to deal with what the sociologist Mary Blair-Loy, in her study of work-family balance among female financial executives in mid-nineties Chicago, calls "competing devotions": dealing with the fundamental contradiction between two traditionally gendered schemas in American life, which are the complete devotion to work and the total devotion to family (2003). FWA friendships provided a space for the women to mediate ideas about gender, the meaning of being a professional, and, in Patricia's case, how to be a pioneering professional-managerial class mother. She and other members started a professional working mothers' group in the FWA, where women developed a discourse of professional motherhood. They typically invited speakers who talked (for free) about a range of topics including "stress in the dual-career marriage" (Lubin 1987: 9). The women also advised each other on hiring housekeepers and nannies.

Patricia and Deirdre—individually and together—were the first professional females in financial firms to have babies, take maternity leaves, and return to the workplace soon thereafter. Working within the existing gendered employment system on Wall Street, they drew on and revised existent maternity practices for clerical women. They tweaked the accepted travel schedule a bit within research in order to enable Patricia to travel less in her children's early years, and then to travel more as they grew up and attended school. In doing so, these women helped pave the way for Patricia to perform being a professional mother. They acted as agents, albeit constrained by the existent structure and culture of high finance. This is not to suggest that the two women themselves were wholly responsible—as individual subjects—for bringing these practices into the work arena. Their performances were possible because certain other conditions were in place in financial firms. Notably, there were already women working on Wall Street, albeit not for the most part in professional capacities, but in administrative and clerical ones. Maternity leaves as such existed for this population of women; they were not yet set up for executive women.

The women were not "gender radicals in the sense that they questioned or broke gender rules" in the workplace (Ortner 1996: 184). They were rather "tempered radicals" (Meyerson and Tompkins 2007). As individual and collective actors, they helped create small, potentially incremental change to Wall Street's orientation toward maternity leave and creating jobs that provided some kind of work-family balance. They had internalized the dominant ideologies of the corporate workplace—the devotion to work. But given their exposure to the feminist movement and their own determination to succeed at both work and family, they were also able to imagine an alternative workplace that allowed for the integration of work-family life. Although financial firms were aware of and concerned about being sued for discrimination, an entire tableau of formal work-family policymaking for professionals remained unimagined at the systemic level.

The women's friendship and connection through the FWA introduced elements of support and play into the gender system on Wall Street, allowing the women to be more assertive about their needs with both their female and male peers (Ortner 1996; Marcus 2007). Already by the late seventies the women recognized the importance of female friendship, support, and networking. This shift would later be fundamental to their participation in women's political networks in the eighties and nineties, as well as their subsequent association with female transnational networks engaged in bringing about change and gender equity to corporations worldwide in the twenty-first century. In the meantime, the women firmly believed in the culture of meritocracy on Wall Street—that with the proper determination and talent they would succeed.

Wall Street Women's Networks: Finance, Feminism, and Politics during the Eighties

The FWA was built around their members' shared identity as *women* in finance. The women not only wanted to unite on the basis of who they were as women, but they also wanted to assert a certain social status and to insist on the particularity of their industry. Historically, they did not add issues of race, class, or ethnicity into the mix; their self-definition was thus extremely narrow. Indeed, prior to the nineties, the women in the organization tended to publicly portray themselves as members of a female financial elite, rather than as feminists per se (Fisher 2010). But, as women they could not have entered the work-force without the liberal feminist movement's insistence on the open-ing up of formally male professions, such as law, medicine, and man-agement. Indeed, as professional-class women, they incorporated mainstream feminism's strategy for assimilation. As a result, during the seventies and eighties, they primarily focused their energies on "making it" in the business world (Ehrenreich 1989: 216). However, the tradition-ally more radical agendas of the movement—revolution, overthrowing the corporate order, supporting women's reproductive rights, as well as improving the plight of poor, African American women and, indeed, women in poverty throughout the world—proved far more problematic for financial women and their networks to incorporate into their iden-tity and mission—at least until the nineties and 2000s (Fisher 2006, 2010).

The first generation of women on Wall Street traditionally preferred to be faced with the challenges of individual achievement and growth, rather than with publicly participating in or actually forging a social movement. The women's uneasy relationship to the more radical dimensions of feminism influenced the politics of financial women's networks. The history of the FWA can be understood as a series of identity reformation and political alliance making. Notably, FWA lead-ers in the eighties—members of the first generation of Wall Street women—attempted to strategically incorporate parts of the women's movement into their organizational mission without taking a public stance on their point of view.[27]

Patricia, Mindy, and other female financiers attended the first FWA board meeting of the 1981–82 calendar year. It started off with debates over the public and private relationship of the organization to wom-en's politics. Officially, the association took the standpoint that the FWA was a professional, not a political or feminist, group. Dealing with women's issues, however, became increasingly complicated in the wake of the feminist movement including the growth of women's organizations, as well as antidiscrimination suits on Wall Street in the seventies and eighties. During the meeting on September 2, 1981, FWA women confronted decisions regarding their public support for the Equal Rights Amendment (ERA): "[Mindy Shapiro] relayed to the board the fact that [Linda Brown] from [a city organization for business and professional women] had contacted her to ask if the FWA would help to sponsor a November march on Washington in support of the ERA. A brief discussion ensued during which it was pointed out that in 1978 the Board decided not to take a stand on the issue. It was concluded that this activity was too political and had the potential of a disastrous outcome" (FWA board minutes, September 2, 1981: 1, 3).

The women's talk about the FWA's relationship to the ERA reveals their anxieties about deciding which facets of their multiple identities they were going to continue to build their network around. Having initially chosen to construct it around women, they were then pulled toward the ERA and feminist politics. Yet, by electing not to take a public stance on women's political issues, they attempted to control the ramifications of drawing on "femaleness" as a foundation for solidarity. Making sense of their decision requires examining the conservative national and political forces of the eighties that were shaping Wall Street women. The anthropologist Elizabeth Traube, in her book *Dreaming Identities: Class, Gender, and Generation in 1980s Hollywood Movies*, wrote that, during this era, "Hollywood joined New Right leaders in directing socially rooted discontents against independently upwardly mobile women. Movies, as well as political discourse, attacked uncontrolled, ambitious women in the cause of a moral crisis that, given its definition, called for a stronger authoritarian patriarchy" (1992: 20).

The FWA board engaged in a kind of balancing act. It had to deal with a small but growing membership constituency in favor of pushing a more feminist agenda. Therefore, the board members had to mediate between this group of their female members, and the corporations that helped fund the organization through donations—and might not want their institutions to be too tightly connected with the women's movement. The FWA board "solved" the problem of becoming publicly aligned with women's politics and issues by creating indirect and less overt ways to lend support. In the end, they decided to publicize the ERA march in the newsletter, but they made it clear that the city organization for business and professional women, not the FWA, was the sponsor.

Hiding behind the political cloaks of other women's organizations became a common FWA strategy. The FWA thus found it useful to link with other women's groups engaged in doing the work of the women's movement, work that the FWA, at least openly, could not support. This was especially true of the FWA's early relationship with other national associations of professional women. In October 1981, several other FWA board members participated in a National Women's Executive meeting. They reported to the FWA board in November that the national group "is still substantially less sophisticated and professional than the FWA. Therefore the FWA is placed in the position of sharing its resources with them without the likelihood, at this point, of receiving reciprocal benefits of equal value" (FWA board minutes, November 4, 1981: 2). Notably, they did not suggest that the FWA withdraw its support for or involvement with the group. Rather, they concluded that the network's "potential does seem to be in the area of Washington representation and of being able to take a political stance on certain issues on the national level and thereby reduce the pressure the FWA experiences to take political positions on the local level" (2).

The women's frustration regarding the lack of power, leadership, and resources in other executive women's networks in the nation had some serious consequences for their alliance-building strategies with other women's groups. They used their affiliations with women's national networks to avoid publicly taking political stances on women's issues such as the ERA. This decision (to formally act as a "depoliticized" organization) upset some members of the first generation who by the mid-eighties were beginning to focus their energies on women's issues more broadly, were proponents of the ERA, and in some cases, were considering actually running for political office. Specifically, some women like Mindy Plane found themselves becoming interested in participating in women's political roles, organizations, and activities. Indeed, the FWA was aware of the shift in senior women's career ambitions in moving away from the world of Wall Street toward politics. In a discussion about "politics and government" in 1984, FWA board members noted the following: "Our more senior members are interested in courting government appointments. A criticism leveled against some of these individuals is that a few have 'Potomac Fever.' Most senior members are inactive, although they are responsive when they are asked for help. Our more senior members have learned to use the FWA for their own purposes, which in some cases can be political. The FWA generally gains from this 'use'" (FWA board minutes, 1984).

*Professional Organizations Doing the Work of the Feminist
Movement: The WCF and State Feminism*

From the election of Ronald Reagan in 1980 to the defeat of George
H. W. Bush in 1992, the world of American politics was openly hostile
to female politicians and public policy claims made on behalf of wom-
en's issues. Nevertheless, outside the world of finance an active network of women's political and policy organizations had grown—many
of which were headquartered in Washington, D.C. (Spalter-Roth and
Schreiber 1995: 105). The expansion also included a growing national
network of politically active women who were focused on fund-raising
for female candidates.[28] Women's political groups now ranged from
the partisan fund-raisers EMILY's List (Democratic) and WISH List
(Republican) to bipartisan organizations such as the Women's Campaign Fund, which supported female candidates in favor of a woman's
right to abortion.

During the eighties these women's political groups did some of the
work of the women's movement (Ferree and Martin 1995: 4). They
brought traditionally radical feminist ideas (outsider issues, such as
women's reproductive rights) into the established political system.
They recast feminist ideas about women into a more palpable discourse. Notably, in the absence of formal national state-run women's
agencies such as those that exist in Europe, a large number of American feminist-oriented organizations—including women's political
groups—worked for changes in the laws and lives of women in the
United States (ibid.). In turn, the United States government (sometimes) responded to demands from the women's movements for policies to achieve gender equity in the status of women (McBride Stetson 2001b: 247). And when pro-choice women, for example, were
successfully elected into office, they themselves worked to uphold
women's reproductive rights from directly within the state.

In this context, women's political organizations such as the WCF,
and in turn elected female government officials, engaged in what
feminist scholars have come to refer to as "state feminism"—the advocacy of the women's movement from inside the state (Outshoorn
and Kantola 2007: 2).[29] In the United States part of the "work" of
advocating the women's movement entailed raising funds from various constituents to support women running in local, state, and national elections. In 1974, the first year of the WCF's operation, the fund
contributed $30,000 to twenty-eight pro-choice candidates. A decade

later, the WCF's goal was to donate $500,000 to more than sixty candidates.[30] In a 1984 article in the *New York Times*, Stephanie Solien, the then director of the WCF, described the group in the following manner: "We're venture capitalists. We invest in women."[31]

Capitalism and the monetary investment in women thus appeared, from Solien's point of view, to go easily hand in hand. The challenge for the WCF was which women to invest in and support. By 1984, the thirty-member board was composed of women from a range of professions and political affiliations. During the eighties the board had "established a litmus test that requires all candidates who want help to endorse the equal rights amendment and to support the right to choose abortion."[32] The result was that even if a woman candidate supported women's rights in other areas, the fund would not support her if she herself was not an active proponent of the ERA and the right to abortion.

The WCF's stringent criteria for candidates produced a certain amount of tension within the organization, particularly for the board, and for some female politicians who felt wrongly slighted when the organization did not offer them support. Congresswoman Mary Rose Oaker, for example, did not receive funds because she voted against using federal funds to finance abortions. "My philosophy is Catholic—I won't deny I was raised to be pro-life," Oaker explained in the 1984 *New York Times* article. "But I consider myself to be a leader on feminist issues, and it's really a shame this has separated women." Oaker, who had led the fight to equalize pay and credit for women, felt strongly that these kinds of issues were more important than a woman's right to abortion. "Economic issues are liberating issues for women," she said. "If they have money they can have all the options they want." Solien, as director of the WCF, disagreed. The ERA and the freedom to choose abortion, she argued, "are the very crucial, bottom line rights that are essential for a woman's independence."[33]

Debates about the degree and meaning of bipartisanship also arose within the ranks of the WCF. The WCF, for example, supported several Republican women who were in favor of abortion but who were also proponents of President Reagan's budget cuts. Some Democratic WCF members felt that Reagan's budget cuts discriminated against and hurt women. Beyond this, some conservative Republican women were not even interested in being a part of the WCF. They felt that although the WCF was technically bipartisan that most of the women were really quite liberal.[34] Indeed, by the late eighties the WCF sought the participation and support of Wall Street women, in part to strengthen its Republican membership.

In spite of the tensions within the ranks of the organization, the WCF became an increasingly powerful player within the world of women and politics. Indeed, during the eighties, the fund was one of about twenty political action committees (PACs) in the United States whose primary goal was the election of women to public office. These PACs, most of which had been created within a five- to ten-year period, brought an entirely new dimension to political fund-raising for women.[35] For example, when Ann Richards considered a late entry into the Texas race for state treasurer in 1982, she was concerned about raising enough money to support her campaign. Her base at the time, composed predominantly of women, came through. Within forty-eight hours of her considering entering the campaign, her backers had pledged $300,000. Richards went on to enter the race and win.[36]

During the eighties women (predominantly white, middle-class, and upper-middle-class women) were trying to make it in a range of male-dominated domains including finance and politics. For the most part, each group pursued its struggle individually rather than collectively. The FWA sometimes invited local female politicians to speak to the group. It also began to organize group expeditions and visits to Washington, D.C. Wall Street women were becoming more familiar with the government and female politicians. But as a group, they did not create major alliances with women in the political world.

Professional Mobility on Wall Street Instead of Potomac Fever

Some individual FWA women (mainly first-generation Wall Streeters) began to try to move in a more overtly political direction and to use their affiliation with the FWA as a stepping stone to more traditionally elite organizations (such as the Economic Club of NY). Here, they were able to begin to make links with more traditionally urban, elite actors (mainly men). By contrast, the FWA as an organization chose to focus on making international rather than national connections in order to cement its identification as a group of financial professionals, and to link with other financial women (as opposed to political women) and to bypass dealing with feminist and women's issues at home. In 1978, only six years after President Nixon's historic trip to China, a group of FWA women made their own pioneering trip to China to meet with men and women and learn about potential busi-

3. In 1978 a group of women from the FWA traveled to China to meet with men and women to learn about potential business opportunities. (Photo by Carole Lewis Anderson)

ness opportunities. They were also, according to Karen Tinsely who went on the trip, particularly interested in seeing the ways women "were treated under socialism—if they were equal to men." Carole Anderson, another FWA member who made the trip, made sure to bring her camera. Her slides showed that the women not only visited tourist sites such as the Great Wall of China, but also conducted business meetings throughout their visit (see figure 3).

During a board meeting (in 1981) the organization continued to choose not to pursue national links, and the greater value of international networking became a major source of interest. Kathy Hamilton, an FWA board member, drew the board's attention to its "sister organization," the Hong-Kong FWA, an alliance of the FWA composed of one hundred members, many of whom held financial positions and were associated with the FWA of New York City. She "suggested that the existence of such an organization provides the potential for an international scope which may prove a more fertile direction than the national organization efforts of the National Women's Executive Group" (FWA board minutes, November 4, 1981). The board immediately pursued a tighter bond with the Hong Kong FWA. By the following month, President Hoffman invited Laurie Butler, of Banker's Trust Hong Kong and the founder of the sister FWA organization, to meet the New York board. After the board meeting, the women went to dinner where the "whole issue of national and international affiliation would be explored" (FWA board minutes, December 2, 1981).

During the eighties, the FWA continued to privilege international networking over national alliance building. It also maintained its strategy of linking with women who shared its financial identity. About thirty New York City women traveled to visit the (women's) financial community in London in 1985. The focus of the trip to London, according to the FWA's Government Committee, was "the financial community in London's privatization movement of business, from state to private business." The excursion, according to the FWA's London Symposium Schedule, was packed with activities: a management seminar, a panel on the Euro-market, a tour of the Stock Exchange, a reception hosted by the *Economist*, and even a meeting with Margaret Thatcher.

The FWA's reception in London received considerable press both in the United States as well as in England. In a London *Sunday Times* article, entitled "The Need to Network," the journalist Maggie Drummond reported on her experience "trot[ting] round with the transatlantic high-flyers for a day." Drummond interviewed a number of FWA women for the piece, one of whom explained that "New York is the tip of the financial world and the women you are seeing are at the top of that tip." Barbara Thomas, an American, who was the first woman on the main board of a British merchant bank, explained that women's networking practices in the City of London were "at least five and possibly ten years behind New York." Drummond elaborated upon the differences:

> Barbara Thomas is all for the networking principle—which doesn't seem to have been embraced as enthusiastically over here as it has in America. The City of London does, it is true, have at least two women's network groups—but much smaller and less organized than New York's FWA. British women seem to be more defensive about networking—possibly because men immediately pounce on it crying "sexist." The FWA members, on the other hand, have absolutely no problems squaring this concept with their demands for increasing power and status in the financial world.[37]

The FWA board of the mid- to late eighties continued to promote its association in an international and increasingly global direction. In 1986, the FWA sent an "Overseas Delegation to Tokyo, Peking and Hong-Kong" "to gain an Asian perspective" on the economy and "to increase awareness in the U.S. and Asia of the FWA, its leadership impact, and influence on the financial and business community."[38] Judith Green, who went on the Asian trip, explained to me that the men they encountered found the women to be curiosities. They were "surprised" that the women actually wanted "to learn about" various countries and their "business and financial matters."

The FWA members returned to London in February 1987 for a second symposium, which focused on "deregulation and internationalization of financial markets," with a "Big Ben reception."[39] In 1989, the FWA presented an evening seminar sponsored by Citibank, which took place at the Citicorp Institute for Global Finance. The flyer for the event, entitled "Group of Thirty, Recommendations, and Impact," depicted a map of the world with the FWA of New York City's banner emblazoned across the continents, and it posed three questions: "What is the group of thirty? What impact will it have on my company?" and lastly, "What does globalization mean here in New York?"

The Group of Thirty, established in 1978, is a private, nonprofit, international body composed of very senior representatives of the private and public sectors and academia, which focuses on deepening understanding of international economic and financial issues (according to the Group of Thirty's website). At the time of the 1989 meeting, the Group of Thirty Steering Committee, chaired by the then chairman of Citicorp, John Reed, had studied the issues raised by cross-border investment activity and had provided recommendations. Thus, during the eighties the FWA increasingly provided its members with sporadic but important access to the most powerful and senior men in the emerging global world of finance. In effect, the FWA created a space in which the women's network could potentially form links with men's business networks. Indeed, over time, some members of the first generation leveraged these links in order to help themselves gain access to the highest echelons of power in finance. FWA women thus increasingly focused their attention on the globalization of finance and its impact on their city, companies, and selves. Notably, as a group, they did not particularly consider the impact of globalization on women in their own city, country, or abroad—particularly the growing feminization of labor and forms of inequality that were taking place worldwide (Eisenstein 2009).

The Logic of Women's Network Formation: Continuing to Privilege Finance over Feminism and Politics

As markets and firms went global beginning in the eighties, a new global power structure in finance emerged. The FWA women's decision to favor the international responded to the reality that high-status and well-paid jobs in the higher echelons of management were increasingly concentrated in global cities (Sassen 2012). By the eighties and nineties, New York, Tokyo, and London had become central nodes in the new financial economy, strategic sites for the concentration of top-level control and management of spatially dispersed, global market activity. One effect has been that such cities have gained an importance and power relative to nation-states. Flows of capital, people, and information have bound global cities within networks, creating a global city web whose constituent cities and city-actors become "global" through the networks in which they participate.[40] Given that the overarching goal of the FWA was moving women into positions of power in finance, the women's networking decisions were generated and made in relation to the male-dominated geography of global city managerial power. It is therefore no coincidence that the women found themselves frustrated with the lack of power, leadership, and resources available in the national networks of executive women. Indeed, it is not surprising that they turned their entrepreneurial attention toward connecting with women's financial groups in London, Tokyo, Peking, and Hong Kong. The women working in these financial areas were, after all, also participating in the new circuit of transnational financial power embedded in their global cities.

Preferring alliances with financial women in global cities produces a network that separates wealthy transnational female professionals (those in the "group") from underpaid and poor women to whom they have some responsibility in the public sphere of the nation, and, indeed, the world at large. Through this separation, the FWA built a constituency for the global mobility of women in finance. In this light, the organization's initial move to privilege international over national connections provided a way to bypass feminist issues at home that could be divisive among members or place the FWA in a position where it might not benefit as much from networking. The FWA did not, for example, build alliances with other American women's groups that might potentially force the group to deal with problems facing "other" women, such as poverty. Nor did it create links with women's political groups, including, for example, the Women's Campaign Fund. Furthermore the FWA did not establish links with transnational feminist networks—emerging by the mid-eighties—that had overtly feminist (and sometimes anticapitalist) agendas, such as, for example, Development Alternatives with Women for a New Era (DAWN) (Moghadam 2005: 8). Forming any of these kinds of connections might have pulled the association away from focusing on its agenda to push women up the career ladders in finance. As a result, the FWA in the eighties created new arenas of financial all-female sociality that drew on but extended local forms in elite transnational directions and produced global female financial subjects.[41]

CHAPTER 2

CAREERS, NETWORKS, AND MENTORS

Maydelle Brooks is a friend and a member of Patricia Riley's professional female cohort. At the time of our first meeting in 1994, she was a forty-seven-year-old mother of two young girls (ages five and eleven). She was dating a postmodern painter who lived in SoHo, in downtown New York City, but she herself lived on the Upper West Side, where she had a live-in nanny for each child in order to ensure "there was never any breakdown in childcare." Like a number of first-generation women, she had a summer home, in this particular case, in the suburbs of Westchester, New York. When I first met Maydelle, she wore traditional navy blue suits and tasteful gold jewelry. Like Patricia, she also started working as a research analyst during the seventies. But Maydelle had a different family upbringing, educational background, and career pathway.

Maydelle was born in the suburbs of Maryland in 1947 to a cosmopolitan, intellectually oriented family that traveled a great deal throughout the world. School was important to her parents, and they made sure that Maydelle attended private schools her entire life. When it came time to attend a university, Maydelle, like many of her Wall Street peers, considered going to a women's college. She applied to five women's colleges and an elite coed college in the Northeast. According to Maydelle, "I got accepted everywhere. And then I decided that I did not want to go to a women's college. I decided to attend the only coed school I had applied to." Thus, from the start of her higher education career, Maydelle's educational track differed from many of her female peers in finance.

After graduation, Maydelle was interested in pursuing a career in politics. She found her initial position in government because she had attended an elite school with alumnae with deep connections to government. Her early work experiences took place within the highest echelons of the nation's male power structure. The male interconnections between Washington and Wall Street then further paved her way into high finance. Her career track from the very start of her working life followed the pattern of men, rather than of women. Eventually, through one of her male bosses in government, she found a position on Wall Street:

> In the late seventies I ended up going to New York City. I worked within one of the premiere institutional research firms. They asked me—do you want to be a salesman or a research analyst? I looked around the firm. I noticed that there was one other woman and she was an analyst. So I said, "I'll be a salesman." I learned the business on Wall Street in terms of being an institutional equity salesperson. In those days there were only three or four women in institutional equity sales. The client base—most of them institutional investors—had never seen a woman salesperson. (1994)

Research, and to a more limited degree sales, became more feminized beginning in the late seventies and well into the eighties. Both were associated with new, seductive, performative forms of labor, and also with traditional images of nurture and care. When Maydelle decided to go into sales, rather than research, she recognized the impending shift toward more feminized practices in sales. "Being one of the only women salespeople, I thought I had an advantage. I thought it was a great advantage because I think women tend to be more client service and relationship driven, and this was very much a relationship-driven business. I found it was terrific because being a saleswoman was being a bit of an actress—being able to play differently to different clients, being able to send the client's needs and moods" (1994).

During her first years in Manhattan, Maydelle worked by day at sales and attended NYU's business school at night, where she met Patricia Riley, Mindy Plane, and other women who were paving careers on Wall Street. But unlike Patricia, Maydelle did not remain in one area her entire career. Instead, a few years after being hired into her new firm, she continued to make some highly unusual moves. In the early eighties she made a virtually unprecedented switch for a woman at the time—moving from sales into investment banking. She advanced further and further into all-male territory in investment banking, where she became directly involved in making deals to produce capital accumulation for her firm and its clients. And she did so with the help and support of a very senior male mentor.

The Contest over Women's Place

The contest over women's legitimate place on Wall Street and the transformation of gendered relations played out amid the upheaval produced by global capitalism during the eighties and nineties. The lives, problems, and successes are exemplified by two representative members of the first generation of Wall Street women during the latter part of the twentieth century: Patricia Riley, who remained in research; and Maydelle Brooks, who made some highly unusual career moves for a woman during the eighties and nineties. Their life histories illuminate the gendering of the globalization and extensive growth of the financial sectors and shareholder revolution; the increasingly performative nature of financial labor, including the feminization of sales and research jobs; the intensified masculinization of trading and investment banking; and the introduction of gender and racial diversity efforts within financial firms.

During the eighties and nineties the women's individual and collective biographies continued to intersect, converge, and be shaped by their workplaces as well as by their Financial Women's Association (FWA) networking experiences. In the male-dominated structures of power on Wall Street and the female financial space of the FWA, both women constructed new understandings of what it took to be a successful woman on Wall Street. However, Patricia's career path and sense of self, like many other women in research, continued to be predominantly shaped by her relationships with female FWA colleagues as well as with her female and male bosses. She often turned to her women friends in finance (working in other firms) for career support and advice. These women, for example, shared information on how best to deal with difficult male colleagues.

Maydelle's climb up the corporate ladder and subjectivity, by contrast, were much more influenced by her strong relationships with very senior-ranking male mentors. She thus followed the more traditional career paths of executive men and women who advance with the help of a male patron who, for example, showcases his protégé's abilities, cues his mentee to critical political developments, and helps arrange his employee's promotions (Jackall 1988: 61). In this respect, Maydelle's career path via male mentors is similar to other groups of women who broke glass ceilings early on in finance and other industries (Kanter 1977; Epstein 1981; Vianello and Moore 2000, 2004; Schipani et al. 2006, 2009).[1]

The Second Gilded Age:
The Shareholder Revolution and the Emergence of Diversity and Work-Family Policymaking in the Midst of the Bull Market

Just as the first generation of women was on the brink of receiving major promotions, Wall Street again changed significantly (Fraser 2005). Legal changes helped quicken the pace of finance, as did the increasing power of neoliberal ideologies that promoted "free" markets (Harvey 2005; Maurer forthcoming: 3). Globalization, the conversion of nonmarketable assets into marketable ones, and the subsequent introduction of new risk-management technologies to deal with resulting volatility and uncertainty all radically reshaped the institutional landscape of Wall Street (Kaufman 2000). There was, as a result, a huge expansion of employment in the financial-services industry in the United States, as well as in Britain and Japan (Sassen 2012). Firms dramatically expanded their research, trading, and banking departments and capabilities (Geisst 1997). For example, when the financial economist Henry Kaufman began his career in 1962 at Salomon Brothers, he joined a new six-person research department. By the time he left the firm, in 1988, he was managing a research staff of more than 450 employees (Kaufman 2000: 148).

In the context of continued growth and internationalization of the industry, institutions enlarged their managerial structures and initially emphasized leadership and partnership (Eccles and Crane 1988). As markets and firms expanded globally, a new global power structure in finance emerged. High-status and well-paid jobs in the higher echelons of management became increasingly concentrated in global cities such as New York, London, and Tokyo (McDowell 1997; Sassen 2012). This new professional-managerial class was still, however, composed for the most part of men, particularly at the higher echelons, and, in the case of Wall Street, in the male-dominated areas of trading and investment banking (Zaloom 2006; Ho 2009).

Indeed, the last two decades of the twentieth century witnessed the emergence and solidification of a new category of professionals:

"super elites," increasingly transnational workers that included financial managers, advisors, and corporate consultants (Leyshon and
Thrift 1997). These elites were highly mobile, and they embraced
lifestyles and even politics far different from their predecessors (Lind
1995; McDowell 1997). They were more focused on consumption,
with their ubiquitous luxury automobiles, iPhones, and other nifty
electronic goods. And, frequently, they were also highly educated and
often self-made individuals who had worked their way up the corporate and class ladder rather than being born into wealth (Ortner 2003;
Callahan 2010).[2]

As Wall Street grew—in personnel and profits—the world of finance
witnessed higher activity in mergers and acquisitions, also called
"M&A mania" (Ho 2009: 7). For example, J. P. Morgan began to
morph from a commercial bank into a global financial-services firm.
In the wake of massive governmental deregulations of finance, including the late 1990s Gramm-Leach-Bliley Act, which rolled back the
Glass-Steagall Act dividing commercial and investment banks, J. P.
Morgan and Chase Manhattan merged to create J. P. Morgan Chase in
2000 (Ho 2009: 7). These kinds of rearrangements entailed the restructuring of many banks. Thus, by the nineties, the culture and
structure of Wall Street were radically different from how they were in
the seventies, the decade in which the first generation had initially
entered the world of finance.

One of the most important transformations in finance in terms of its
culture was the shareholder revolution: shareholder capitalism is the
doctrine that companies exist exclusively to make money for their
shareholders (Ho 2009). A company will downsize, firing employees
purportedly not a part of the corporation's central purpose, in pursuit
of stock price appreciation and profits. Shareholder capitalism is distinct from an earlier form of stakeholder capitalism after the Second
World War, which held that companies existed for the benefit of their
customers, workers, and communities—not just their investors.[3] However, in this new form of capitalism employees rarely benefit and
sometimes even suffer when the corporation makes a profit (Ho 2009:
3).[4] Indeed, "the delinking of corporate profit from employee compensation has pushed rising numbers of Americans into poverty and
created an increasingly insecure world for the working class, the working poor, and the very poor" (Gusterson and Besteman 2009: 8–9).
Accordingly, only a few shareholders, CEOs, and high-level profes-

sionals actually gain, and they thereby contribute to the ever-widening abyss between the very rich and the rest of American workers.

Other equally important shifts that came along with the Reagan revolution to restructure firms and financial culture were, I argue, the introduction and rise of diversity management, and work-family programs and policies in corporate and financial America (Laird 2006; Dobbin 2009). During the eighties and nineties, more and more women and minorities entered the corporate workplace, increasing legal and cultural pressures on Wall Street companies to implement more formal procedures with respect to gender, diversity, and in-time work-family policymaking. But financial firms were extremely slow to create actual programs and policies designed to bring about equality in the workplace. Wall Street was at least five if not ten years behind the rest of corporate America when it came to managing equal opportunity (Dobbin 2009). In corporate America, "new recruiting and training programs of the 1960s, formal hiring and promotion systems of the seventies, diversity management programs of the 1980s, [and] work life and harassment programs of the 1990s" all became part of the toolkit of human personnel professionals (Dobbin 2009: 10). By contrast, brokerage firms and investment banks did not put recruiting and training programs into place until the seventies, and it was only when Wall Street faced a series of discrimination lawsuits and a round of bad press in the early nineties that consultants began to advise companies to form task forces to study how to expand hiring (Dobbin 2009: 155). According to the sociologist Frank Dobbin in his study of the implementation of equal rights policies and programs in corporations,

> By 1994, only 57 women and 38 minorities could be found among Merrill Lynch's 564 directors. Goldman, Sachs, counted only 7 women and one African-American among its 150 partners. Salomon Brothers had just one black trader. *Business Week*'s "Is Wall Street Finally Starting to Get It?" pointed to diversity task forces as the most promising remedy. Roger Vessey, a "heavy hitter" executive vice president formerly in charge of Merrill's fixed income department and now in charge of a new task force with a $1 million annual budget, reported, "This program has teeth." Morgan Stanley hired a full time diversity consultant, and put its new diversity task force under the charge of William M. Lewis Jr., an African-American managing director in investment banking. (2009: 155)

Wall Street was thus not completely unaware of the growing critique on the part of the public, including shareholders, regarding the lack of diversity in firms (Bose and Lyons 2010). It is therefore hardly a coincidence that firms implemented diversity and work-family policies in the wake of the shareholder revolution. Furthermore, firm announcements of diversity initiatives and work-family human resource policies have been shown to often influence shareholder reaction favorably (Arthur and Cook 2004). Not everybody within a company necessarily took advantage of such policies: this was usually out of fear for their job security and career advancement. But hiring and promoting more women and minorities, as well as implementing work-family policies such as flextime, could conceivably have very positive effects on the everyday lives of workers from the secretarial level on up. Such programs could, for example, provide a way for men as well as women to deal with work and family conflict (Blair-Loy 2003: 195).

The individual and collective career biographies of the first generation of Wall Street women during the nineties thus intersected with the reconstruction of corporate workplace models and managerial policies that promoted the value of a diverse workforce. As the women were promoted to senior levels, some found themselves in the role of putting the ideology of equal rights (associated with their belief in liberal feminism) into actual practices and policy (Dobbin 2009).[5] More often than not, as the token women, they (whether they were interested or not) were asked to participate on specific task forces or committees focused on women, diversity, and work-family issues. The women (and some men) interacted with the human resources department; they were often also the managers who had to implement policies into the everyday workplace and try to make such practices work effectively. And "because Washington never codified fair employment regulations, companies inscribed their own regulations in their human resources manuals" (Dobbin 2009: 5). The women thus contributed to the mainstreaming of gender diversity and work-family practice into financial America at a larger scale and in a more systemic manner than Deirdre Parliament and other individual women had been able to achieve during the seventies.

Gender, Generation, and the Making
of Market-Feminist Subjects

The first generation of Wall Street women entered the world of finance at a different historical moment in the marketplace from the
gilded eighties and nineties of celebrity investors; they thus inhabit a
very specific subjectivity. The women bridged a historical moment
between an era of organizational loyalty and the expectations of building a career within a single firm, and an era of enormous job mobility
and downsizing. Their careers straddled a period between the introduction of affirmative action into the American imagination in the
seventies, and the shift toward a focus on diversity management by
the eighties (Squires n.d.: 2–3; Dobbin 2009). The particular set of
women I followed had their share of concerns about whether they
were being promoted quickly enough, and they worried that men were
being hired over them and at a faster pace. However, they were more
often than not the "exceptions"—the "high flyers," the "token" women
on Wall Street—who, in the wake of public and shareholder pressure,
Wall Street sought to symbolically and materially showcase. Their
particular market subjectivity was, in part, I argue, shaped initially by
the much more conservative, less prestigious, bear market world of
seventies Wall Street, and it was shaped later on by the combined
culture of smartness, hard work, and insecurity that bred bankers
during the nineties (Ho 2009).

Indeed, the women themselves were extremely aware of the differences between their generation and the generation following them
and of the work worlds that had respectively shaped each generation
as market subjects. The women's early experience of a difficult market
environment shaped their long-term attitudes toward decision making not only about stocks and bonds, but about their career paths.
Mindy Plane, for example, began her career in a commercial bank in
the late sixties, and she became a very successful investment banker in
the eighties and nineties:

> It is a different world. I grew up in 1969. I did not know anything.
> But by 1971 I had been made an officer of the bank. At this point we
> had tricky dicks where you had price control so I could not get a
> salary increase. I just got the title. But then the market cratered
> through 1972, 1973, 1974. So I grew up in a period that was a difficult

market environment. And we tend to be . . . more conservative because the market was always going down. I think that people that were brought up in the last ten years tend to be more willing to take risks because they have always seen the market go up. But I am reminded of the long term, long term, long term. (1994)

One net result of such an orientation toward work among the first-generation cohort is that many built their careers during the eighties and nineties within a single firm. For example, after Patricia began her position in the area of research with Deirdre Parliament's help in the late seventies and eighties, she remained in the same firm until her retirement in the early 2000s. Similarly, Deirdre worked within that same firm for nearly thirty years. Notably, Patricia, Deirdre, Maydelle, and others also entered Wall Street during the last days of firm-employee loyalty, an organizational ethos that shaped their expectations as well.

Patricia and other first-generation women were also aware that the women following in their path came from more privileged family backgrounds and universities. They recognized the younger generation's easier access to finance, increased opportunities for advancement, and overall sense of entitlement:

> The women that came in seven, eight, certainly ten years after us got into main training programs. I had lunch with two women—both had MBAs from Columbia. One was twenty-eight; the other twenty-nine. One went to Yale; the other went to some other very good school. They always had everything. They assumed they would go to the best colleges. Some of these schools weren't even coed when I was going. They assumed they would go to business school. And they assumed they would get a good job at a good firm. (Patricia Riley, 1995)

The gendering of market and corporate conditions contributed to the shaping of the first generation of women: of their careers and sense of self, and their relationships to the women and men following in their footsteps, as well as their views of the men in senior positions above them. Indeed, the male hierarchical authority structure of finance dominated the ways the first generation thought about their work worlds, themselves, and what it took to move upward within the corporate ranks. They did not experience structures of gender and power in an abstract way. These gendered hierarchies were embodied in, for example, their ongoing relationships with their bosses and superiors (mainly men) and their experiences of the ways male-male alliances and networks worked—both within and outside the firm— from the very beginning of their careers.[6]

Elite, Male-Dominated Hierarchies

At the top of the pyramid in financial-services firms, there are several layers that sit above the vice president position, including senior vice president, principal, or director. Above them are partners or managing directors (Ho 2009: 86). Few women or men for that matter make it to the managing director level—even today in 2012. Indeed, by the nineties women had worked their way up into the top tiers of financial firms, but at the highest level they were a distinct minority. At the close of the twentieth century, only 5.9 to 13.6 percent within specific firms were managing directors.[7] Although EEOC data reveal that 29.6 percent of managers were women by this same period, many of these women still occupied lower-level positions. By title they were listed as senior officers, but most were in staff positions in personnel or administration, rather than in line jobs. Line positions are those jobs seen as making a direct contribution to the company's profits. Line people, by the nature of their jobs, usually have more power than staff people; they tend to advance more quickly and further up the corporate hierarchy than those in staff positions. And, almost without exception, line people are paid more.

Many women during the eighties continued to occupy research positions.[8] Barely a handful of women had gone on to become executive research heads at firms, the first being Margo Alexander at Paine Webber in the early eighties. Most investment banks began promoting their first female managing directors and partners by the late eighties (Roth 2006: 4). The nineties witnessed an increasing number and proportion of women entering Wall Street, as well as the promotion of small numbers of members of the pioneering generation of women (Fisher 1990: 7). Goldman Sachs, for example, named Abby Joseph Cohen as a partner in 1998—a year before the company went public in 1999 (Roth 2006: 13). From time to time small groups of women decided to strike out on their own and form their own firms. Robin Wiessmann, for example, is a founding principal and president of Artemis Capital Group, the leading women-owned investment banking firm in the United States during the nineties. She went on to become the state treasurer of Pennsylvania in 2007.[9]

Yet in spite of the overall improvement in the numbers of women advancing to higher positions, there was still gender inequality in pay on Wall Street during the eighties as well as the nineties (Roth 2006: 8). Most Wall Street executives received a fixed salary, but the majority of their pay was in the form of a bonus based on performance reviews. According to the sociologist Louise Marie Roth, who has studied gender differences in compensation on Wall Street, "Among the men and women who still worked on Wall Street in 1997, total compensation ranged from $100,000 to over $1,000,000 with a median of $410,000. There were substantial gender differences within this range: women's media earnings were $325,000, while men's were $525,000" (2006: 88).

When men and women move to the vice presidential level and higher, access and inclusion to the key social circles of financial executives, corporate managers, and sometimes government officials become increasingly important. This is particularly the case in the male-dominated domain of investment banking, where "one is promoted only when one begins to sell and generate deals to various corporations and institutions. As such privileged social networks are more obviously required for the 'second stage'" (Ho 2009: 113). Thus, investment bankers are expected to network continually from the boardroom, to dinners, to the golf course.

The type and style of people Wall Street banks covet the most, particularly at the senior echelons, are executives who can project an image and understand the elite world beyond the work milieu. Since top financial circles often mesh with high political, civic, and intellectual social circles within New York City and other global cities, a person's poise and conversational ability become increasingly crucial. White, pedigreed males—married to trophy wives—form the typical image of the financier that matches these kinds of criteria. They have developed dispositions that will be advantageous in the world of finance (Bourdieu 1984; Ho 2009). Historically, women do not fit the profile. This was particularly the case during the seventies, eighties, and even nineties as the first generation forged their careers in high finance.

Carol Johnson: The Only Female at the Boardroom Table

Carol Johnson is another member of the first generation. She grew up in a middle-class family, attended a women's college, and then, after a stint in a PhD program in mathematics, moved into the financial-services industry. From that point on her career has crisscrossed the business and public sector. The more Carol was promoted, and experienced being the only woman at meetings, the more she understood the liquid boundaries between more senior male executives' work and social lives. She thus became aware that her male colleagues often engaged in deal making in a variety of after-work male social spaces: the university club, the golf course, and various dinners and events.

Men are very structured in how they do things. Let me talk about tennis and structure. . . . When I became appointed to [a particular financial-oriented position in the New York State government] I found myself going to meetings of credit unions, savings banks, and to the New York State Bankers midwinter meetings. I used to call their meetings the midwinter carnival. It was black tie. It still is black tie and has been for a hundred years. It takes place at the Waldorf Hotel . . .

I used to admire how someone could come and be chairman for a year. The chairman would come and be elected—upstate, next downstate, small, big—they had a whole pattern. I was just really impressed with how the person could get up and make the remarks. I mean granted he had a little script. But he knew people. I thought this guy is hot stuff! . . . Well, I started realizing after about six months, that the person that is responsible for the tennis appointment (in the bank) will be the chairman in ten years. Now what does this mean? It means he does tennis for a year, and then he organizes golf for the next year. And then he is the program committee chairman. Then he becomes secretary, then he becomes treasurer, and then he becomes vice-chair.

This man is moving, but each time he is moving, he is suddenly invited to the dinner. The first year he is observing. The next year maybe he plays a minor role. By the time he is chair he has seen things for five or six years. He knows the players. He knows the legislature. He knows the various people. He knows exactly at what point you knock the glass and say, "All right. Let me say a few words."

It is a game. But once again I never knew the rules. There was no one there to go and say to me. . . . Instead, suddenly I walked in and I am saying to myself—Oh, my God. I have been on board for three months. How do these people know all of these people? I realize that it has been bonding and training—instituted all along. The gestalt is there. That is a very masculine thing. Women do it in terms of the home. They teach the kids in the kitchen. This is how you wash. But I am not certain if women in general are as good about thinking about how you have to pattern, do the imprinting, and start it early on. (1994)

Within the ranks of the professional-managerial class, bureaucratization throughout most of the twentieth century has traditionally affected criteria for advancement (Traube 1992: 73). Hard work is a necessary but not sufficient means for successfully advancing in the corporate hierarchy. Mastery of the techniques of self-presentation, particularly at the top echelons of institutions, is equally essential. Properly managing one's external appearances—face, dress, and speech—provide crucial signals to one's peers and superiors that one is willing to undertake other forms of self-adaptation required in the business world (Jackall 1988: 46–47). Body image and maintenance are increasingly an essential part of performance in financial and all kinds of service-oriented work (McDowell 1997).

Normally, one learns the managerial codes in the course of repeated, long-term formal and informal social interactions with other managers and with one's superiors (Jackall 1988: 61). Men in finance who eventually become chairs of institutions are groomed for such positions from the very early stages of their careers from within their respective firms. As these men advance in their careers, they acquire knowledge on how to carry themselves within the financial world, including how to host major events. Their apparent ease at such spectacles may appear natural, but it is actually learned. Knowing when and how to tap a glass at a dinner, for example, requires experientially learned knowledge—knowledge acquired by participating in various bank occasions over time. Men who ultimately reach the top therefore engage in corporate masculine rituals of initiation as they move through their career paths. These rituals are training sessions. They introduce the men to key corporate players as well as teach them how to prepare speech scripts. Such training is, as Carol keenly observes, starkly different from traditional domestic female rituals—rituals that teach children, particularly girls, for example, on how to take care of the home.

Hierarchies not only differentiate senior from junior executives but also separate people within the same rank (Ostrower 1995: 7). Within a single group of senior executive men, for example, slightly subordinate men must symbolically reinforce their own subordination to higher-ranking men. When I first met Carol in the mid-nineties, she had recently become the first woman to be head of her department, a traditionally male bastion of power in the banking world, where she had interacted with CEOs, CFOs, government officials, and the like. She described her ongoing experiences in an all-male board meeting of top executives associated internally and externally with her new firm:

> Now there are certain things that may just be in this group. But I have seen this in male groups. I think we can use them as a model. There are certain rules of behavior in the group which are so totally ingrained that you need the Rosetta stone. I see that women's behavior is totally upsetting, startling to men—not because they are women, but because it is just that someone comes out and starts playing basketball in the middle of a football game. One of the things that makes it interesting, is that they are becoming more comfortable with me—or maybe they are realizing that they need a change—they are willing to take the castor oil. I relate myself to castor oil. . . .
>
> For example, the way people get seated in the boardroom. The men always sit in their seats in a particular order. When there is a change in chairman—people come in and they are like homeless. They do not know where to go. They have no clue where to sit because instead of the person sitting over here he was not at the head table—upsetting the arrangement! I'll use different names here. Lowell was going to sit on Jed's lap because Jed was sitting in the chair that Lowell had sat in for the past two years. . . .
>
> The men identify with their bank or institution. There are some that sit at the top of the room, and those that sit at the bottom. That is number one. Number two, those at the bottom do not speak. . . . One of the little-ler guys told me that he had been at the meetings now for three years and he thought that now he could start to speak up. I was floored. This is someone that is CEO of a major bank, but he was waiting for his three years before he could start to participate in the discussion. I feel like I am Jane Goodall. I am seeing glimpses of behavior. I think that so much of it is genderless. I mean he is one of the guys who had gone through the right schools, had come up through the right ranks, and was now a CEO. . . . So, here is your peer

in every respect—I mean back to almost the same genetic pool at some point coming in, and this person knows, because he has got his little male gene that he's got to wait to speak. Now that would have never dawned on me in a million years. As a matter of fact, I would have thought, I am sitting at this table. I should speak up sooner rather than later—say something. . . .

When you are in an organization there is a pecking order that gets reinforced every single day—there should not be a pecking order in these meetings. So you have here in this institution—sealed almost —is a culture and a way of life that doesn't really exist anymore. Have you walked down this hallway? [pointing to individual portraits of white mostly protestant men who had held her job] I call them the ancestors! (1994)

Through their daily and long-term interactions—making decisions in executive boardrooms—men build a male-dominated atmosphere of meaning and power (McDowell 1997; Zaloom 2006). For male executives, finding and knowing one's material and symbolic place in the boardroom is crucial. Understanding one's place means understanding the hierarchical relations, the authority structure that exists among men within a single, very elite board. This includes knowing where to sit and when to speak. In this way the men acknowledge, embody, and thereby reproduce the traditional hierarchical order within financial institutions. Year after year the men wait and eventually find as they move up the hierarchy that they can address the group.

These traditions are, as Carol so aptly observes, handed down to the men by their "ancestors." The rigidity of the hierarchy of the boardroom reflects the rigidity of hierarchies that once existed within the earlier, older banking elite—men born into wealth, the "inheritors" of their positions within the financial world and broader class landscape (Bourdieu 1984). This old-money culture is reproduced each and every time the men attend a board meeting. As Carol points out, the men essentially come from the "same gene pool" and have "gone through the right schools, the right ranks, and are now CEOs."

Institutional rituals and everyday practices in the financial world, particularly at the highest echelons, often position women as the "other." Women are marked as different from the idealized versions of masculinity (McDowell 1997: 138–40). Carol's presence at the boardroom table appears to disrupt the order of things. Carol, however, argues that her behavior "upsets" the men not because of her gender per se but because she is "different" from the other players at the table because of her class origins and path. Carol is different because of the way she has worked her way up the corporate and class ladder. She was not born into a financial family, and she did not attend the "right" Ivy League schools. In Carol's narrative she moves between drawing attention to gender differences and erasing her own gender and the impact of her female performance of leadership in relation to the men's board-meeting rituals.

Female Spaces on Wall Street

Carol is one of a small minority of women to have moved along in her career far enough so that senior men are becoming, as she puts it, "sufficiently comfortable" with her presence. Throughout her career Carol had a series of male mentors who helped her advance in the ultra-senior ranks of the financial world. Historically, however, women have encountered difficulty in securing a mentor to show them the corporate ropes, to showcase their abilities, and to introduce them to powerful corporate players. They have traditionally found it very challenging to gain entry, let alone acceptance, within exclusive "old-boys' networks" (Kanter 1977; Schipani et al. 2006, 2009).

Formal mentoring and the creation of internal female networks within Wall Street firms did not gather much force or momentum until the nineties.[10] Participating in FWA events, for Carol and other members of the first generation, therefore provided an alternative means for the women to attempt becoming proficient in the rules of survival and success required to move up the executive ladder on Wall Street. It also enabled them to begin to build their own female networks.

During the eighties, the FWA contributed to creating the first cohort of female financial-market subjects. Specifically, the network provided a space for women to slowly take on a female corporate habitus. Through participating in FWA events, the first generation gradually developed a system of bodily movements, gestures, eating habits, and ways of dressing that helped distinguish them as professional-managerial class women (Bourdieu 1984: 192). For example, Linda Super, a high-ranking financial professional, said:

There were no women role models for the corporate paradigm. There was no one around to tell you if it was okay to wear nail polish to the office, what office dress meant, if black tie meant your dress could be cocktail length or if it had to be an evening gown. There were no women to show you how to stand, to watch what they did, to explain and define all of the cues. There were no women to tell you how much to drink, to order white or red wine, or if you should laugh at a bad joke. You did not have someone to talk to about all these things. But the FWA is great because you have women to talk to, to be around. You can find out where something fits in, what is corporate behavior, and things that are not easy to define. Subtle cues make a difference. The glass ceiling revolves around these issues. (March 1996 fieldnotes)

In the flexible, increasingly uncertain corporate environment of the nineties, mentoring and networks became even more central to working practices. The Street's increasing emphasis on creating alliances not only commodified networks, but it also placed an increasing emphasis on the presentation of self for women as well as men (Gray 2003; Larner and Malloy 2009: 46–47). By now, senior-ranking Wall Street women no longer participated actively in FWA events, except when invited to speak as authorities on women and finance. They spoke to FWA audiences of predominantly younger women—women in their late twenties and thirties—often providing them advice on what it took to become successful Wall Street women. Thus the only times I saw members of the first generation at FWA gatherings were at anniversary events or on panels in which they engaged in gendered performances of successful women in finance: they appeared polished, well groomed, and very much at ease with giving public presentations.

The FWA's Fortieth Anniversary

In the spring of 1996 I attended a panel about women's leadership to celebrate the FWA's fortieth anniversary. Five first-generation, very senior Wall Street women talked about their career experiences. For younger women (like myself, at the time), attending FWA events can feel a bit high-pressure. Many often start with a cocktail hour (or half hour). The anniversary event began with an extensive buffet filled with hors d'oeuvres including sushi, French bread with pâté, and tiny, finger-sized chicken wings. There was also a rather extensive bar with three male bartenders pouring wine into glasses.

A great deal of networking typically went on before FWA panels. We were all almost always given name tags. The night of the fortieth anniversary panel, after I had signed in and put my name tag on, I went into the ladies' room, where I bumped into one of the women in my research, Sharon Martin, who was in the process of fixing her hair in the mirror. She said, "Oh. You are back." I said yes, but was unsure of what she meant by "back." She followed up by asking me if I had taken time off to have a baby. I told her no, that I was busy enough working on my dissertation research. She seemed confused and then told me that she must have mixed me up with another woman "who looks like you and has long brown hair" who works at Paine Webber. She apologized, said that her "mind was elsewhere" because they (the FWA) were in the midst of "trying to get more women members." We exited the bathroom and went our separate ways.

Part of the networking that went on at FWA events occurred between women, mainly between, as I discovered over time, younger women who were looking for help in finding jobs from more senior, more established women. But the other function of networking was for the FWA itself, which was always in search of new members. Sharon (in and out of the bathroom) was "working the room" in such a manner. She had begun her career in finance in the sixties and had been active in the FWA during the seventies. But she had also taken time out during the eighties to marry and live on the West Coast. Her re-entry and active participation in the FWA by the time we first met was, as she explained to me during one of our talks, part of her plan to move back in and up the ranks of Wall Street. Unlike most first-generation women (who had not taken time away from finance for family), Sharon felt she needed the FWA, that participating and meeting people through the FWA could potentially help her career.

Sometimes I partook in the networking at FWA events; other times I observed from a chair or a corner. My tendency to withdraw into observation was not only part of my anthropological training. There were times when I still felt a bit out of place hobnobbing with professional-managerial women, even though I was dressed up in a suit and heels, with my hair done. After the Celebrating Women's Event, I wrote in my fieldnotes:

> I did not feel especially sociable last night. I would have preferred that I talked to more people during the earlier part of the evening. And I would have liked to have said hello to Bonnie Jackall [not her real name] who I think only half recognizes me. I still am not crazy

about Sharon Martin [not her real name]. I think she is basically a fake and a self-promoter. . . .

Also, I did not feel completely polished and groomed last night. I feel when I attend these events, an awful lot of social pressure to conform precisely to a very feminine, polished mode of dress, appearing and behaving. I feel that my body language needs to be especially forceful and that I need to exude a sense of importance and confidence—always. And mostly I do. All of the women seem to be actively holding themselves together in such a manner. To some though it seems to come more easily—for example, the woman who is on the board of a seven sister college is the real McCoy. For others it all seems much more forced, more stylized, more self-conscious. Sharon, for example, rubs me this way. Her whole manner seems less genuine. (March 1996)

Fashion, as Georg Simmel observed long ago, signals the cohesiveness of those belonging to the same social circles, at the same time as it closes off these circles to those of inferior social rank (Simmel 1971: 296–300). On Wall Street, professional women have worked hard to distinguish and present themselves as members of the financial elite. During the seventies and eighties, this entailed wearing navy blue suits and ties, which emulated the conservative suits of professional male executives. By the nineties, the dress code for women had relaxed, but only a little. Women still tended to wear power suits, but in a variety of colors, styles, and fabrics. Their hair was almost always coiffed and cut no longer than shoulder length. The women wanted to be taken seriously, and not mistaken for a secretary or a member of the more lower- and middle-class back office (Ho 2009: 117–18). They disciplined themselves and each other at work, and at various FWA events, to ensure that they individually and collectively presented a professional-class performance. The pressure I felt from women at FWA events to be groomed, polished, and exuding confidence is a tribute to their effectiveness.

Between Women: Female Mentorship, Friendship, and Competition

When the first cohort of professional women entered Wall Street, terms such as "networks," "mentors," and "role models" were not part of America's general vocabulary.[11] However, by the eighties and especially the nineties, the language of social capital was an unremarkable part of everyday business, especially among women (Laird 2006: 265). Here the FWA was instrumental in teaching women how to get on boards, network, and find mentors who would make them more visible and, hence, potentially promotable. In fact, the organization pioneered women's use of these types of strategies of visibility. During the nineties the FWA, for example, invited speakers—including first-generation women on Wall Street—to talk about networking, mentoring, interviewing strategies, and career planning, all techniques designed to help their members succeed. For some first-generation women, this meant shifting their expectations and understanding of the FWA as a place where they themselves mentored each other, to a place in which they were now the mentors to the next generation. As Mindy Plane explains:

> I think that senior-level women have an obligation to mentor women because if they don't, some people won't be mentored. But I think that you have an obligation to mentor people who are interested in being mentored. In fact that is probably one of the reasons why some of my peers have not stayed as members of the Financial Women's Network of New York—because frankly the organization doesn't do much for us. However, I think that we have a responsibility as members to do things for the organization because there are a lot of thirty-year-olds that need our help. I am going to be a moderator on a panel on how to get on government boards. I did a panel for them about responsibilities of directors of municipal funds. I could do that without being an official member. But I think that if you do it with it being a member, people feel a bit more comfortable asking you questions. (1994)

Another way in which senior women (former active members of the FWA) acted as mentors was by providing younger women with access to powerful people in the financial and political worlds. Carol Johnson, for example, helped provide FWA members with opportunities to meet with government officials:

> I am supportive of the FWA. They are doing a trip to Washington next week. I have contacts in the Department of State—so I set up the contacts for the group's trip. But I realize that I don't have an interest anymore in the things the FWA are doing. But the younger women are really excited that they can go down to Washington and meet with so-and-so. Well, I have called so-and-so and asked so-

and-so to do it. A lot of the women's organizations are for network-ing—the outreach, the contact. I already know these people. To show up to a group of fifty people to shake hands with someone that I could go and have dinner with—it's a waste of my time.

Now I would have gone down with the group next week, quite honestly—you know to show the flag. But I am without an au pair for two weeks so I am not going down to Washington next week. I'll continue my membership and I will go to the annual dinner. I'll do one or two things on a committee. I'm willing to make the phone calls to connect things. . . . And I send in my dues because if someone wants to call on me, I want them to know that I am available. (1994)

Although most women were no longer active in the FWA by the nineties, the friendships they forged originally through the FWA con-tinued to play an important role in their professional and personal lives. This was particularly the case for those who, like Patricia, had paved successful careers in the area of research. As Patricia told me, "You know how it is said about women not helping women? Well, I cannot tell you how much help I've had from women throughout my early career. I think that a lot of that closeness was born out of strug-gle. You know in the seventies you were all alone for so long—and then you found these people through Financial Women's Association" (1994).

Patricia and most (though not all) of her cohort are part of a genera-tional network of female friends, which provides a system of support that both is a part of and stands apart from the male-dominated financial workplace. This system, from Patricia's perspective, was borne out of the women's shared struggle in the seventies. Notably her choice of the term "struggle" draws directly on the feminist discourse of the period. However, what is so remarkable is that they continued to sustain these friendships through the nineties, in spite of, or perhaps because of the increasing uncertainties and contingencies of working on Wall Street.

Patricia herself was never downsized, but she and her female cohort were willing and able to come to the rescue of first-generation friends. "Even now we are supportive. A lot of us are at the stage where we are losing our jobs from cutbacks. And every time that happens, the rest of us come in and enclose this incredible support group: 'We're going to find that person a job!'" (1994). The women's ties could serve as a buffer between the women and a male-dominated work world. The women's friendship provided a source of female solace, help, and identity connected to the world of work, but it existed outside the parameters of the corporate workplace. But, for some, the form and meaning of such friendships changed over time. Even within the cohort there were different types and constructions of relationships between women throughout the decades. And even among friends there are different perceptions of the place and meaning of their respective relationships. The women's career advancement experiences within or across particular kinds of firms, including the kinds of relationships they forged with colleagues, mentors, and bosses at work also contributed to women's shifting connections to the FWA and their ties with one another over time.

> I am a big believer in joining organizations and participating in them. I joined the Financial Women's Association of New York City. I think they had a three-year requirement. You had to be in the workforce for three years. I joined as soon as I could. . . . It was a much younger organization in the seventies than it is in the nineties. I was on the board by the age of thirty or thirty-one. People who are now presidents are even closer to my age now. They are in their forties. But we have all matured together. . . .
>
> Women have been isolated in corporate America so that is more difficult for them to network. So, therefore, I believe that organizations like the FWA have played a role. As I have reached a different level in my career, I have also made sure that I was a member of other organizations. I am a member of the Economic Club of New York. Do I think that I needed the FWA when I was younger? Yes. First of all I could not get into the Economic Club when I was twenty-five. I think that people network through these organizations. . . . I think that men do it that way. It is just that I think that women, because they were such a minority, and probably still are a minority in the senior levels of management, need organizations to network with. . . . You know there is no Financial Men's Association —no men's organization for finance. . . .
>
> The women that I met in my early twenties were all members of the FWA. We have all advanced in our careers . . . but we have all mentored and tried to help one another. Now we have all gone off in different career directions now. I bet you interviewed Patricia Riley. I've known Patricia since we were both going to NYU back in the

early seventies. I will give Patricia a call or she will call me—I mean I talk to Patricia like two or three times a year. (Mindy Plane, 1994)

The personal biographies of women (including their family, class, and educational experiences) intersected with their workplace and career advancement experiences in specific areas on Wall Street—the more feminized area of research versus the more male-dominated domains of sales, trading, and investment banking—to further shape their understandings of their connections to one another. Some women, particularly those who remained in the area of research, like Patricia, continued to rely on a combination of their FWA friendships and their internal relationships within their respective firms to help them advance throughout their careers. Female friendships (within and outside their actual workplaces) provided sources of support and advice, even if this meant speaking to one another by phone only a few times a year.

But not all of the members of the first generation viewed their relationships with other women in finance as friends or as confidantes and sources of support or career advancement. Some, particularly those who advanced in the very senior ranks within the male-dominated areas of investment banking, forged different career paths, typically with the help of very powerful male mentors, from their counterparts in research. As a result, these women tended to view and define their relationships with women and men on Wall Street differently.

Maydelle Brooks and Vivian Binder: Breaking Glass Ceilings in Investment Banking

Maydelle Brooks spent the last two decades of the twentieth century working her way up the corporate ladder of a major financial-services firm, becoming one of the highest-ranking women to run an actual business on Wall Street during this period. After becoming a banker, she spent the mid-eighties working in London; soon after, London became a major global financial center in the wake of the Big Bang in 1986 and the deregulation of financial markets. But as financial markets were globalized, she was called back to New York City by one of the partners to take on a position as director for a division within the bank. Her promotion to this position was an example of one of the ways in which the globalization of the financial-services industry contributed to creating new positions, increasing employment, and providing potentially new opportunities for women to move up the ranks.[12] Notably, Maydelle recounted that when she asked the male partner what she would be doing, he replied, "The challenge is that we have all these various businesses in the [xxx] division. They compete with each other. They don't talk to each other. And the world is getting such that all these parts are fungible in the minds of the buyers. We have to put this all together" (1994). Maydelle was promoted to a principal during her tenure in the position, and she then became one of the first female managing directors of her firm in the late eighties. She joined a small group of women on Wall Street who were beginning to make it to the very highest positions in the world of investment banking, a heady experience (Fisher 1990). As Maydelle remembered, "I had been made a principal. I'm chugging along, having a great time. Out of the blue I am made one of the first managing directors. That was quite extraordinary. I did not expect the promotion at all. I had been on the fast track, but being promoted to managing director was overwhelming" (1994).

A number of other women were also (finally) promoted to managing director, and this all happened just at the moment that Maydelle's firm went from being private to being public, and accountable to shareholders. As Maydelle notes, no one "missed the irony" of the timing. Firms were, by that point in time, well aware of the growing call for diversity in the business, particularly at the higher ranks. It was hardly a coincidence that Maydelle and other women in her firm joined small numbers of women throughout all of Wall Street that were paying closer attention to gender diversity. Maydelle's high-flying career continued to soar during the nineties.

She said, "One day I got the knock on the door by this partner who said, 'Well, I want you to run the [xxx] business.' You could have picked me up off the floor—since no woman at our firm ran a business! But here was another challenge, another opportunity. When something is run into the ground all you can do is make it look better! And I've been here ever since. It's been quite successful. That is basically the story" (1994). Maydelle's reaction to her promotion—that "it was another challenge"—reflects a particular value system, in which engaging in hard work, taking something that someone else has "run into the ground" and making it work, is a badge of honor, a sign of successful work in the higher echelons of investment banking (Ho 2009: 74). Indeed, Maydelle had a great deal of ambition and determination to succeed throughout her career. However, upon reflecting on her overall career pattern, Maydelle also attributes much of her success to a series of very powerful male mentors. In this respect Maydelle's work experiences are similar to the career paths of many women who broke glass ceilings in a variety of male-dominated industries, including, for example, the legal profession (Kanter 1977; Epstein 1981; Schipani et al. 2009).[13]

> But I think that the threads you see through my career is that I have had three or four very strong male mentors throughout my career. It's interesting because I don't know if the mentors would have viewed me as the mentee. They were very strong figures. But at the same time, I always worked hard for them. Yet they were very strong in their own right not to feel insecure or threatened. In fact, they thrived by being supportive of a woman. But they weren't doing anything out of the ordinary because it wasn't as if I wasn't working for it. . . . These guys were just treating me like every other guy—just dealing with me on the merits of my work—beating on me, you know, just as tough as they were on the other guys. And, in that sense, I don't think that they did anything different. And that is why I don't know if they viewed me as their mentee in that sense. But I viewed them that way. . . .
>
> I probably learned more from them than they ever know—from the man in government in terms of how to deal with organizations, and how to you know, as a twenty-three-year-old write decisions memos for [high-ranking federal government officials]. . . .
>
> I would say that in terms of this firm, this person is now very senior within the firm. It's fair to say that people do associate me very closely with having worked very closely with him over the last seven or eight years. And he tends to be a person that works with a few number of very close people, and I guess I would be considered one of them. (1994)

Maydelle's narrative about her experience with male mentors reveals the ways in which hegemonic cultural values on Wall Street are inculcated through structures of power, including boss–employee and mentor–mentee relationships. The process of one-on-one mentoring is one of the ways that investment banks teach employees what it takes to be a successful subject in a global financial institution: for example, to be successful one has to work extremely hard; people are judged via their merit (Ho 2009: 41). On the one hand, Maydelle acknowledges that the men seemed to thrive on being supportive of her as a woman. On the other, she claims that they only viewed and treated her as "one of the guys." Gender as such appears and then disappears within her narrative.

Senior-ranking people typically identify and align themselves with other senior executives within the corporation (Jackall 1988). Maydelle's relationship with one of the highest-ranking executive men in the investment bank thus brought her into everyday proximity with power. By forming and continually performing such an alliance she was known by others as someone who worked closely with this particular individual and she was affiliated with the elite male hierarchy. But being the only woman at the top is not necessarily easy. It can be rather lonely. Breaks in key gendered alliances, for example, even if they are temporary, can be extremely difficult to handle, requiring stoic performances, as the investment banker Vivian Binder explains.

Although Vivian had grown up in a professional-oriented family in New Rochelle, New York, her father, a lawyer, had not been particularly supportive of Vivian's quest to enter and move up the ranks of Wall Street. Even when Vivian got into an elite business school directly after college he told her she should simply go to New York University's business school, which she subsequently did. And when Vivian, who at the time was working in sales, had the opportunity to learn more about investment banking, her father thought she was better suited for sales and should remain where she was, rather than take a chance trying to create a career in a male-dominated domain. This time, however, Vivian decided to make the move anyway. She has done well for herself. Her relationship with her male mentor, however, has not been without its difficulties and tensions either:

> I remember a situation where [*pause*] my mentor here came down very hard on me because he felt that I had beaten up on some people. Those were not the facts. I always try and defend myself. But you can only go so far. You just have to have a stiff upper lip and go on from there. But, six months later, and to my mentor's credit, he came back to me and said that he had presumed the wrong thing. That is fine. But those six months were hell—internally—because of this whole issue to prove yourself! . . .
>
> I find as a woman that I cannot differentiate the personal from the professional. And you have to be able to do that. I do not know if that is gender based. The men usually don't talk about it. But I find that with me it is very difficult. . . .

The other part is that you really cannot talk to many people about this, because they are your friends, or they see you as being exceedingly successful without really knowing. They cannot imagine that you would have problems. . . . So, you are really very isolated. (1994)

In contrast to Patricia Riley, and many women who work in more female areas of finance, Vivian does not feel that she has a female network of support within her firm: "Women are very mistrusting of other women. They are more likely to align or familiarize themselves with a man than they are another woman. Women tend to be back-stabbing." Moreover, even though Vivian was somewhat active in the FWA earlier on in her career, working extremely long hours advancing to the top has, from her perspective, limited her ability to see, sustain, and build female networks and friendships outside of her firm:

I do not know if women's networks exist. They may. But I have not had too much time to spend in terms of developing them. I think they do exist out there. I often say to myself that if something happened to me tomorrow, I do not think that five headhunters would call because I have never developed the network. Now they may all know of me, but from what I see of how other people work the network—they are out there really working in it. And I do not do that. . . .

I do not have much time other than working, sleeping, and spending time with the children so I do not socialize much with people in the industry. Unfortunately, I have tended to have fewer close friends as the years have gone by. That is one of the prices you pay. Sitting in the corner office is very lonely. You cannot chit-chat with everyone about everything. These are the hidden costs that no one tells you about when you become a manager and much more senior. I think they take a greater toll on women because we are naturally more expansive, communicative, and want to share. You become very isolated. (1994)

For managers and executives the devotion to work was the "symbolic dimension of the late-twentieth, early twenty-first century American capitalist firm" (Blair-Loy 2003: 21). Promotion into the ultra-senior ranks requires longer hours and close involvement with colleagues, thereby leaving less and less time for family and leisure. Vivian, like many career-committed executive women in finance, has to deal with the countless meetings, travel, and so on and so forth that it takes to be successful, thereby limiting her time with her five-year-old twin boys and thirteen-year-old daughter.

Like other Wall Street women in her situation, Vivian recognizes that many of her male colleagues have "traditional" stay-at-home wives who take care of their husbands and families full-time (Blair-Loy 2003: 118). The classically gendered structure and norms of executive men, including their families, also contribute to senior women's feelings of isolation. To most men, very senior corporate women are cultural anomalies. Highly successful working women do not fit into typical socially accepted categories of female personhood:

> Most men do not know if they are supposed to deal with you like their mother, their wife, their lover, their sister. Whereas you can always invite the male boss and his wife to dinner, it is very rare that you are going to invite the female boss to socialize. You cannot take that personally. For years when I was not in this position it would bother me that the men would come in on Mondays and talk about the parties. And then one day I brought this issue up and said to this guy, "You know it's very lonely and depressing—Have I done something?" He said, "No. But Vivian, you have got to realize that it is the wives that organize the men's social lives. Am I about to tell my wife, please invite Vivian to come to our house for dinner on Friday? Vivian is the woman that I just spent three nights in the Philippines with." When he put it in that perspective I realized that it was not me—that is the social network and fabric here—and you have to deal with it. (1994)

Conclusion

Wall Street women tend to come from two kinds of class backgrounds. Some, like Maydelle and Vivian, came from more cosmopolitan, privileged backgrounds, had attended coed schools, and had more highly placed contacts (men and women) who can help introduce them to others in the business world. Some women, like Patricia, came from more solidly middle-class homes; had attended small, nonelite female colleges; and had found their jobs at least initially through newspaper ads, rather than through a close family member or school tie.

The two types of classed female personhood that exist among the first generation of women in finance are, of course, more ideal types.

In reality, individual women have more diverse, complicated backgrounds and career pathways. Nevertheless, there do appear to be some overarching differences between the women who made their careers in the more feminized area of research from those who moved into the very male-dominated areas of investment banking and management. Women in research tended to depend upon a mix of their female FWA friends and internal bosses to advance in their careers. By contrast, women in investment banking moved up the corporate ladder via their alignments with powerful male mentors. They relied far less on their female colleagues, friends, and ties formed in the FWA and at work.

In part we can attribute the differences between women in research and those in investment banking to the particular gendering within certain areas within financial firms. But there is also a class element at play that should not be missed. Although the FWA served a number of different roles in the women's lives, first and foremost it provided a key space for the women to develop a female corporate habitus. In general, many of the women who participated in the FWA, like Patricia, did not come from backgrounds in which they had learned what it took, including how to dress, act, and speak and how to navigate the financial world, especially at the higher echelons. The FWA provided a necessary training ground.

Women who did not participate as much in the FWA, like Maydelle and Vivian, tended to come from slightly more privileged backgrounds. Thus they came to the financial world with a distinct advantage—they already had acquired much of the elite habitus required to hobnob within elite circles. In the end, however, in spite of such differences, the two "classes" came together on Wall Street to help form the first professional elite cohort of women.

CHAPTER 3

GENDERED DISCOURSES OF FINANCE

In 1975, long-standing restrictions on stock brokerage commission rates ended, ushering in an era of financial deregulation. In the wake of these changes, Muriel Siebert helped to pioneer the concept of the discount brokerage house. Seeking to distinguish herself and her new company, Siebert took out a full-page advertisement in the *Wall Street Journal* that showed her using scissors to cut a $100 bill in half. At the moment in which fictitious capital (electronic money) began to threaten to displace paper money, Siebert literally and metaphorically cut commodity money in half. At the dawn of an era in which it seemed increasingly possible to conjure up enormous sums of money by engaging in risky market practices, her scissors cleaved the portrait of Benjamin Franklin that adorns every $100 bill, destroying the icon most closely associated with the American Protestant work ethic linking hard work to success.

Twenty-one years later, on a cold Manhattan night in March 1996, approximately 150 well-groomed professional-managerial-class women gathered in the ballroom of the Phillip Morris building to meet Muriel Siebert and other well-known women. They and I, in the midst of my initial fieldwork, were there to attend an event entitled "Celebrating Women's History: Defining Moments in the Lives of Five Leaders." Organized for the fortieth anniversary of the Financial Women's Association (FWA), it invited women to consider the following:

At what point in your career did you first know you were successful? When did you realize that you had power and influence? What, so far, has been your greatest moment? Has it all been worth it? You've probably been asked these kinds of questions from time to time. If you're curious about how other women would answer, then join us for a panel featuring five, prominent, accomplished, history-shaping women. Each will candidly recount "herstory": The pitfalls and pinnacles, roadblocks and opportunities, choices made, challenges undertaken, resulting risks and rewards.

The evening began with women filing past metal detectors into the ballroom. Even prior to 9/11, security in buildings in New York City was tight. Women received name tags, with gold, red, or "no" stars; no stars indicated that you were not an FWA member. Eventually, after everyone was sitting down, the president of the FWA greeted the audience. She stated that FWA members averaged forty-four years of age; earned an average income of $160,000; and possessed an average household net worth of $1,000,000 or more. She then introduced the panelists and presented Muriel Siebert. Siebert, she said, attributed her meteoric success on Wall Street to the following formula: "work, risk, luck, and pluck," echoing a constellation of attributes and meanings I was picking up in interviews with members of the first generation.

Siebert's prescription for success (for herself and women on Wall Street more generally) bridges a divide between older traditional ideologies that link hard work and pluck to material reward (ideologies that still exist on Wall Street) and newer ones connecting risk-taking practices and luck to producing wealth in the new global economy—often without perceptible production (Comaroff and Comaroff 2000). Each of these ideologies turns out to be gendered. Meritocracy emphasizes individual achievement and gender-neutral discourses about professional work and success in American culture and the marketplace, ironically fitting into one set of feminist arguments for the inclusion of women in historically male-dominated fields. But newer discourses of risk emphasize differences between women and men.[1]

American and liberal feminist ideals about hard work and meritocracy were central to the subjectivity of the first generation (Chase 1995). Women working in all areas within financial firms elaborated discourses of individualism and meritocracy, linking their mobility and success to gender-neutral economic images and American entrepreneurial practices of hard work, production, and performance. These ambitious professional women believed that people achieved success as individuals, not as men or women, whites, Hispanics, or blacks. At the same time, influenced by mainstream actors of the liberal feminist movement, the women carried up the career ladder the idea that women's equal access to the workplace, including their own, could be accomplished through the system, with sufficient adjustments and reforms to allow women access to all areas of economic and public life. In part through their work, it was primarily this version of feminism that gradually became mainstreamed within Wall Street in the eighties and nineties.

These versions of meritocracy resonated with neoliberal rhetoric celebrating deregulation as freeing financial markets and citizens from the state (Sassen 2001; Ho 2009), and with neoliberal doctrines that held "that human well being can best be advanced by liberating entrepreneurial freedoms and skills within an institutional framework characterized by strong private property rights, free markets, and free trade" (Harvey 2005: 2). Neoliberalism "as a technology of governing" relying on "calculative choices and techniques" pervaded everyday conduct in finance (Ong 2006: 4). As such, it provided the concepts that "inform[ed] the government of free individuals," in this case Wall Street women, "who were then induced to self-manage according to market principles of discipline, efficiency, and competitiveness" (ibid.). Wall Street women thus enacted and in many respects became the "ideal" neoliberal subjects of the nineties.

At the same time, in deploying gendered discourses of risk, the women also contributed to further inculcating a more cultural and, indeed, essentialist feminism into the world of finance—an ideology of "female nature" that revalidates undervalued female attributes such as conservative thinking and thereby commends the differences between women and men. Both forms of corporate feminisms on Wall Street would provide much of the framing of the gendering of the financial crisis of 2007–9.

Risk is an important feature of global finance (Porter 2005: 174). Prior to the financial crisis, risk taking became increasingly important within the major business units of firms, including investment banking and sales and trading. To work with risk was (and still is) to engage with fate and play with future uncertainties. Both men and women on Wall Street closely associate risk taking with masculinity (Porter 2005: 164). In the trading pit, male traders "use risk-taking as a strategy for gaining status and securing access to the physical positions and social standings that are crucial trading resources" (Zaloom 2006: 100). Risk-taking strategies were played out between and among men, who did not view women as players in the game.[2]

Women in different areas of financial work performed and amended discourses of risk in different ways in order to insert themselves (with varying degrees of success) within the male-dominated world of Wall Street. Their specific professional identities and practices emerged out of necessity, agency, and innovation, and the particular area in which they forged their careers. In research and brokerage, women tended to draw on supposedly natural attributes of American femininity, such as conservative, risk-averse behavior. Women in these fields invoked and reframed the figure of the financial "consumer" in order to sell themselves as professional subjects of economic expertise. They mobilized their feminine identities as they emphasized the importance of women's ways of buying and understanding value. In this way, women researchers and brokers constructed themselves as authoritative financial subjects. Wall Street, as a result, tended to accept such feminine women working in research, because they fit into the heteronormative gendered order of firms.

Women in investment banking provided a different articulation about risk. Their narratives more straightforwardly echoed prefinancial crisis discourses of white heterosexual masculinity, celebrating cool, calculated rationality; adventure; and risk taking (McDowell 1997: 182–90; Assassi 2009: 125–26; Ho 2009). Investment bankers were directly responsible for capital accumulation, in contrast to women in research and brokerage who were still, for the most part, not directly generating revenue for the firm.

Risk-taking performances that can reap tremendous profit in finance inverted all that is traditionally proper about American femininity. What happened then to the relatively few women working in risk-oriented senior positions within investment banking? Wall Street treated them as the "anti-mothers" of the professional-managerial class. Female bankers—who engaged in risk-taking behavior—became demonic mothers who did not care about their employees or, in some cases, their real-life children. Men's risk-taking predatory market machismo and cool, calculated banking behavior legitimated financial agency in masculine terms (Guthey 2001: 114). Wall Street women who dared to engage in hypermasculine performances thereby threatened the gendered order of firms as well as men's agency and power.

All of the Wall Street women of the nineties, regardless of the particular area in which they worked, were thus negotiating historically constituted financial discourses (such as globalization and neoliberalism), economic models and concepts (including the value put on risk), as well as American discourses of gender, professional work, and "success" (Ortner 2003; de Goede 2005b; Zaloom 2006; Ho

2009). Their talk about themselves and their careers shared part of their logic with the logic of global financial capitalism; women performed the ideas and values of the free neoliberal market. By the nineties, a variety of images and performances of gender, feminism, and the market thus structured the first generation of women's expectations of themselves and others as they advanced into more senior positions. They also produced legitimacy for certain kinds of corporate and managerial activity in offices, on the trading floor, and inside executive boardrooms.

As predatory market machismo increasingly became the hegemonic masculinity in finance, this type of masculine behavior became further legitimized in the name of shareholder maximization during the eighties and nineties (Guthey 2001: 129). Managers' "sole duties were to maximize shareholder value, not to serve as the trustees of the public interest or as guardians of an autonomous corporate entity" (137). In the atmosphere of increasing competition for clients, faster and more transaction-oriented deal-making practices—what the political scientist Susan Strange calls "casino capitalism"—all but replaced any vestiges of traditional long-term "relationship banking" or paternal concern for corporate employees and their well-being (Eccles and Crane 1988). As the feminist scholar Cynthia Enloe observed at the dawn of the new global economy in the eighties, "risk taking" was now at the core of masculinized conceptions of banking. "Just as travel to exotic regions was once imagined to be a risk and therefore a particularly masculine form of adventure," she wrote, "so risk-taking is thought by many financiers to be integral to competitive international business" (1988: 158–59). More than a decade later, the anthropologist Anna Tsing similarly argued in her ethnographic study of a gold-mining company that the "frontier story" of capitalist investment and exploitation requires that male explorers "wander alone in the empty landscape" (2005: 173). These gendered performances of masculinity, she argued, actually bring about actual, real, capital flows. This is the financial capitalism that set the stage for the economic crisis of 2007–9. Indeed, in the decades directly before the financial crisis, it was clear that "risk reap[ed] reward—in money, status, the elaboration of social space of markets, and the construction of a masculine self" (Zaloom 2006: 93; see also McDowell 1997; Thrift 2001; de Goede 2005b; Tsing 2005).

Patricia Riley: The "Caring Mother"

Women in research and brokerage used risk-aware, conservative strategies for gaining status and securing their social standing as females in Wall Street firms. They deployed their "natural" feminine abilities to develop and maintain strong relationships within the firm and, in some cases, with clients. While men engaged in risk-taking strategies that played loosely with the contingencies of the future, women were more concerned with the long-term consequences of their financial recommendations and actions. Being risk aware requires the performative elaboration of a particular female economic self that plays upon gender difference to women's advantage. The concerned, sympathetic female research analyst at work is not a natural outcome of women's "biological" female qualities. The emotions of sympathy that appear to be the result of her personal feelings are one kind of performance that women engage in to successfully engage and interact with the late twentieth-century market (Hochschild 1983). Consider some of Patricia's thoughts about what it takes and what it means to be a successful woman on Wall Street:

> There is an advantage and a disadvantage [to being a woman broker]. The disadvantage is they don't have a lot of women friends and contemporaries making a lot of money. Just because of the way things are. On the other hand, some of the most successful brokers are women. You can see why. Women tend to be sympathetic. They are not afraid to spend time with the client. They really listen to what the client wants. They tend to be very service-oriented. You can build an incredible amount of business by just caring about your client. Women tend to be much more conservative, more long-term *oriented* than "let's buy the hot technology stock." So when I look at successful women brokers here, I see a consistent pattern. They are very conservative. They don't take too many risks. They have long-term relationships.
>
> You know it is funny. Oppenheimer—an investment management services firm—commissioned a study of women investors to see if there is a difference. In fact, there are. One of them is that long-term, conservative, risk-averse thinking helps you in the market. I think that women, just the way things have been, tend to balance a lot more. I think that women have always had so many responsibilities

that it almost in an easy sense translates to stock. I mean as corny as it sounds, let's say that you decide to buy a new blazer. You can walk down the street to Saks. You know you are going to pay full price. You know that you are going to get good quality. You know if you go to Loehmann's. You know what you are getting at Filene's Basement. I mean you are constantly making decisions of price and value.

I think when women look at stocks they have a lot more respect for the concept of risk. This serves them well. Men are classics. I constantly get this—they are at a cocktail party, and they get a hot tip. If you suggest electronics they want to buy it. But women will sit there and say "like my family's IRA account" or whatever. The women want something conservative, something long term, something they can hold onto for a couple of years. Meanwhile, the men always want something that is going to double the next week. I don't know whether it is good or bad. But, in terms of outcome, I think that women's attitudes are better for investing. (1994)

In the newly global market, Patricia's evaluation (and celebration) of women as more conservative departed strikingly from the fetishization of risk underlying new economic practices in the "second gilded age." At the same time, her gendering of risk invoked American debates about gender. Indeed, purportedly feminine attributes of serving and caring have historically provided a rationale for women successfully occupying a range of traditionally female positions such as nursing, teaching, and even in selling insurance in the earlier part of the twentieth century (Kwolek-Folland 1994). So we can understand women's performances of femininity—of risk aversion—as one way they creatively inserted themselves in male-dominated financial practices. They subtly transferred the womanly qualities that they demonstrated in advising and selling to the stocks they endorse. Their performance suggested that similar traits would be attributed to their clients' portfolios and future market successes.

Even Patricia's shopping example is a play on gender, imaginatively drawing on the historical identification of femininity with consumption.[3] While such associations have been used to dismiss women as fundamentally unserious, here she uses it to distinguish women as especially well equipped to participate in financial markets. There's even a note of hearty common sense here to combat the implied arcane math of the male economics whizzes. By equating buying blazers with buying stocks, Patricia arguably illustrates how, as Arjun

Appadurai argues, "consumption has now become a serious form of work" in which "the heart of this work is the social discipline of the imagination, the discipline of learning to link fantasy and nostalgia to the desire for new bundles of commodities" (1996: 82–83).

Notably, Wall Street women's career stories and discourses are local and historically specific instances of global capitalism (Sahlins 1988; Ho 2009). More particularly, their narratives illuminate the subjectivity of the particular segment of American society—the professional-managerial class—most fully engaged in market activity at the end of the twentieth century. Producers and marketers of stock advice like Patricia constructed apparently objective research products (embodied in reports and in their performances of selling) that actually drew on, reworked, and incorporated structures of feelings operating within their clientele, primarily the professional-managerial and upper classes. One of the major structures of anxiety for that class in this historical moment was whether or not it could pass on its status to its children (Newman 1988: 14; Ehrenreich 1989; Ortner 1999). This anxiety appeared to be in some ways operating across the class board, in spite of vast differences in resources between professionals and managers and the very wealthy. Women like Patricia were especially successful in research in the nineties because they performed acceptable forms of womanhood. They acted as mothers who cared about the future and reproduction of their client families in an age of enormous economic and cultural uncertainty.

Images of motherhood and female success in the financial-services industry were not entirely new (Kwolek-Folland 1994). As women resurrected and revised American gendered discourses to fit into Wall Street, they reconfigured an earlier gender-business ideology that imagined relationships between executives and clients, and managers and employees, as those between mother and the family as nation. Female narratives about risk aversion, particularly those elaborated upon by women positioned in research, drew on an earlier corporate domestic discourse that viewed educated, middle-class businesswomen as "motherly" saviors of the nation. However, in the case of 1990s finance, the nation as such referred only to the professional-managerial and upper classes. In Patricia's narrative we can see how Wall Street women reiterated and elaborated a set of gender norms derived from an earlier turn of the twentieth-century financial management ideology identified by the business historian Angel Kwolek-Folland (1994) as "corporate domesticity."

According to Kwolek-Folland, male life insurance executives adopted a gender ideology of "social motherhood" to incorporate and provide a means for educated women to symbolically and literally help advertise and sell life insurance products to the public. Building on images and discourses associated with the late nineteenth-century social motherhood movement, executives tapped into the argument that "women's place should expand into the realms of politics and public welfare because the unique qualities of womanhood would bring sympathy, nurturance, and enlightened responsibility to the public arena." Just as "educated women became the mothers or guardians of the whole society," insurance companies imaginatively portrayed the corporation as a benevolent mother, watched over by "fatherly" executives, all of whom were collectively responsible for ensuring the safety and future of the nation through placing and selling a monetary value on every individual's life (Kwolek-Folland 1994: 17, 136). In Patricia's reformulation of this earlier gender ideology, Wall Street women are no longer the mothers or guardians of the whole society. Instead they watch over their own class.

Patricia's articulation of Wall Street women's gendered qualities can be understood as a further legitimation of the privatization and commodification of risk protection in place of protections traditionally associated with the welfare state (Dean 1997, cited in Lupton 1999: 99). Behind her caring corporate motherhood lurks a class ideology designed to maximize the power of the new American oligarchy, the white overclass (Lind 1995). Images of social corporate responsibility, nevertheless, continued to refer to women's natural orientations to the home and emotions. Even at a time when women like Patricia were participating in an economy of radical individualism, high risk, and instability for many workers, her narrative revealed a key means by which Wall Street subsumed women into the workforce without explicitly rejecting the old connections between femininity, motherhood, and work. Thus, women gained entry at the price of accepting traditional gendered roles and norms.

Vivian Binder: The "Monster Mother"

But what happened to women on Wall Street in the nineties who exceeded the norm and were identified as risk takers? To address this question we turn to a different narrative of risk. Vivian Binder's "herstory" exists alongside Patricia Riley's risk-averse account. Engaged in a career in which she was the exception to the norm (and often the very first exception), Vivian articulated anxiety over the ways Wall Street attempted to identify her as a masculine risk taker in the nineties. In our first interview, she proudly presented herself as a "risk taker" in a variety of professional guises. In descriptions of her publicly performed self she typically occupied the more masculinized subject position of a measured "risk taker." She seamlessly attached to herself dominant neoliberal American values of choice, calculation, self-responsibility, and agency. For example, this was her response when I asked her to tell me more about her unusual career move into investment banking: "I have always figured that sometimes you have to take a half step back to take three leaps ahead. But my risks are real calculated. People do view me as a risk taker. But, I usually know that 51 percent of the time it is going to work out." Vivian's meteoric career depended on, in part, her ability to project a "masculine" risk-taking performance that produced recognition from her employees and peers. Moreover, her indication that her risks were calculated reveals the extent to which she constructed herself as the ideal neoliberal subject whose "abilities" can be measured.

Yet the firm's perceptions of her also illuminate how Wall Street viewed risk-taking performances in women as the dangerous and negative forces of sexual excess, especially in women occupying top leadership positions. Consider Vivian's discussion regarding the "hard times" in her career:

> There were times, especially after I made the transition into investment banking that, because I wasn't from Harvard, I was assumed not to be as bright, good, or successful. All the intangible and perception stuff is hard to deal with. Over the years, I got a reputation in this firm as being very tough and very aggressive—and, therefore the assumption is that I will always be a ball buster. Even in the last few years, the people that know me well assume that I kept this place in order—got the business turned around—because I must have been shooting people. (1994)

Vivian's description, suffused with images of violence and sexuality, provides an important glimpse into the masculinization of powerful Wall Street women in the nineties. Her reputation as a "ball buster" reveals male corporate fears of emasculation that also accompanied the rise of women into the ultra-moneyed executive ranks. There is an important class, ethnic, and status subtext lurking in her narrative. Vivian alludes to the cultural obstacles she faced in the 1980s in making a set of unusual career moves for a woman into investment banking. Indeed, she mentions the difficulties she faced switching out of what was typically perceived as the rough-and-tumble, white (Irish or Eastern European Jewish, depending on the firm), "working-class," and "middle-class" world of trading and sales, into the traditionally prestigious closed universe of investment banking, occupied by predominantly blue-blooded Harvard men.

For Vivian, dispositions perceived as firmly rooted in her outsider, less polished, aggressive, salesman, middle-class habitus appear to follow her throughout her career trajectory. This perception works to both her advantage and disadvantage. On the one hand, Wall Street branded her with the "iron maiden" stereotype imposed on tough and strong businesswomen in the seventies (Kanter 1977). On the other hand, Vivian fortuitously entered into banking at a moment in which, under deregulation, "predatory market machismo" began to partially usurp earlier forms of WASP paternal and gentlemanly deal-making practices.

Just as the notion of benevolent social and corporate motherhood is not completely novel, neither was the creation of the masculinization and demonization of powerful women on nineties Wall Street. Indeed, highly agentic women in Grimm's fairy tales are often subject to particularly horrible violent deaths (Ortner 1996). What is novel, however, is the way in which images of powerful women register with the celebration of risk taking and risk-management techniques.

Throughout our talk, Vivian moved back and forth between taking a more masculinized professional position of celebrating risk and a feminized private position of avoiding risk that more closely matched Patricia's motherly narrative. When I asked why she thought some women manage to break through career barriers, while others do not, she had the following response:

> I think that some people, men or women, still wait to be given an opportunity basically. And sometimes you have to take a risk and basically go out and do it. You are either going to succeed or you are going to be told, "No, no. Stay back." But if you don't try, nothing ever happens. Now some will tell you that these are some of the fundamental qualities of good leadership, but they first have to come from within you before you can try and instill it in others. I

don't know because I am not a risk-oriented person. I don't like to ski. There are certain things that in my normal life I would never be seen doing . . . never consider myself a risk-taking person.

Throughout Vivian's narrative, she worried about "the inner plays in the mind between the personal and professional." She articulated a divide between public risk taking and private risk avoiding, and she moved nervously back and forth between two contrasting versions of her publicly and privately imagined self. She noted that she was perceived professionally as a "demonic" mother, in relation to both her employees and her real-life children. Notably violent gendered images often accompany her self-description as a risk taker. Yet she simultaneously reiterated her subjectively understood private reality as a caring mother and as a self-described "non-risk-oriented person" in her "normal life." Indeed, throughout our first interview (and occasionally throughout our conversations over time) she expressed a deep desire to convince everyone in the firm, as well as me, that she was a "good mother." This concern, in the end, produced the most unease for Vivian. Throughout our subsequent meetings, she repeatedly told me about how people in the firm imagined her, for example, as an "ogre who beats her husband and kids." After nearly two decades of working in the same firm, Vivian decided for the first time, in the nineties, to invite her entire department to her country house for a day. She held the event for two reasons: "team building" and to show everyone that she was "pretty down to earth" and that she had a healthy life outside the office.

She isn't paranoid. My discussions with other executives—men and women—indicated that Wall Streeters did nervously link her aggressive speculative practices to her mothering behavior. Although managers rarely spoke to me about her private life, they most often drew on evocative physical stereotypes of masculinity—her "swagger," that she is a "big, swinging dick"—to conjure up images of her body and corporate style. The masculinized stigma stamped on very high-level women, the potency attributed to Vivian, derives in part from the tension between such figures' crosscutting of gender (masculine and feminine) and of class (working-class and professional) identities.

In the end, the image Vivian tried very hard to portray was close to the picture articulated by her counterpart, Patricia, of the caring mother. Patricia's narrative, however, assured us that professional working women will still take care of and reproduce the nation's children—or at least those of the professional-managerial and upper classes. By contrast, Vivian's account enacted deep neoconservative concerns about the current and future state of the American family. The masculine tropes she drew on reveal structures of what the anthropologist Elizabeth Traube (1992: 123–67) argued were classwide anxieties at the end of the twentieth century about "who will do the caring" in an era of a small but growing presence of financially and culturally independent women.

The "Gender-Neutral" Discourses of Corporate Neoliberalism

While Wall Street women's career stories about risk constructed gender difference, their narratives also elaborated upon discourses of neoliberal individualism and the associated rhetoric concerning the efficacy of deregulation in freeing the market and citizens from the power of the state. Here, they linked their experiences of career mobility to supposedly gender-neutral economic images and entrepreneurial practices of work, production, and performance. In particular, they invoke the traditional American dream of success—that any individual if he or she works hard enough will be rewarded. They continued to believe strongly in the culture of meritocracy, much like they had as younger adults first entering Wall Street. But, by the nineties, they inserted this more classic ideology of success directly into their accounts of the marketplace. Below Maydelle Brooks elaborates:

> Glass ceilings are made to be broken. I think that too many people sit and wait for the ceiling to break. You've got to figure out how to break in. In this business it's easier to do because it is a business where performance and production are nongender-specific and nonrace-specific. I know that is very different from working in corporate America. . . .
>
> If you are a producer, performance is evaluated in terms of securities bought and sold, transactions done. If you are a banker it is in terms of deals brought in, executed, and business developed. That is production. That has tangible numbers and measurable results. It is how many calls have you made this year, whereas being the brand manager at Procter & Gamble is very different. . . .
>
> Corporations and banks are more of a bureaucracy. I mean, on

Wall Street you are talking about loose organizations and affiliations and individual entrepreneurs with real measurable results, results that can transcend race and gender. (1994)

Maydelle's account of gender neutrality and race neutrality resonates with the heightened emphasis on transparency, competitive individualism, and entrepreneurial values in celebrations of the free market. Indeed, her reference to "tangible numbers and measurable results" is predicated upon the idea of objective disclosure within financial markets. Here, the idea of number of calls made is stripped from the social context of unequal access of opportunity and systems of meaning and interpretation (Zaloom 2006: 141–60).

Beyond the notion of transparency, Maydelle's assertion also fits within a long history of the American belief in the work ethic. Individuals, regardless of gender, race, or ethnicity, are able to control their occupational and class identities (Bellah et al. 1985). Her account of Wall Street in the nineties, however, unmoors this success ideology from its traditional berth in the workplace and the nation. In an era of corporate neoliberalism, she located the entrepreneurial American self *directly* in the global marketplace of "loose organizations and affiliations." This is Wall Street's notion of a "money meritocracy" in which the only color it sees in the marketplace is green. Here the financial world's enormous greed for making money purportedly overrides sexism and racism in American society at large (Ho 2009: 107).

Maydelle differentiates Wall Street firms from old-fashioned, slow-moving bureaucratic corporations. The underlying implication in this part of her career narrative is that the financial world is perhaps less caught up in hierarchical relations and the "old boys' network" (Ho 2009: 208). Success, from this perspective, depends on one's objective performance, not on subjective perceptions of gender or race. Maydelle truly believed in what she said about investment banks, production, and success. What is remarkable is that she also spent an enormous amount of time during our talk, as Vivian had also done, lamenting the ways Wall Street views her as a masculinized woman and an unfit mother. These deeply gendered perceptions of Maydelle affected her ongoing relationships within and outside the firm with men as well as with women.

Similarly, while on the one hand Patricia attributed women's success in research to their feminine risk-conservative qualities, she, too, also elaborated upon discourses of objectivity and gender neutrality. Accordingly, she said, "I think you find a lot of women in research because it was one of the few areas on Wall Street where competence was proven by the prices in the marketplace, and not by a subjective boss who liked you or didn't like you, or denigrated your work" (1994).

In Maydelle's, Vivian's, and Patricia's narratives we can see the ways in which they, like many other women I spoke to on Wall Street at the time, moved between discourses about gender and risk that distinguished women and men from one another and discourses of meritocracy and gender neutrality and race neutrality in the professional workplace. Women were caught up in this discursive disjunction: the connection (and disconnection) between gender and success. They continually shifted back and forth between these two discourses, often at times without being fully conscious of such shifts.

There was another gendered discursive disjunction at play here. On the one hand, earlier on in my talk with Maydelle she attributed much of her success to the senior male mentors in her career. Men helped open doors and made opportunities available. In that particular part of her career narrative, Maydelle was clearly aware of the structures of gender and power that exist in financial firms. The fact that she, Patricia, and so many other women I spoke to in the nineties also believed strongly in gender neutrality—the erasure both of structures of gender and power and of the advantage of having a male mentor— is a tribute to the strength of the moneyed meritocracy ideology and a complete faith in the objectivity and transparency of numbers within the world of finance.

Maydelle's discussion also offers significant insight into the ways Wall Street female elites articulated an ideology of gender neutrality in the American public sphere, again grounding global capitalism in its particular iterations. However, feminist theorists have argued that seemingly neutralizing discourse is still gendered, classed, and raced (Ortner 1991; Chase 1995: 19). As Sherry Ortner argues, Americans lacking a strong class discourse tend to displace "class frictions into the discourses and practices of gender and sexual relations" (1991: 17). As Maydelle stated, "This business breeds insecurity, especially among women. But that is what makes people more productive. That is what makes people more competitive. And like most women, even not in this business, but most successful women, I look at the bag ladies, and say, 'There but for the grace of God go I.' You can call it immigrant mentality, but I never was born with a sense of entitlement" (1994). This is striking language from a woman standing at the very top of the corporate ladder, making millions of dollars. Yet, nonetheless, she, like a great number of women I spoke to in the nineties, imagined their fears to be mirrored within female figures and "others" positioned near or at the very opposite end of the class scale. Their observations suggested that in an era of economic and corporate restructuring, anxiety about massive capital losses and about spiraling downward mobility registered even among elites (Ortner 1999; Ho 2009).[4]

Being Women Leaders

As the women advanced in their careers, they achieved positions of power and leadership that sometimes made them feel conflicted between their status as elites and their identity as women. For example, they found themselves having to balance their goals as managers in charge of ensuring the bottom line, with at times their desires to open up the playing field in finance to women as well as minorities. As senior-level executives on Wall Street, the women were interested in building their own corporate careers, individual status, and power. They understood the importance of their firms seeing them as dedicated profit-seeking "team players" whose first priority in life was work and the corporation's success (Jackall 1988; Ho 2009). Family and other seemingly personal or moral concerns were to be kept under a tight lid or (better yet) behind closed doors (Blair-Loy 2003). Witness the amount of time it took for Vivian to invite her colleagues home to meet her children before she decided it was "all right" not to "always separate" her personal and professional worlds.

While corporate bureaucracies tend to bring together people with very little in common with one another, the first generation of women had shared certain experiences. Most had been brought up in middle-class to upper-middle-class households. Many had gone to women's colleges during the beginning of the modern feminist movement. They had all also experienced being among the first women to enter into and succeed on Wall Street and to fight certain forms of discrimination. Many had met one another at NYU's business school and had participated in the FWA in the seventies and eighties. Many went on to be active in the Women's Campaign Fund in the nineties. And, as they advanced in their careers, the women continued to be shaped by the liberal women's movement, particularly the movement's focus on putting women into positions of power. They also shared experiences of discrimination.

Perhaps most important, their ongoing experiences of straddling competing visions of gender, work, and success shaped their perceptions of themselves as bosses and members of executive committees. They believed strongly in the financial culture of meritocracy, hard work, individualism, and gender neutrality. They also believed in gender differences not only in terms of risk taking, but women's needs for mentoring and networking relationships of support, advice, and promotion. Understanding how the women came to serve as high-ranking senior executives in this ambiguous yet highly gender-charged atmosphere helps illuminate their performances as the pioneering group of female leaders on Wall Street.

Moreover, Wall Street women's dual, shifting, and conflicting understandings of gender were deeply shaped by a long history of debates within American feminism that views equality and difference as antagonistic aims (Pateman 1989). Like many liberal feminist-oriented women before them, they shared a belief that women should pursue equality within the framework of existing institutions. This perspective affirmed their belief in gender neutrality on Wall Street. On the other hand, the women also adopted a "difference" perspective in which they affirmed gender particularity in high finance. During the nineties, the first generation of women were caught up and constrained by these two ideological poles. As the feminist historian Joan Scott notes, "When equality and difference are paired dichotomously . . . they structure an impossible choice. If one opts for equality one is forced to accept the notion that difference is antithetical to it. If one opts for difference, one admits that equality is unattainable" (1997: 765).

Affirmative Action and Affirming Difference

Affirmative action–influenced policies and programs were the favored equality strategies prior to the incorporation of diversity management in the mid- to late nineties on Wall Street. Under affirmative action, policy preferences were to be given to individuals who were members of underrepresented groups in education, business, or government (Squires n.d.: 12). Such an approach did not sit easily with neoliberal beliefs in individualism, meritocracy, and efficacy of the free market as

Patricia's narrative about whether to start a minority management firm in the mid-nineties illustrated:

> I am midway through a research process to determine whether it's worthwhile to start a minority management firm. Women qualify as minorities. [Some] state localities have a certain amount of money that they set aside and give to minority firms. Some of the private-sector companies, like Colgate and Palmolive, give portions of their pension plan to minority money markets—minority money managers. One of the problems is that a lot of minorities do not have a track record. The woman I would team up with has a track record. Between the combination of her track record and my visibility—I think we could really do a good job. . . .
>
> The reason I have moral qualms is that I think these plans should be going to the best money managers they can find, not minorities —set aside. The other thing—on the one hand, I mean to put myself into a minority category as if I am disadvantaged seems to be taking advantage of the system. On the other hand, legally I qualify. Women are minorities under these programs. (1994)

Patricia does not perceive herself as being at a disadvantage in part because of her class. She is wealthy. Her moral qualms about starting a minority management firm actually reflect widely held critiques of affirmative action during the eighties and into the nineties: these effectively elevated the opportunities of targeted groups via quotas, offering them special treatment at the cost of discriminating against equally qualified or even better qualified majorities (Squires n.d.: 12). In short, Patricia and others found affirmative action to be an affront to their ideals of meritocracy. Maydelle echoes a similar sentiment in her talk about the creation of gender task forces in the mid-nineties: "I personally do not believe that just because the workforce is 50 percent women that therefore that means that everything else has to be 50 percent. I do not think that if you are black, green, or blue that that should be that way. There are a lot of people that think that way. In that sense, I am probably a bit of a renegade" (1994). Such discomfort with affirmative action–oriented policies was rampant in American business and finance in the eighties and nineties. Indeed, some Wall Street women became increasingly critical of such practices, particularly as they became managers in charge of hiring and promoting employees. They believed that (some) women blamed discrimination for their workplace problems and lack of mobility, while they should, in fact, put the blame on themselves as individuals. Here are the perspectives of two other members of the first cohort of women, Susan Laird, a senior investment banker, and Pamela Driscoll, a senior research analyst:

I think affirmative action is sometimes a hindrance in terms of management hiring because we are such a litigious society. I had a case where I thought I had the most diverse workforce in the firm. In the end, I had to terminate someone for cheating on their expense accounts. This professional had an MBA from Harvard, happened to be black and a woman, and filed an EEOC complaint. But, in fact, the issue was cheating. I know from some of my male counterparts who have problems that [when] they see two qualified individuals [*long pause*] they pick the white male. (Laird, 1994)

I think that if you are willing to work hard, this was true even in the seventies, even in what was an environment that was not open to women—you could make it on Wall Street. I think that if you persisted there were enough of us who showed that you could do it. I think that a lot of women, even now, continue to have ambivalent feelings and will sometimes cite discrimination as a reason for not making it, when it really is their own fault. We have a woman analyst here—a single mother—who has a beautiful house in Fairfield County, Connecticut, and she had twins. She would not move back into the city because she loved her house in Connecticut. . . .

And then about less than a year after her babies were born, she quit her job. Now she tells everyone it is because she cannot work now as a working mother. She says they [her firm] were not flexible enough. Well, the bottom line is that she left home for work before the babies were up in the morning because she had to start pretty early here at the firm, and the kids were asleep by the time she was home at night. And I say that she self-sabotaged. I am ten minutes, door to door. And I do that because I am a working mother of one. Every single working mother we have in research and sales lives in the city. (Driscoll, 1994)

The first cohort of Wall Street women typically figured out individual strategies to successfully advance up the corporate ladder. In the end they may have been aware of the challenges facing women in male-dominated workplaces, but they felt that other women like themselves could ultimately overcome discrimination and be promoted based on their own merit. Senior women in finance thus made these types of issues secondary to their commitment to professional work (Chase 1995: 183; Blair-Loy 2003). Wall Street's culture of individualism and politics of hard work thus led the women to construct individual solutions (like deciding to live in Manhattan to be near to a workplace). They did not engage in collective action that directly challenged the system of gender and power on Wall Street. In fact, the more they moved up the hierarchy in finance the more they found themselves "on the other side" of the elite, male-dominated system.

The Feminization of Work-Family Programs and Finding Oneself on the Wrong Side

In 1993, Congress legally required firms to offer twelve weeks of unpaid leave to new mothers and fathers, allowing them to return to their jobs after giving birth. Most corporations, including Wall Street, by this time already had maternity and medical leaves in place, but Congress made such leaves legal requirements rather than options (Dobbin 2009: 174–75). Maternity leave was the first work-family program to be introduced to the world of finance, but it was not the last. Flextime and job sharing became part of a new system of work-family practices designed to recruit and retain female employees (176). Personnel departments were increasingly dominated by women. Firms hired them because they felt they would help target, attract, and recruit women and minorities into the firm (169). Here, the goals of newer work-family policies and older diversity management policies (from the eighties) were folded together.

Corporate America had started to take heed of the call for work-family policies starting in the eighties. However, by the mid-nineties, experimentations with flextime and other work-family policies were still in their embryonic form in finance. First-generation women by this point in time were in their mid- to late forties. They did not for the most part participate in these programs. Younger women in their thirties tended to be work-family pioneers, but more senior women like Patricia and others were sometimes the supervisors or bosses of these younger women. They were, at best, ambivalent about the new system:

> Maternity leave is now six weeks. A male could take it, too—I doubt if any male does. There is good news. And there is bad news. The

good news is that there is a great deal of flexibility for professional women who are valuable to the firm, much less at other levels. The firm has a huge investment in some people. If you are talking about a receptionist or secretary who wants something, it is much less. Now, if they had a baby, don't want to work full-time—then somebody else has a baby and the two of them hooked up together and asked if they could split the job, we do a lot of that. I think that on an informal basis then we have been very good. . . .

There is a dichotomy going right now which is that some of the older women, like me, are very annoyed with the younger women. A woman that worked for me got pregnant and took her six-week maternity leave. When she called up to come back, she said, "I am coming back to work either Monday or Tuesday. I am not sure which day because Memorial Day occurred when I was out on my maternity leave—I think that I am entitled to an extra day."

I said, "You are going to quibble with me over an extra day? I doubt if our firm policy gives you an extra day because there happened to be a holiday when you were out on maternity. Why don't you call human resources if this is so important to you?" Of course, human resources said absolutely not. You do not get credited for holidays when we are paying you for your maternity leave.

. . . Then she arrives back to work—about a week later she says that she is taking a vacation the first week of August. I said, "You cannot do that. I am out on vacation that week. You should have checked with me." She said, "I have nonrefundable airfare. I have to do this." I said, "No. You have to check with me. I don't vacation when my boss is out. You work for me. You don't take vacations when I am out." She says, "But I paid for airfare." And I said, "You forgot a crucial thing. Our publication deadline is August fifteenth. You are responsible for that publication. It has to be out the first week of August."

We went back and forth. Finally, I said to her, "All right. If you are going to insist on taking this vacation, which I think is incredibly poor judgment—if you miss the deadline it is your total responsibility. If you screw up this publication as far as I am concerned you have screwed up your job." . . . She took the vacation. I was staggered. When I was out with my kids I would have never dreamed of coming back here and immediately taking a vacation. . . .

We have had several women cause major disruptions over the last year in the firm. And Deirdre and I think—who is going to hire these women when this is what happens? It's nothing but headaches. It is going to be a subtle form of discrimination here—because in my mind when I am considering hiring someone I am going to think I need coverage—What if I have no coverage here?

What is wrong with these women that they do not feel that they have any responsibility? Deirdre and I would have never dreamed of acting like that when we were their age. There is definitely a change in the younger women. It is now an entitlement—What am I entitled to as opposed to what are my responsibilities to the client?

I do not think our policies are going to get any more generous. I think the firm has faced too many problems that have been created out of these new policies and programs. . . . There are senior male executives that are furious about several women and the situations they have created when it comes to maternity leaves, job-sharing. . . . And the ironic thing is that I find myself in the men's camp. I have no sympathy for these women! I feel like I am on the wrong side! (Patricia Riley, 1995)

Patricia's strong, even negative, feelings toward younger women taking advantage of new work-family policies, including part-time work, echo the sentiment of many executives (female and male) in finance during the nineties who considered part-timers to be "uncommitted second-class citizens" (Blair-Loy 2003: 92).[5] Cultural values shape people's experiences and expectations of dealing with work and family life while working within corporations. But a financial subject's generation, market experience, and particular position within the corporate hierarchy also produce that actor's understanding of work, success, and what it means to be a good boss or employee.

Generational differences were also generational fissures between senior- and junior-level women on Wall Street. Notably, the women following in Patricia's footsteps had attended college, entered the workforce, and went to business school during the eighties and early to mid-nineties. They entered the world of finance during the bull market. Wall Street's culture of hard work, macho risk taking, and being super smart produced a sense of superiority and entitlement among its trained professional workforce (Ho 2009). Moreover, these workers began professional life in an era in which any expectations of building a career for life in a single firm, being loyal to the corporation and, in turn, having the corporation be loyal to you had vanished; people expected that they would eventually be downsized. And they also entered Wall Street at a point in which having women work in a male-dominated environment was becoming more commonplace. The younger generation thus also built their careers during an era that many have come to label (in contrast to the feminist period of the seventies) postfeminist (Faludi 1991). This meant that some of these women believed that feminism was no longer needed. Women could have it all—a successful work and family life—without becoming or identifying themselves as feminists (McRobbie 2009: 8).

From Patricia's point of view, however, some of the younger women working for her in the firm felt simply far too "entitled." They appeared to focus more on their own needs than that of the clients. This behavior was not only bad for businesses, but it also damaged women's overall reputation in the financial world as professionals. Patricia was hardly the only woman to talk to me about the next generation of employees, particularly women, in this manner. Deirdre Parliament spoke in even more depth about her female employees:

> One of the disappointing things is that over time, you find, or I have found that, in the end most people try to take care of themselves. They want things. They want more stock coverage, more accounts, and more money. They will let you invest in them, and that all seems quite fair. But, in the end, it is usually a one-way street.
>
> Now there are other times when people will pay you back in a personal way. But you have to be clear that you know you are doing it for reasons that you know why you are doing it. Don't expect too much back—that is part of your job—or that is your style of dealing with people. Don't expect that people are going to be indebted to you forever.
>
> Actually the women have been the worst. The women who are close to my age here have been horrified by the way some of the young women act. They are even more calculating and callous. We older women have all discussed it. We think that it is partly because they are young and that they think that by being open, responsive, and warm about things that they are not being tough. They think the way you should act in business is screw you. I got a higher offer. I am out of here. . . .
>
> I am not sure what the young women want. I would be very interested to know what a thirty-five-year-old woman wants. When younger women tell me they do not want to work that hard, that they want children but do not want to work long hours . . . well, then

they are not going to get the jobs—because men who get the jobs, they always work hard. (1994)

Liberal Feminism and Financial Markets: Some Paradoxes

Work-family and affirmative action–oriented policies and programs on Wall Street during the nineties did not, for the most part, sit comfortably with senior management in charge of the bottom line, whether these managers were women or men. Borne out of the liberal feminist and civil rights movement of the sixties and seventies, these programs did not translate easily or without resistance when it came to professionals putting them into everyday practice. Moreover, some of the premises of these programs—using quotas, being labeled a minority, making exceptions—did not fit particularly well with many of the first cohort of women's notions of professional success: theirs and others. From their perspective, allowing minorities to qualify for special programs did not necessarily mean that jobs were going to the best, hardest working, and deserving workers. Working mothers who took advantage of the new work-family flexible job programs were often less committed employees. In the end, then, creating and implementing many programs designed to advance women and minorities in finance went against the dominant worldview of the moneyed meritocracy.

All of this is not to say that senior women like Patricia, Maydelle, Vivian, and others were not sympathetic to the plights of their female employees. Indeed, many of the women acknowledged the need for Wall Street, and their own respective firms, to create gender and diversity task forces and to develop programs that would facilitate the recruitment, retention, and advancement of women and minorities. But the path to accomplishing these goals was not always clear-cut. Nor did they fit well with the pressures that executives experienced to think in the short term and to pursue profit for the firm and themselves. This was the paradox that most women found themselves working within as they advanced in their careers.

The institutional culture of Wall Street constrained and generally forced the women to bracket their personal or professional concerns about gender inequality and discrimination from what was best for the corporation. The first cohort of women thus focused most of their energies on their own careers and the general professionalization and cultural acceptance of women in leadership positions. Taking such a depoliticized position had also been translated into their work within the FWA during the eighties. However, by the nineties, instead of seeking collective solutions and gender change on Wall Street, some of the women turned their energies toward the national stage and the broader world of women and politics. They became deeply active in the Women's Campaign Fund.

CHAPTER 4

WOMEN'S POLITICS AND STATE-MARKET FEMINISM

In April 1994, Mindy Plane and I sat down in her midtown office after hours to chat. By that time, Mindy was a partner in a small boutique investment bank. She also spent a great deal of her time helping women candidates get elected to state and national office. During our talk, we chatted about her current deal making, the Knicks and the pending playoffs, as well as Mindy's day at work:

> Who did I have lunch with today? A female senator. I was told to bring some women. I brought Vanessa Eccles, who I have known since the late seventies. She was head of one of the FWA [Financial Women's Association] committees when I was on the board of the FWA. Now she is head of a major business at a premiere investment bank. I invited Fiona Jacobs, who is senior vice president of human resources at a major insurance corporation. And I invited Wendy Tinker, who founded a woman's financial firm. The three of us, the senator, plus Steven Clips, who is head of a major financial-services firm, and a bunch of other men went out to lunch. These are my friends. If I want to check out somebody in city government in Boston, I know that Ellen Hall's husband works in Boston—I will just ask Ellen and she will go out for me. . . . But I think that I am unusual—I do not know too many women who do what I do that combine business and politics the way I have. Men have done it. But I don't see women doing it.[1]

The world of American elites had begun to change by the time Mindy invited her financial female friends to the luncheon meeting with a female senator and several high-ranking executives from Wall Street. The constructions of class, power, and gender were shifting. As men who had historically not been excluded from Wall Street's power circles, the businessmen at the luncheon were used to their "work" and "social" and "political" lives intersecting. "Power lunching" was a part of their daily lives. But for members of the first generation, attending such a luncheon was a relatively novel phenomenon, albeit one that was becoming more familiar to women like Mindy, who by that point in time was active in the Women's Campaign Fund (WCF) and national politics more generally.[2]

By the nineties, after decades of keeping their feminist concerns largely under wraps, some of the members of the first generation became quite active in the formal world of women and politics. They openly supported pro-choice women running for elective office. In doing so, they effectively combined their two major feminist interests: advancing women's equality and leadership, and ensuring that women continued to have reproductive rights. Other changes were at play at the 1994 luncheon. Chief among them was the primary guest at the event—a female senator. Her presence, along with those of the women in finance, suggests that the idea of interacting with small numbers of women in positions of power in the financial and political arena was becoming part of the fabric of Wall Street institutions. The luncheon thus provided an informal occasion for Wall Street executives, for the women as well as the men, including one CEO of a financial firm, to network with the senator (Benoit 2007: 70). On the one hand, government officials—at various levels and in both parties—seek the financial support of wealthy individuals and corporate political action committees (PACs). On the other, executives, particularly those working within the area of public finance, seek the business of government. State and city governments need huge sums of money to keep running, and much of that cash comes from investors. Part of the work then of public financiers is to work out complicated fund-raising practices in cooperation with government officials (Fisher 1990: 55). Thus, while the men at the luncheon may have been supporters of women in finance and politics, they (as well as their female colleagues) were likely also there to socialize, to discuss public policy issues (particularly those pertaining to markets) and business, and to create stronger ties with the senator, ties that might be useful in the future.

Notably, none of the Wall Street women at the luncheon had been born into blue-blooded upper-class families. All were from middle-class backgrounds, had worked their way up the corporate ladder, had made significant sums of money, and in doing so had become members of a new professional-class elite in New York City (Ostrander 1984: 10). They had done so through their initial involvement and networking in and through the FWA. Their individual goals and aspirations, and indeed their political parties, did not always match one another. But, for the most part, they shared an interest in making sure that women were able to successfully move up the ladder in a range of traditionally male-dominated professional domains.

Beginning in the late eighties and well into the mid-nineties, some first-generation women were dissatisfied with the FWA's lack of a political agenda; others—like Mindy Plane with political desires of their own—left the FWA and began pulling one another into joining the WCF. Upper-class female members on the WCF board, unable to draw donors and participants from their old-money, elite women friends, went in search of and found women with new money. This meant women working on Wall Street (Democratic and Republican), including Mindy, Maydelle Brooks, Vivian Binder, and Patricia Riley. Mindy and others then subsequently continued to invite other women from Wall Street into the WCF, and into various forms of political engagement, including, for example, helping to raise funds for political candidates. Mindy officially became a WCF board member in the early nineties, and, in time she recruited her female financier friends—both Republicans and Democrats—and others to the organization.

The first cohort of women had not for the most part collectively embraced and helped incorporate feminism into the private world of the financial workplace as they ascended within the corporate hierarchy. However, by the nineties the women had broken through glass ceilings and were more assured of their place and stature. Moreover, as senior corporate actors on Wall Street, they were now in positions that bridged the state and the corporation, the political landscape and the marketplace. While elite men's circles in business and government had overlapped for years, this was the first time that there were sufficient numbers of women to form the first generation of a female financial and political professional-managerial elite in the United States (Ostrower 1992). As such, they incorporated aspects of liberal feminism into American political life: namely, advancing women who supported women's reproductive rights into leadership positions.

By the nineties then, the women were engaged in a feminism that went beyond aligning liberal feminist interests with the state. Theirs was an emergent kind of feminism—one that was not entirely mediated by the state but, in this particular case, also the WCF—a market-oriented organization of female venture capitalists who supported female political candidates. The women achieved their liberal feminist project through carefully designed first-generation networks—beginning with the FWA (during the eighties) and subsequently with the Leadership Circle of the WCF during the nineties. During the FWA years, the women did not collectively take a public, political stance toward feminist issues such as sex discrimination, equal rights, and the right to abortion. Their stance toward politics and activism, however, began to shift in the nineties, particularly as they became more involved in the WCF. The diversity of the feminist movement itself, over time, forced the women initially in the FWA and then in the WCF to negotiate, debate, and make decisions about the mission of each network, the organization's relationship to feminism, and the ensuing work that needed to be done (Ferree and Martin 1995: 6).

Making State-Market Feminism via the WCF

By the time the FWA began to initiate such changes, some of the members of the first generation were at very senior levels in the world of finance. They were no longer directly active in the FWA. Many, but not all, still paid dues. However, even then, they did not partake in the daily running of the organization—nor had they done so for some time. Still, on occasion, some, including Patricia, Maydelle, Vivian, and, on rare occasions, Deirdre Parliament, returned to talk to the younger women following in their path about such topics as "breaking glass ceilings."

For the most part, members of the first generation were now actively building their own increasingly senior careers. Mindy had, for example, begun her career in commercial banking, spent some time in corporate America, and entered the world of investment banking in the late eighties. During the seventies and eighties she had been a very active board member of the FWA. But by the early to mid-nineties, she had become increasingly active in state and national politics. She was also known to be a major networker and fund-raiser in the world of women and politics. Thus, in addition to her full-time job in banking, she served on the advisory committees of several governors and mayors within northeastern states. And she was also on the WCF board: "I am mainly viewed as a political person right now because I do so much in politics. The advice people want from me—women and men —is to give them advice on dealing with state agencies. I am viewed as a resource. I serve on a variety of financial committees of various individual campaigns. And as I become more involved in politics I think I might, at some point, go into someone's administration or just continue to do what I do now in investment banking and serve on corporate boards" (1994).

The WCF board was founded in the eighties. For the next two decades, the WCF, as a bipartisan organization, traditionally made sure to have one Democrat and one Republican act as co-chairs of the board. Since 2005, however, the WCF has had only one chair. During the nineties, Madeline Winters, a well-known, upper-class female activist, actively helped to recruit women to serve on the board. During this period of time it became increasingly difficult to find female pro-choice Republicans interested in being board members. When Madeline had exhausted her usual contacts, she decided to pursue a small but growing group of Republican female "newcomers" on Wall Street. A Republican congresswoman told Madeline about Mindy, who was already known in certain circles for her participation in the world of politics. According to Madeline, "Everyone wanted to pitch Mindy to me. It was always important to be bipartisan because women have so much in common. I said to Mindy, 'I really want you because you have a love of politics and you have to love politics to do this kind of work.' If you have the combination of love and politics then seeing these young women going places is one of the best rewards. There are really few rewards in life, but this is one—Mindy had that combination. And she became active in the WCF" (2008).

Once Mindy became active on the board, she began recruiting other financial women into the organization.[3] But while some first-generation women became quite active in the WCF, others did not. When I spoke with Deirdre in 1994, for example, she informed me that as a working mother and senior-level executive she "had no time for the FWA or other women's groups." Her focus was on work, her teenage daughter, and her husband. She might write a check on occasion, but she did not attend WCF events. Maydelle, on the other hand, said that she participated in a range of industry networks as well as the WCF: "I was a board member of the Financial Women's Association ten years ago when that organization was sort of getting off the ground. In recent years, I have been involved in groups that have tended to support or help women politicians, not just in terms of fund-raising, but in terms of giving their technical expertise—as a Republican or Democrat. And that has been very satisfying" (1994).

Finance and economics are traditionally conceived of as depoliticized domains of activity.[4] Modern finance is thought to be objective, knowable, and certain, hence the women's strong belief in the gender neutrality of performance (e.g., the numbers of deals made). If Wall Street women and the FWA had begun to deconstruct the boundaries of the acceptable and the normative in the world of finance, including gender inequities, they might have begun to actually disrupt financial discourse and practice. They might have revealed the system to be filled with historical struggles, political strife, and cultural ambiguity about what and who legitimately belonged in the financial sphere. But the women and the FWA—like the overwhelming majority of Wall Street actors—accepted hegemonic economic notions of the financial system as a coherent, bounded system with rules of its own. For the women, changing the political order of society, including the gendered order, required becoming active in more traditionally accepted forms of political organizations and activity, including the WCF.

The women's participation in the WCF signaled that by the nineties the women were part of what I am calling "state-corporate feminist" or "state-market feminist" networks. "State feminism" is a term that has emerged to describe women's policy agencies, national machineries for the advancement of women, or gender equality machinery within state bureaucracies (Outshoorn and Kantola 2007). European governments, in the wake of demands from the women's movement (from the sixties onward) for policies to achieve gender equity and women's lives, formed women's policies agencies. However, the United States has never created a national agency assigned responsibility to oversee women's equality, issues, and status (McBride 2007).

In the absence of a formal national women's agency, women in the United States have created a large number of feminist organizations, including NGOs, in order to work for change in the law, courts, corporations, local communities, and lives of women (Ferree and Martin 1995: 4). While some politically active feminists work exclusively within such organizations, a fairly large number of women in favor of making change to women's lives do not necessarily work in full-time occupations directly focused on advancing some form of feminism. Instead, these women tend to identify in some way with the women's movement.

The first generation of women who became active in the WCF in the nineties did so because they identified sufficiently with the specific feminist-inspired mission of the WCF: namely, the organization's commitment to supporting female candidates who favored a women's right to abortion and, in earlier years, the Equal Rights Amendment. Through their participation in the WCF, Wall Street women made connections with female political candidates who shared their views on women's power and reproductive freedom.

Women in finance and women in politics, affiliated with the WCF, did not necessarily share political views on other issues, such as the economy. This would be a source of some tension within the organization. Moreover, although Wall Street women shared some of the same objectives of female candidates, they themselves were not formally full-time members of any state bureaucracy as such. Some women, like Mindy, did and continue to, from time to time, serve on the budgetary advisory and other committees of some officials in New York, New Jersey, and Connecticut. And some eventually came to serve on advisory committees for presidential candidates. Wall Street women, like Mindy and others, came to occupy multiple identities and affiliations within the private and public sectors.[5]

By the nineties, the primary decade in which Mindy, Maydelle, and other first-generation Wall Street women became involved in the WCF, the organization had given $1.2 million to 242 candidates in 41 states and the District of Columbia, a 308 percent increase in contributions since 1985.[6] Their donors, approximately 20,000, made contributions ranging from $5 to $5,000. For female candidates who were often unable to receive funds by established sources, even small amounts of money were vital to their campaigns.[7]

The year 1992 was a record breaker for women in politics, and pundits and politicians alike called it the "Year of the Woman."[8] The number of women in the United States Senate had tripled from two to six. Twenty-four new women were elected to the House of Representatives, bringing the total to forty-eight; there were over fifteen hundred women in the country's state legislatures. Nevertheless, in spite of such progress, women in politics still had a long way to go. They only made up 7 percent of the U.S. Senate and 11 percent of the House. There were still only three women governors at the time, and women did not hold even a fourth of the state legislative seats.[9]

The WCF's primary mission during the nineties was "electing pro-choice women to public office." Specifically, according to WCF promotional materials from the period, in order "to earn the endorsement of the Women's Campaign Fund, a candidate must be pro-choice, support public funding for abortions for low-income women and be running a viable campaign."[10] The expenses of running the organization came from PAC funds. Half of the assistance—financial and technical—was given to help women running at the state and local level; the other half to women running at the federal level.

The WCF's mission reveals the ways in which, by the nineties, some of the more traditionally radical dimensions of feminism were being absorbed into more mainstream organizations. Indeed, the use of "insider tactics" among feminist organizations to bring about gendered transformations grew significantly in the eighties and nineties (Spalter-Roth and Schreiber 1995: 105–27). The WCF's strategies incorporated "insider tactics" within the political world—having the Leadership Circle, fund-raising events, and the like—to bring about structural change to gender relations in the United States.

By 1993, the WCF board was composed of forty directors. The board was responsible for setting organizational policy, approving candidates, raising funds, and recruiting new supporters. The WCF raised money through three fund-raising programs: direct mail; events, including a major dinner party in cities including New York, Washington, D.C., and, for a brief period, San Francisco; and the Leadership Circle, a circle of high-level donors who each donated between $1,000 and $5,000 annually. Contributions from corporate PACs were accepted during this period. According to the Federal Elections Commission, political contributions to the WCF were not tax deductible. However, contributions to the Women's Campaign Research Fund (WCRF), the WCF's nonprofit political education arm, were tax deductible. The WCRF provided regional leadership training and conducted research and polling projects on key campaign issues. It also sponsored interactive exchanges among women who were elected officials, business leaders, and academicians.[11]

The WCF Women Leadership Circle and Women Leaders Breakfasts

During the late eighties and early nineties WCF members began to realize that they had two groups of women affiliated formally and informally with the organization: a growing number of female donors (mainly business and financial women), and female candidates (from all over the country) who visited the WCF to raise money for their campaigns. The WCF formed the Leadership Circle and held Women Leaders Breakfasts to bring the two groups together in what Madeline Winters calls an "exchange." Those who gave large donations to the WCF therefore gained access to female candidates and briefings, while the candidates gained funding and access to female politicians. According to a 1993 WCF brochure,

> Held at least eight times throughout the year and generously sponsored by the Leadership Circle contributors, these events [the Women Leaders Breakfasts] introduce our New York donors to a diverse group of candidates. Frequently, a candidate will address the Leadership Circle early in her political career, and we are able to follow her successes as she climbs up the political ladder. This was the case with Ann Richards, who first spoke to the New York Leadership Circle while Texas State Treasurer; in 1994 she is running for re-election as Governor of Texas.

Female donors to the WCF who gave between $1,000 and $5,000 (the maximum allowed to be given to PACs by the law) thus became members of the Leadership Circle. Like most women who participated in women's political PACs and contributed more than $200, the women who became part of the Leadership Circle were "highly affluent, highly educated, and disproportionately white" (Day and Hadley 2004: 33). Donors are always seeking information about the persons and projects they fund and how their money contributes to actual on-the-ground action and activism (Riles 2001: 154). One way in which the WCF exposed Wall Street women donors to the persons and campaigns they were funding was by inviting the women to Women Leaders Breakfasts. Indeed, during the past several decades, money needed for campaigns has increased and along with that so has the access to policymakers that money can buy (Day and Hadley 2004: 9). Leadership Circle women were thus, in effect, "buying" access to female politicians and the information that the women in government provided at the breakfasts and other similar kinds of events.

The women who attended the breakfasts were meeting and, in some cases, influencing female politicians. However, it would be unfair to characterize the attendees' motives as purely utilitarian and self-promotional. Wall Street women felt they shared a great deal with the women attempting to move into the male-dominated world of politics. Consider part of my correspondence with Maydelle:

Some of us got very actively involved in supporting women running for public office and were active in the bipartisan Women's Campaign Fund (we helped Barbara Boxer, Olympia Snowe, among others) and also worked with older more socially prominent women (who did not work but were married to chieftains) who were among the first to be put on corporate boards for their genders, not experience. So it was not a question of finding other role models, but more focused on helping other women achieve in other areas to break the glass ceiling. Most of us were active in founding the Financial Women's Association which continues to this day. So without role models, we unconsciously worked to bring other women along, and we were all active in the pro-choice movement, which our teenage daughters are completely ignorant of and take choice for granted. (June 2010, email correspondence)

The WCF became a site for the alliance making, merging, and blending of upper-class and professional women (in business and politics) who shared an interest in electing women politicians. As such it became a new site of normativity for the continued creation of a professional, elite female habitus.

I attended several Women Leaders Breakfasts each year during the early to mid-nineties. A significant number of first-generation women also attended the breakfasts. In each and every case, speakers discussed their experiences as women in the male-dominated political realm. In each and every case the speakers invoked references to "the needs of women," "the role of women," or "the importance of women." The term "feminism" as such was, by contrast, rarely mentioned. But the speakers and attendees often evoked traditional feminist issues through a discourse of individual liberalism and equality (Spalter-Roth and Schreiber 1995). Thus, rather than use more radical terms such as power and domination, they spoke about gender difference and the inequalities women faced when running for office in terms of money, skills, and contacts. During one breakfast briefing in 1993, for example, a female pollster spoke about the "gender gap" in terms of the issues concerning female and male voters. "Women," she explained, "are more likely to look to government for solutions than men." When it came to women voters, "women connect the economy to values." They feel that "no economic security means that they have no ability to protect their kids, or to teach them values." Men, by contrast, "separated the economy from values." Wall Street women and their speakers thus used the breakfast briefings as spaces in which they discussed and worked through the discourses and images of gender relations, the economy, cultural values, and the political realm.

In January 1993, I attended a breakfast for the Leadership Circle, contributors, and friends. Our speaker was Lynn Yeakel, a woman who had run for the Senate in 1992. The meeting was held on the fiftieth floor of the McGraw-Hill Building at 122 Avenue of the Americas. The corridors of the floor were painted in light, airy peach, foam, and gold. The breakfast room was large and impressive, with thick royal green carpeting, light blue walls, enormous picture windows, and several soft pastel abstract drawings on the walls. Seven circular tables with white linen tablecloths had been set up in the room. A podium for the speaker was in front of the tables.

I arrived at the breakfast a few minutes after eight. By the time of my arrival most of the attendees were sitting down with their cups of coffee and croissants. The majority of guests, predominantly white women, were in their forties, fifties, and sixties. I sat down next to a well-coiffed woman wearing a smart white suit and Chanel bag. We exchanged pleasantries. I waved hello to Madeline, who was standing by the podium in the front of the room speaking with several women and one man. I also recognized several members of the first generation: Maydelle, Mindy, and a number of others sitting at various tables throughout the room. Everyone appeared impeccably dressed.

Lynn Yeakel arrived around 8:30. Yeakel, a Democrat, had run against Republican Arlen Specter in 1992, the year after Specter had accused Anita Hill of "flat-out perjury" while testifying during Clarence Thomas's Supreme Court confirmation hearings. Yeakel, a previously unknown fund-raiser for women's charities, responded to Specter by deciding to run against him. She almost succeeded, but in the end Specter was re-elected.[12]

The Yeakel-Specter campaign had been particularly brutal. As one journalist observed, the campaign "made Yeakel a folk hero to millions of women who saw themselves in her, the political novice who'd finally had enough of the 'boys' club' in Washington and who took it upon herself to do something about it. It also, for a time at least, cemented Specter as a villain to these same women, a clueless insider who resorted to the same brutal tactics against Yeakel he'd used on Hill."[13] Yeakel's very public drama against Specter thus also resonated with members of the first generation. Her story, including her reaction to the Hill-Thomas hearings, put on display a more mass experience of sex discrimination and gender inequality in the workplace and nation. It turned her into a gendered icon, one who had gone up against, struggled, and eventually lost access to the male hierarchy of power in the nation.

Yeakel's and other women's experiences running for office provided the means for Wall Street women's personal and often quite private gendered struggles to be given a public voice and audience. As FWA members and often within their corporate offices, the women had to carefully navigate the extent to which they publicly acknowledged and spoke about gender inequality, sex discrimination, and overall discontent. By providing support (financial and otherwise) to women in government, members of the first generation were giving voice to their own, lesser-known career stories. The WCF politicized businesswomen's concerns with gender, power, and leadership, concerns the women historically could not fully act on within the FWA and within their respective firms. Indeed, during Yeakel's talk, she proudly displayed a "shatter the glass ceiling" pin given to her during her campaign. She told us that the pin provided a "picture" of women pushing through the glass ceiling, women pushing through the power of the political arena. Women had shuffled some of the panes in 1992, she said, though she added she wasn't sure if she meant "pane" or "pain."

WCF Annual Dinners

During the seventies, the WCF had created what turned out to be a rather successful fund-raising device—a cocktail reception with celebrity bartenders, followed by a dozen or more small dinner parties in various swanky apartments in Washington, D.C., each featuring a well-known chef and celebrity guests.[14] By the nineties, the period of time in which Mindy and other first-generation women were participating in the WCF, some of the women were not only "celebrity" guests at the dinners but had also actually hosted or cohosted these private parties in their own homes in Manhattan. Notably, while the breakfasts provided the women with an opportunity to network with city, state, and national female candidates and government officials, the dinner parties allowed the women to rub elbows with a wide range of members—both women and men—of the predominantly white professional-managerial elite, from many different industries. Here, the women could also perform their elite status by demonstrating their knowledge and appreciation of fine wine and food and a wide range of conversational topics. The women were now members of the new financial nobility (Bourdieu 1998).

Evidence of Wall Street women's (relatively) new reality and habitus was thus palpable to me when I attended WCF fund-raisers and strode through the ballrooms of various cocktail receptions followed by intimate dinners within (some of) the women's Upper East and Upper West Side apartments. The first such fund-raiser I attended was in October 1995. The evening began with a reception at the headquarters of Pfizer Pharmaceutical on 42nd Street between Second and Third Avenues. It was a cool fall-like evening. By the time I arrived at the event with my then partner, there was already a line of people waiting to be signed in to the party. Virtually everyone was dressed in suits and formal officewear.

The majority of attendees at the event were women, but about 25 percent of the guests were men. Women were mostly present on their own or with female friends and colleagues, though a few had come with spouses. Nearly every man who attended had a female spouse by his side. As soon as I entered the ballroom area I could see Madeline and many other women I had come to know. Mindy, dressed in a bright yellow suit, was moving about the room with skill, embracing, warmly shaking hands and greeting various people, speaking with them for a few minutes, and then moving on to the next group. As I watched I was amazed at the ways in which small circles of people opened up around her so that she could introduce the female politician by her side. Maydelle was also moving around the ballroom. All the meeting and greeting was like a polite dance. I was transfixed by the women's dress, their demeanor, and the way they moved through the crowd, exhibiting ease and comfort within the party setting.

Eventually I sat down with a small group of women who were active at that point in both the FWA and the WCF, most of whom I'd interviewed as part of my larger research project. We politely sipped our wine spritzers. A few of the women talked about upcoming FWA events. The talk show host Sally Jessy Raphael eventually took to the podium where she rapidly introduced thirty female candidates who were each given about thirty seconds to express thanks and say something about their campaigns. All of the women were sure to talk about the importance of electing pro-choice women.

As soon as the last speech was over, everyone scurried out of the ballroom to try to catch a taxi to get to respective dinner parties by 8 PM. These WCF dinner parties provided one with a rather intimate glimpse of the lives and apartments of a variety of wealthy individuals in New York City, including that of several Wall Street women's. The dinner party I attended was, indeed, hosted by a woman in finance. Below are some of my initial impressions of the apartment and dinner party based on my fieldnotes (with some changes in names and details):

> Lucinda Beekman lives in a very grand penthouse apartment on Riverside Drive. The interior of the lobby is quite small—but filled with deep, dark wood furniture, ivy green, regal red and gold carpet. Lucinda lives on the top floor of the building. Her apartment is decorated in a style that is reminiscent of the Hollywood of yesteryear. The bedroom is especially grand—painted royal blue with just a tint of gold. The duvet on the bed matches the blue walls perfectly. Four small golden angel statuettes are attached to the wall behind the bed, as if they are flying over the bed's occupants. One feels enveloped in grandeur, in a world away from all worlds. Next to the bed is a photograph of several women sitting together. They look like old time movie stars. . . .
>
> The rest of the apartment is decorated in cool colors—beiges, pink hues, white marble, and a remarkable collection of artwork that adorns all the walls. The living room has an enormous window looking onto the Hudson River where one can see some of the new apartment buildings sprouting up in New Jersey. At the back of the apartment, there is a staircase leading to a second floor—one large music room with black and white tiles. There is a door leading out onto the roof of the building. Everything on the first floor seems very regal and majestic to me; everything on the top floor, more modern, casual, and family-friendly. . . .
>
> About twenty-five guests attended the party—a smattering of young, old, financial, and political people—some well known; others not. Prior to our sitting down to dinner one of the female politicians stood up and informed us that she was the only freshwoman Republican that is pro-choice. She wanted to make sure that we all knew that there were Republicans in the room. . . .
>
> Dinner itself was catered by an Italian restaurant. We ate salad, pasta, salmon, meat and potatoes, and drank wine. After the dinner was over, Lucinda began to introduce the celebrity guests at the party to everyone. She introduced Patricia Riley—informing us that Patricia was "a very well-known figure on Wall Street." Lucinda then asked Patricia if she wanted to say something to the group. Patricia

got up and spoke eloquently to us about the importance of supporting women candidates for election. And then she made an interesting and telling analogy: "The place of women in politics today is
similar to the place of women on Wall Street twenty years ago, a
time when women were few and far between, and the road and
knowledge of that road was far less travelled." She then added that
"in spite of the similarities in their situations, women politicians
were less fortunate compared to women on Wall Street. Wall Street,"
she explained, "acts as a 'meritocracy' which allows good people to
succeed and do well. The fortunes of and successes of politicians,
including women politicians, operate in and under a slightly different system." Patricia ended by giving a soft pitch to continue
supporting the WCF.

Conclusion

During the nineties members of the first generation—as female market actors—entered into new associations with state actors, and they
increasingly engaged in political arenas and issues. They provided
individual (or collective, as in the case of the WCF) expertise, strategic
management advice, education and training, and platforms for research; they also actively attempted to influence the political decision-
making process, particularly when it came to advancing women's issues or women into leadership positions. The women, through their
networked practices, like power-elite men before them, bridged corporate and political life (Mills 1956). And like the men, they did so for
business as well as political purposes and the pursuit of their own
power (Wedel 2009). But, unlike men's networks, Wall Street women's
networks had a strikingly women-focused, gendered agenda. Through
their political-market tie making, the women mediated the spaces
between and among both state and market feminism. They contributed to making a new gendered public domain and were focused on
the re-gendering of American government and practice.

Through their participation in the WCF, the first generation became
situated within a multilevel, overlapping network of city, state, and
national female elites. Wall Street women's political networks in particular, like the WCF, became spaces in which women worked out and
produced new discourses, images, and tactics of gender relations,
politics, feminism, finance, and a professional-managerial classed hab-

itus. Women in both the Democratic and Republican parties united in their support of liberal feminist issues. Most who got involved in the WCF did so in order to ensure that women were elected into decision-making positions within government, so that they could hopefully alter some of the priorities of government institutions, including women's reproductive rights.

CHAPTER 5

LIFE AFTER WALL STREET

Deirdre Parliament sat in her glass-enclosed Manhattan office over-looking the trading floor of a Wall Street firm. It was March 1994, and she was one of the most senior women in the world of global finance. I sat across from her on this weekday afternoon. She asked me if I minded if she smoked, and though I did, I said it was all right. Soon we were deep in conversation about her life and career. As she looked out onto the floor of mostly male traders, she recalled her early days in finance and her youthful ideals: "I was one of the only women that graduated from an 'Ivy' business school in 1970. I had this philosophy that business was the heart of social change—that somehow if more people with the right liberal ideas would be part of corporate struc-tures then the world would somehow be a better place. I thought I'd be a force for social change going into business onto Wall Street." Accord-ing to her, her goals were now more modest. "I think that I bring with me a certain fairness and support of individual growth that, in a modest way, affects the people I work with—but I don't have visions of social change—at somehow hiring vast numbers of different classes of people and changing the structure of Wall Street on my own."

Fourteen years later, on a cold March afternoon in 2008, twenty-five well-dressed women in their fifties and sixties gathered in the board-room of a major law firm in Times Square to hear Laura Sharp, a former investment banker, reflect on her life in high finance. Laura first told us that retiring was a "hard decision."[1] She described a slow process of revelation, a tectonic shift in her beliefs about women on Wall Street. When she started working in finance in 1976 she firmly believed in meritocracy, "that cream always rises to the top." Now, nearly four decades later, she told us, she had lost some of her faith:

"In the seventies my failure was not being realistic about my work environment. I did not want to be too aggressive. Then I looked around and realized that misogyny was alive and well—and hidden. There is culture on Wall Street that you have to fit into. There is a network—men with connections. We still can't underestimate that culture and network."

Over the years women had often talked to me about the challenges they experienced being one of a few women in a male-dominated environment. But then Laura said something that made me sit up. "Women," she said, "are the only group of people that as they grow older get more radical, opinionated, and political. . . . My dream today is to work with women to help them be successful in a man's world." Many other members of the first generation had been telling me about becoming more politicized as they began to entertain the possibility of life after the world of finance. Indeed, some women described their retirement as a professional or personal crisis precipitating a period of revelation. They remembered the everyday activities of their work lives in finance as they drew their careers to a close, particularly feel- ings of disenchantment with the meritocratic work ethic. They talked about watching others—mostly men, but in some cases women, too— moving up in the senior hierarchy of the firm while they remained "stuck" in the same position.

Others described key events that became turning points in the way they saw themselves and the world. In particular, they talked about the 2008 presidential election as a transformative moment for them as women. Hillary Clinton's rise, her fight for recognition, and the ways she was demonized by some in the press altered some of the women's perception of the state of gender and feminism in the United States.[2] For some, Hillary's campaign experiences brought up their own ques- tions about gender, power, leadership, and the success of the women's movement (Traister 2010).

Their decision-making process about the "next stage" of their lives entailed a rethinking of their identity as women in finance and their relationship to other women in the world. In some cases this entailed dealing with and accepting their diminished agency as professional women operating within a male-dominated world. The women also began to reorient their understanding of the place and meaning of the market, gender, philanthropy, politics, and feminism within their lives. They drew on their knowledge of business, finance, and being women in order to analyze their present and assess and plan for their future

(Miyazaki 2006: 150). Through their decisions to leave or change their line of work, the women signified that they had reached a moment in their careers in which they reordered their work and political as well as philanthropic priorities and their definition of themselves as professional career-focused women.

Some women, like Sharp, began to "dream about helping other women" as they slowly abandoned their belief in meritocracy, the dominant cultural framework of Wall Street and of their own youth. Now instead of individual ability, talent, and dedicated service to the corporation, they felt that self-presentation, networking, and politics were critical to moving up within the corporate hierarchy. Not only equal access to the workplace and hard work, but also women's leadership, the market, and investment power, were now the real keys to women's individual and collective advancement, equality, and empowerment.

Veronica Keyes herself now spoke in these terms. When we sat in her home office on the Upper West Side of Manhattan in July 2008, I had not seen or spoken with her for nearly a decade and a half. Her narrative about her youthful ideals now had a strikingly different endpoint: "When I first left college, as an undergraduate, I had this idea that business was going to change the world—and that this was a way that women can get hired. . . . But that did not necessarily happen. . . . Now that was a different moment. But here I am—forty years later applying business to investing in people. I thought, gee, I have come full circle."

"Applying business to investing in people," for Veronica, means fundraising for women political candidates and sitting on (among others) the board of a venture capital firm that provides microfinancing to women and to the poor nationally and internationally. She uses investment techniques that she honed during her long tenure on Wall Street, bringing them to the worlds of women's politics and philanthropy. Here she joins others in a broad new movement called "philanthrocapitalism"—a movement that promises to save the world by applying market-based perspectives to various social and economic challenges (Bishop and Green 2009).[3] Specifically, Veronica is participating in what I am coining "feminist philanthrocapitalism"—a hybrid of a capital-driven manifestation of the women's movement and a women-driven manifestation of the philanthrocapitalism movement. Feminist philanthrocapitalism is a form of market feminism in the contemporary era, one that is paving the way for the feminizing of capital and markets.[4] In this emergent domain, market actors, like Veronica, work for corporations and nonprofit global ventures in order to provide expertise and strategic management advice and therefore influence political decision making, particularly for issues that affect women. Twenty-first-century venture capitalist organizations dedicated to advancing women in national politics are another form of contemporary market-feminist activity that is feminizing markets and politics. Gender-focused corporate social responsibility is yet another manifestation.[5] These various projects embody a more inclusive neoliberalism that is moving away from an earlier embrace of pure privatization and marketization (in the eighties and nineties) to purportedly more socially interventionist and ameliorative projects, including the rise of corporate social responsibility (Peck and Tickell 2002; Garsten 2008; Lewis et al. 2008).[6]

Not all of the members of the first generation are engaged in these types of projects. However, they are all influenced by a professional-managerial feminist discourse that promotes phrases like "self-empowerment" and "women's empowerment" not only in the domestic sphere but in the market as well (McGee 2005; Fisher 2006; McRobbie 2009). This discourse is circulating in the popular and business press in various modalities. For example, Linda Tarr-Whelan, a distinguished senior fellow at the national think tank Demos, and a former ambassador to the UN Commission on the Status of Women in the Clinton administration, recently wrote a book entitled *Women Lead the Way: Your Guide to Stepping Up to Leadership and Changing the World* (2009). Tarr-Whelan identifies women's distinctive approaches to leadership. She contends that when women's representation at the top of institutions is 30 percent, real changes will begin to happen—changes that have "demonstrable positive effects on the bottom line of business and government" (21–24). Her argument elaborates upon a particular form of market feminism, linking gender and leadership to the marketplace. She and other similarly positioned gender experts provide a new discursive space for female professional subjects, including Wall Street women, to assume and perform a new kind of market agency in the world. Women leaders, like themselves, come to understand themselves as empowered beings, as agents of change (McRobbie 2009: 6). And some female leaders are, as a result, engaging in interventionist projects that seek to feminize corporations, including corporate boards.

Wall Street women are clearly not engaged in radical projects in order to fully destabilize capitalism. They are not participating in any of the organized labor movements against corporate globalization (Juris 2008). They are not identifying themselves with the more radical versions of contemporary feminism—for example, the work of scholars who advocate putting socialism back on the feminist agenda (Eisenstein 2009: 201). And they are not participating in more alternative forms of finance that can be seen in the representational politics of art, poetry, and comedy that de Goede (2005a) characterizes as the "carnival of money." But some Wall Street women, like Veronica and a few others, are participating in forms of "dissent" from the normative order of global finance. They are engaged in an example of what the political scientist Paul Langley argues is "well established financial dissent that seeks to inscribe explicitly moral and ethical concerns into everyday investment" (2008: 114).[7] The women are at the forefront of attempting to destabilize and replace hegemonic forms of financial capitalism. They are drawing on traditional ideals about social change and gender equality in an effort to bring about transformation in (and by means of) the marketplace. They are creating a narrative with performative force in which they and other female economic actors are bringing about gendered changes in capital, the corporation, and the marketplace (Gibson-Graham 1996; Rosenblum 2009).

Four Post–Wall Street Identities and Projects

For describing the women's senses of themselves after leaving Wall Street, I see four possible identities. They are the "feminist financial manager," "the feminist philanthrocapitalist," "the elite feminized subject," and the "elite masculinized actor." These emerge as possibilities for new elite gendered performances. They are also linked to the women's projects "after" neoliberalism. These projects are global, gender-focused social responsibility; international, capitalist-driven feminist philanthropy; national, female elite philanthropy; and national, corporate-government, masculine political networking and alliances.

All of the women's projects work to uphold and in some cases further their positions as national, even international, elites. Their agency continues to be not only gendered but classed as well. The women continue to create and reproduce a female elite through their everyday and project-oriented practices. Indeed, by the time I encountered the women individually and as a group, they had achieved significant upward mobility on Wall Street and within American society. They were all bona fide members of the corporate-financial elite. Some were also participating in feminist-oriented, elite, activist-oriented transnational networks. And a few were even members of what David Rothkopf (2008) calls the "superclass"—the new global, male-dominated power elite. The women were thus all elites, but they occupied different positions within the structure of elites. Their particular positions depended on their careers and networking histories as well as their contemporary engagements in various types of networks and projects.

Andrea Dirks: The Feminist Financial Manager

Andrea Dirks is a senior executive working within a socially responsible firm. In 2008, she told me that—in retrospect—she views her thirty-plus-year career in finance as having "three blocks, three stages." The first is her early career when she felt included and had believed in meritocracy. She had confidence in liberal feminism's ideals and social objectives, and she had thought that equal access and opportunity can bring about gender equality. The second stage took place during her mid-career years. This phase was characterized by a period of "awakening"—of revelation and crisis. Andrea lost faith in the dominant cultural frameworks of meritocracy, equal access, and gender equality in the workplace.

This second period, I would argue, is one in which Andrea (like many of her first-generation female peers on Wall Street) engaged individually and collectively in the process of figuring out women's "rules for survival and success" in the corporate workplace. It was sparked and shaped primarily by their experiences working in Wall Street firms and by their interactions with, for example, their mostly male bosses (good or bad) as well as their friends, allies, and rivals (both women and men). In women's spaces such as the Financial Women's Association (FWA), women attempted to become proficient in the rules of survival and success that are required to move up the executive ladder (Fisher 2006: 220). Some, like Andrea, hired female career coaches to help them learn to wear the "right clothes" and network with others in order to advance up the corporate hierarchy.

As the women reached their mid-careers and beyond, they began to recognize that their future chances on Wall Street were not exclusively dependent on hard work, competence, and performance. They saw the importance of the social and cultural criteria established by the male-dominated structures of power in finance: networking, alliance making, and the proper presentation of the gendered self. This is the period in which the women become class agents in their own right. Some joined women's organizations such as the FWA and the Women's Campaign Fund (WCF) and created their own networks of money and power. Some, like Patricia Riley and Deirdre Parliament, developed female mentoring relationships within these networks in which they worked together to strategize ways to deal with difficult bosses and navigate the financial corporate hierarchy. Still others, like Maydelle Brooks, developed key mentoring relationships with powerful senior male executives who advocated on their behalf.

In the third stage of her career, Andrea decided to leave the traditional world of Wall Street and to join a firm invested in corporate social responsibility (CSR). CSR refers to operating a business in a manner that accounts for the social and environmental impact created by the business. In Andrea's case she decided to work in a firm with a "mission" to "make a difference for women and minorities." She thus redirected her career path from one trajectory to another in order to start feminizing the marketplace.[8] She professionally and personally converted from "conventional investment management" to "corporate sustainable and responsible investing":

> I grew up in a conventional investment management with my prior [Wall Street] firm. When I came to help run my [present] firm, I felt I had a lot to learn about social investing before I decided to take the job—because I was not going to get involved in something that I did not believe in as an investment philosophy in the process. I decided at the time, and still feel now, that what we look at in corporate analysis beyond the financials—the workplace practices, the environmental practices, diversity, human rights policies—is actually getting at quality of management because they are all factors that show up in the stock process in the next ten minutes . . . you know? . . . Corporate social responsibility is a movement. I think it is woven into the fabric.

Andrea's turn toward CSR is an example of financial dissent. Ethical investments, as she points out, open up the everyday routines and practices of everyday investment. Her work thus is part of a larger project engaged in re-shaping the discourse of investment, one that seeks to combine the financial and the moral (Garsten 2008; Langley

2008: 116). In this manner, Andrea can be viewed as "the feminist financial manager." Here, social movements (such as CSR) disrupt and partially remake the habitus of professional female financial elites.

Recently, Andrea's firm has begun to take gender into account, evaluating, for example the number of women on boards of corporations in their overall investment strategy. In this sense, the firm, spearheaded by Andrea, is engaging in what is, I would argue, the feminizing of markets. On the one hand, the firm engages in (liberal) feminist practices that can work with a market agenda. On the other hand, Andrea and her coworkers embody a feminist ethic that challenges normative representations of investment.[9] Veronica is also engaged in a form of financial dissent that attempts to take ethical concerns about gender into account in order to insert poor women (and men) into the free marketplace.

Veronica Keyes: The Feminist Philanthrocapitalist

I met with Veronica in the downstairs office of her three-story brownstone on the Upper West Side of Manhattan in July 2008. She asked her assistant to get us salads and Diet Cokes for lunch. Soon she caught me up on the nearly fifteen years that had gone by since I had first talked to her. For decades, she noted, men on Wall Street became active in city, state, and national politics through their business practices and connections (Mills 1956). And, since the eighties, Wall Street women had been developing strong women's political networks such as the WCF. Veronica had pioneered her own pathway from Wall Street into the world of women's politics and power. Unlike some other women who moved into the political arena vis-à-vis the WCF, Veronica's initial route into politics was through her firm; subsequently, as a result of her political activities, she met Hillary Clinton:

> It was great fun. President [Bill] Clinton was in office. I met Hillary —the instant I met her she was my hero. I met lots of people who became very good friends. It was a very different circle than I had been part of, just my being a little worker bee. Once you are involved, you go to more meetings, meet more people, and it becomes a community.
>
> Then in the early 2000s I decided to stay on in the firm for a few years to see the firm through some more transitions. . . . And, in the meantime I started working for Hillary's senatorial campaign. . . .

Then I got involved helping women running in smaller races. I fund-raised. It was really a selling job. It wasn't work. It was fun. It was something I believe in, so it was much easier to be a persuasive salesman when you are bringing a lot of energy and enthusiasm.

Veronica drew on her selling skills, honed initially on Wall Street, to fund-raise for women. She found herself loving the process and the female candidates. Her crisis and moment of revelation occurred during Hillary Clinton's campaign for the presidency. As for other women (and some men), Clinton's race—the fact that Hillary was the first woman to be taken seriously in a run for the presidency in the nation's history and the way in which Hillary faced misogyny throughout her candidacy—forced Veronica to rethink her thoughts that feminism had won.

I have run into women of my age, professional women in their sixties. They are just horrified at what has been going on in the presidential campaign with Hillary—the young ones are not paying attention. That is yet another failure of the women's movement. . . .

The women's movement had been out of my mind for years. I was busy working. . . . I guess I thought that the women's movement kind of chugged along—I had not given it much thought . . . until now. And now I realize that the whole thing has been—not a complete failure—a failure would not have gotten eighteen million votes.

Many scholars argue that we are living in a kind of postfeminist moment.[10] Indeed, many members of the first generation believed that the goals of liberal feminism—access to the same opportunities as men, the right to abortion—had been achieved at the point that the 2000s began. However, Clinton's candidacy brought sexism in the media, American workplace, and political landscape to the fore. It forced women, like Veronica, to re-assess the success (or lack thereof) of the women's movement: "The fact that forty-plus years after, *Roe vs. Wade* is a political issue in this campaign is unbelievable to me. But there we are. The fact that women were treated with demands to iron my shirt kind of thing. . . . Someone, actually a friend of mine, gave me one of those Hillary dolls—the nutcracker dolls for Christmas. I was so angry."

Veronica, like other women, was shocked by the brazen misogynistic attacks on Clinton (Traister 2010: 66). She felt sad and angry that discrimination against women was alive and well. Her experience with

Clinton's campaign brought about a kind of conversion experience. After not thinking about the women's movement for many decades, the campaign actually repoliticized Veronica. Veronica found herself questioning and rethinking her assumptions about the success of the liberal women's movement (Kornblut 2009; Traister 2010). But while Clinton's campaign repoliticized Veronica in terms of the women's movement, she did not expand her fund-raising work into the traditional political arena for women or in the form of classic activism either.

Veronica decided to step back from fund-raising and supporting women candidates for a while; instead, she turned her attention toward her work as a board member of a nonprofit global venture fund. The fund uses market-based techniques to address the problems of the poor and women. Veronica has now joined other elite business and government leaders and experts that are coming together to find solutions to major world problems (Rothkopf 2009: 281). The Clinton Global Initiative of 2005 is another example of such a project. The initiative's stated mission is to "increase the benefits and reduce the burdens of global interdependence; to make a world of more partners and fewer enemies; and to give more people the tools they need to build a better future" (281). Philanthrocapitalism draws on "private wealth primarily to advance public good by applying entrepreneurial skills" (Clinton 2009). Veronica, like many other business leaders today, believes in using neoliberal market-oriented techniques and solutions to help save the world's poor women and men, though her own emphasis is on women. She, like other Baby Boomers, brings earlier feminist ideals and notions about social progress (learned in the sixties in college) to the marketplace.

A friend of mine who I had met through politics said to me that I had to meet this woman, Rhonda Westbrook, who was setting up a fund. I met her—I just fell for her! Through all my years of working, I thought I was good at identifying young talent out of school and recruiting them and keeping them. When I met Rhonda I felt that this person is going to make a difference.

I did not quite understand Rhonda's philosophic idea, but I said I am following her. Rhonda had an idea that philanthropy—particularly international philanthropy—as it is normally practiced had limited impact in lots and lots of way. It tends to go in big chunks to infrastructure and big programs. A lot of money gets lost along the way. Worst of all, it is handouts. It is, by definition, not sustainable.

Rhonda's idea was that we have to create a mechanism by which people can take charge of their own lives. It comes from the bottom, not the top. The top is I look at these people and I say what their needs are—aid clinics, camps. . . . Whereas the alternative way is to say what can we learn about what these people actually want through a market mechanism. I thus understood that we were bringing an investment perspective to entrepreneurial opportunities and that if we were successful they would take on a life of their own.[11]

In moving toward philanthropy, Veronica did not move entirely away from the market. She deployed mainly economic rather than political discourse to frame the new field of international philanthropy. She suggests that it is primarily the market, rather than the state or some other entity, that can help poor people around the world. Her project, like Andrea's, seeks to reshape the discourse of investment, to combine the economic and the moral, the market and feminist ideals. Here the morality is a distinctly neoliberal one in which an individual takes charge of his or her own life and destiny through entrepreneurial means. The idea is to remake the "social networks and cultural practices of the poor as part of the free market" (Elyachar 2005: 5). Veronica believes that integrating women from the global South into the marketplace will alleviate poverty and empower women.

Not everyone would agree with Veronica's general position. There is a heated debate among academics and policymakers alike about the benefits of microfinance practices. As the feminist and political scientist Libby Assassi points out in her recent overview of the gendering of global finance, some have "argued that the expansion of a highly volatile, crisis prone global financial system has already added a further dimension of risk and insecurity to the lives of specific groups and societies, within which structures of gendered inequality further impact on existing processes of subordination" (Assassi 2009: 130; see also Elson 1995, 2001; Goetz and Gupta 1996; van Staveren 2002; Bornstein 2005; Karim 2011; Maurer forthcoming).

Lily Franklin: Classic Elite Femininity Revised

By participating in corporate socially responsible and international philanthropic endeavors, Andrea and Veronica are making new professional-managerial feminist organizations and networks. But not everyone in the first generation has followed these types of paths. Other women have actually retreated from both the old and new worlds of politics. They have chosen, as Lily Franklin has, to follow more traditional gendered elite paths in which women most frequently give to social services, education, and culture (Ostrower 1995: 72). But while traditional elite women have tended to focus on services for youth and women, new financial elite women have included other populations and causes. Moreover, unlike classical elite women who viewed and approached philanthropy as a joint husband-wife activity, Wall Street women tend to make their own philanthropic choices independently of their partners or husbands.

I found out about Wall Street women's participation in a range of philanthropic projects when Lily and I got together for a chat in the spring of 2008. Lily and I had first met in 1995 when she had a senior position in research within one of the major firms on Wall Street. Like many members of her generation, she had moved to New York City in the seventies to pursue a professional career in finance and while doing so had met other Wall Street women via the FWA. In terms of her career, she had had, as she put it that spring day in 2008, "a spectacular run."

It was about four in the afternoon when I arrived at a major foundation where Lily was a board member. We met in one of the executive offices, sat on black leather chairs, and drank coffee. Our conversation began with a discussion about her retirement from Wall Street. She had revved up her career during her later years in the financial world, but to little avail: "I was working extremely hard, traveling nonstop, and I knew I was going nowhere. I mean I had a big job ... but I think I should have been given a more global job, and that job went to a much younger man. I really had to accept I was going to be going nowhere. I mean I was very happy with what I had achieved, but I didn't want to keep working at that pace without a carrot."

Going from a career in which she continually climbed the corporate ladder to finding herself at a standstill was really frustrating for Lily. After several other instances in which younger men were promoted over her, she felt "that was like three strikes and I am out." She began sharing her discontent with other women from her generation on Wall Street:

I remember having lunch with my friend Alice Stacey—talking about our disappointments. And Alice said to me, "Lily. You are naïve. Don't you know this? The women getting the big jobs on Wall Street are at least ten years younger than we are—if not fifteen. No one is giving us opportunities. You know we fought the battles." . . . You know I have always had really good friends to sit down and talk to—I talked to Mindy Plane when I was thinking about retirement. I asked: "What do you do all day—besides being very interested in politics?"[12]

As we sat drinking coffee, she described her increasing anger at the time:

> It took me a lot longer to get to where I should have been. There was incredible discrimination against women in the seventies. It lightened up somewhat in the eighties. And the pioneering thing—I was always at the beginning. The things that were adopted—there were just never any openings for me. By the time they had adopted training programs on Wall Street, I had already fought my way into doing what I was doing. I had a lot of anger over all this. . . . But I found as I started verbalizing my frustrations, I found that other women—my contemporaries—were thinking about retiring, too. And I realized that it wasn't just me. There were a lot of us in that kind of age group going through the same thing. And I think that also we worked so hard that we were ready to retire earlier than most. And for this I credit the FWA—the FWA was always having women involved in the community and being very activist across a broad range. So I say that I am retired: you know that I am on several boards.

Like Veronica and Andrea, Lily experienced a kind of crisis in her late career as she bumped into glass ceilings time and time again. By that time, she had already lost much of her earlier faith in a meritocratic workplace. For Lily this revelation eventually coalesced in pent-up anger and frustration. She lost a sense of belonging, of being rewarded for her efforts. In response, she chose to retire, and in retirement she has constructed a lifestyle that she tells me she loves and that seems to involve a certain amount of work. "I am on the board of a university. I am on the board of a hospital. They wanted a financial person. That has been very educational for me. I'm on the board of an arts foundation. I'm also on the board of an insurance company—that is the only for-profit board where I get paid. The others are all volunteer. But it is a wonderful portfolio. It keeps me active and engaged. Sometimes it is a little overwhelming but it has really worked out very nicely for my retirement."

Being active on boards is a considerable change for Lily from working full-time on Wall Street. She does draw on her financial and market expertise for her board work. None of the boards she is on are focused on women and gender equality per se. But Lily's presence and participation are contributing to the slow feminizing of boards. Given this, I asked if she was still involved in the WCF. I had noticed that most members of the first generation were no longer on the WCF board or in the Leadership Circle. Based on my discussion with a number of women, my sense was that a division had occurred among them. They no longer were as interested or invested in working within a bipartisan organization such as the WCF. Instead, women who identified as Democratic were working directly with and for Democratic female candidates, and women involved in the Republican Party, as we shall see, like Mindy, were deeply involved in supporting Republican women only. As Lily recounted, "I stopped being active a couple of years ago because the WCF is supposed to be nonpartisan—just supporting women's candidates who are pro-choice—and funding them early on in their careers. The last event I attended was totally political —about how much 'we hate George Bush.' . . . I got up and said, 'This is not a political evening. This is about supporting women candidates. This is not to bash Republicans. It's not the Democratic Campaign Fund. This is the Women's Campaign Fund.'"

Lily's withdrawal from the WCF demonstrates the contours of an increasingly hostile bipartisan political world and its impact on women's bipartisan-oriented political practices. During the nineties, when many first-generation women got active in women's politics, gender trumped formal politics. The women felt tied together by their belief in liberal feminism and their desire to advance women in the general, overall political sphere. They felt united in their support for a woman's right to abortion. But, in the 2000s, other issues—for example, how to run the economy—were splitting the women apart so that they identified more with particular political parties rather than through their shared identity as women. Moreover, Hillary Clinton's entrance into the presidential race, followed later by Sarah Palin's run as the Republican vice presidential candidate, signaled that American culture was more willing to accept women in the political arena than it had been in the nineties. Given all this, Lily now donates her money directly to candidates, not to women's political organizations, and she has chosen to withdraw from the world of formal politics just as she withdrew from the world of finance.

Even while Lily appears to be moving in the direction of female elites before her—engaging in volunteer and board work—she is doing the traditional work of elite men. Through board work, Lily is involved in the governance of a university, a hospital, an insurance company, and an art foundation. The boards she is on are "high-powered" and prestigious. They have an impact on policy decisions. Lily was recruited onto these boards in large part because of her financial background, traditionally a male domain of knowledge and expertise (Ostrower 2002: 7). Lily is now a bona fide member of New York City's and the nation's elite. But while Lily has withdrawn from active work in the formal world of politics, her friend Mindy has moved in the opposite direction.

Mindy Plane: Elite Masculinity in Politics and Philanthropy—with a Twist

In the spring of 2008, Mindy invited me to meet up with her at a women's political club, where she was a member, in midtown Manhattan. Mindy, now fully retired, used the club as an office and meeting place. When we first sat down to chat, it was almost as if no time had passed since our last conversation. Mindy's passion for politics was as strong as ever, and it had become even stronger than her interest in investment banking.

> [When we first met I] was helping good Republican women get elected. And, since I was on Wall Street, I had the ability to help them. Not so many did—so I did. And, so, ultimately I retired from Wall Street in the late nineties. I just sort of gradually retired out. I got to one level and said to one of the partners, "You know what I want to do? More politics. I would be happy to do things for you part-time." And he said, "No, you cannot do that." And so I said, "Fine. I retire."

Mindy seems happy with her decision to leave full-time investment banking behind her. Indeed, during the first half hour of our talk she spoke enthusiastically about various Republican women she was supporting. She also told me about her growing involvement—over the past decade or so—with several Republican transition teams, through which she advised newly elected officials on financial matters, such as preparing budgets.

Politics is only one of Mindy's new post–Wall Street projects. Since retiring she has focused her attention on being a member of nonprofit and corporate boards. She is now an advisory director for a private equity fund. She continues to be a board member of a mutual fund.[13] Through her board work, Mindy continues then to reproduce her elite investment-banking habitus. Throughout her career, Mindy has operated by and large within the professional and political worlds of high-powered men. This continues in her current capacity working on boards and advising politicians. Mindy's pathway to her involvement in politics and boards occurred through contacts with business associates, mainly men. But while she herself was pulled in by men, Mindy consciously made sure to draw on her group of female financial friends by recruiting them onto boards. She thus actively works to feminize corporate boards. Recently, for example, Mindy recruited Penny Edwards, a female financial retiree she has known from their FWA days.[14] Thus, Mindy is breaking glass ceilings in the world of boards in two ways: first, by being one of a handful of women on such boards; and second, by acting as a "board mentor recruiter" and bringing other women into the world of corporate governance. Here, in the highest echelons of boards, elite female networking in finance— borne from the women's shared experiences on Wall Street and the FWA—is alive and well.

By moving into and remaining primarily within serious elite male games of power, status, and success, Mindy's project is in many ways the most traditionally "political" and liberal feminist of her entire group of Wall Street friends. Her individual project has been to enter into and become part of the dominant financial and political elite. Her broader project has been to bring other women into such elite spheres over time. In our conversation in 2008 Mindy told me that she still considers herself to be a feminist; part of being a feminist for Mindy is helping other women move up the power hierarchy.

While Mindy is clear about her identity as a feminist, her sense of herself as an elite is a more complex matter. Initially when I asked her if she was part of an elite, she hesitated. Eventually, however, she reconsidered what being an elite meant and how she fit into the larger picture of financial elites in the world. Consider our exchange about elites, prompted by Mindy regaling me with stories of her well-known famous friends and her own recent travels throughout the globe for business and pleasure. It is worth quoting at length because it provides insight into her definition of herself, elites, women, and friendship.

MINDY: So between June and July I will be traveling a lot. . . .

MELISSA: I am curious. When academics think about transformations globally, they sometimes talk about the new global elite. I am curious—how do you see yourself?

MINDY: You never consider yourself an elite.

MELISSA: I am sorry. Maybe I should not have used that particular terminology. I don't want to put words in your mouth. But I consider myself a kind of elite as an academic.

MINDY: No. I know. I consider myself very fortunate because I am on the board of a company on an [International] Stock Exchange. So I get to travel. The company insures properties all over the world so I have to pay attention to the world for lack of a better word—so that is intellectually stimulating. . . . My business keeps me intellectually stimulated. I really enjoy doing the financial reports.

Our discussion veered away from discussing Mindy's board and political work to 9/11, the abortion debate, and then back again to politics. About twenty minutes after I had asked Mindy if she herself was an elite, she had the following thoughts:

MINDY: I changed my mind. There are elites. I think I am a small elite.

MELISSA: You are a small elite. What does that mean?

MINDY: Let me say this. There are two types of elites. The elites are the people that work at Merrill Lynch and Citibank who have two-million-dollar severance packages. I don't go around in that circle—but I know people like that—I probably know more of them because I am introduced politically to them. . . . But I am an elite just because I am on the board of an NYSE-traded company. But I call that a small elite compared to the other kind of elite. . . .

MELISSA: And is there a gender composition among elites?

MINDY: We can call them the small elites, I think. But a lot of them are younger. I am sixty years old. Meg Whitman is in her fifties. Carly Fiorina is a little younger than I am. I mean, women past seventy didn't have the same opportunities I had—Muriel Siebert is about seventy-five. She is up there.

MELISSA: She is unusual though . . .

MINDY: The reason she is unusual is that she did not go through the corporate world. She did it by herself—and she had her own firm. She is an outlier. I mean I did it through the corporate world. I was with a corporation. I was with a major bank. Patricia Riley went through the corporate world, Maydelle Brooks. . . . We all got our MBA—went to business school at night. . . . A lot of us went to women's colleges. . . . I think the difference you are going to find here is that the women that came onto Wall Street during my period were the first group in which a decent number of us had the same education that our male counterparts got in that we got the MBA; we got the law degree. I mean going into NYU business school there were other women there already, you know. . . . And [as a result] there were more people to network, to mentor each other for lack of a better word. We all had that benefit. I still think we did it through the corporate model. We all banged and made breakthroughs at all different levels. You know you don't have to be the CEO to have broken the ground. . . . You know, like my friend Julie Nolan. Her goal has always been to be the CEO of her corporation. Well, she got to be number two. You know there are still a lot of men who would kill to be a number two? Right? . . . Now, I will be a little biased here, but I think that some of the breakthroughs that we made, even though we did not make it to the top per se, made it easier for the next round of women.[15]

Viewing Wall Street women's networking from the vantage point of forty years provides a new way to analyze Mindy's group of female friends and colleagues ethnographically and historically. We can see the ways in which certain key female actors within the group, in this particular case Mindy, can act as "brokers" for female financial friends, bringing in and connecting the women to various systems of power, over time, including most recently on corporate boards. The FWA of the seventies, particularly the strong friendships born and built within the FWA during that time between Mindy and others, is then the "originary network" of this small stable of successful Wall Street women now entering retirement. Mindy and the other women are not only engaged in their individual political and philanthropic projects, but they are also, as an ensemble, involved in a collective class project —the "classing" of Wall Street women. Understanding their individual career and networking paths provides us with insight into the diversity within this small group of highly successful elite women. Understanding the ways they formed bonds with one another, how they sustained those bonds, and the meaning of those bonds over time, provides us with a broader picture of the classing and gendering of the first members of a female financial elite.

CHAPTER 6

MARKET FEMINISM, FEMINIZING MARKETS, AND THE FINANCIAL CRISIS

In September 2008, a series of collapses in bank and insurance companies—including the bankruptcy of Lehman Brothers—triggered what would become the biggest financial crisis since the Depression (Tett 2009b). The subprime disaster that had begun to dominate mainstream news in the summer of 2007 had, a year later, turned into a global economic disaster. The crisis effectively halted global credit markets, created record home foreclosures, and produced massive job losses on and off Wall Street (Ho 2009: 298, Ortiz forthcoming).

The effects of these events on women working on Wall Street were devastating. As the crisis evolved, the financial world, in the words of Michael Lewis, a long-time chronicler of Wall Street, "purged women from senior Wall Street roles" (2010). After a decade and a half of gaining ground in finance, the ranks of women began to quickly thin.[1] Zoe Cruz, who had been the apparent heir to John Mack, the CEO of Morgan Stanley, was abruptly fired by Mack on November 29, 2007. Her sudden exit dashed the dreams and expectations Wall Street women (and some men) had that Cruz—just in her early fifties—would become the first female CEO of a major financial firm.[2] Half a year later, Erin Callan, the chief financial officer (CFO) of Lehman Brothers, was fired, four months before the firm filed for Chapter 11.[3] Two months later in August 2008, Sally Krawcheck, age forty-three, one of the senior-most women in finance left standing, was forced out of Citigroup.[4] In less than a year, the three highest, most powerful, and best-paid women on Wall Street were out of a job.[5]

Cruz, Callan, and Krawcheck were part of the generation of women who followed in the paths of the first cohort of Wall Street women. Many believed that a woman from their generation was poised to break through the ultimate glass ceiling in finance and become a CEO. But instead of crashing triumphantly through the penultimate gendered boundary, these women, like the economy writ larger, were in freefall. Younger women in finance followed suit. During the first decade of the new millennium, the number of women between the ages of twenty and thirty-five working in the country's investment banks, brokerage houses, and other financial service–related firms dropped by 315,000, or 16.5 percent, while the men in that age group grew by 93,000, or 7.3 percent.[6] By contrast, women from the first generation in finance were not leaving Wall Street in such dramatic waves. The number of women over fifty-five years of age in the financial-services industry grew by 366,000 or 56 percent, since 1999, outpacing a 234,000 increase, or 34 percent, in similarly aged men.[7]

Amid the gendered reshuffling in the highest echelons of Wall Street, financial professionals, government experts, and the media began to debate the cause of and the solution to the economic crisis (Ortiz forthcoming: 2–3). Just as the majority of women seemed to be leaving (not necessarily of their own volition), journalists, pundits, and executives began to attribute blame for the financial debacle on the greedy, risk-taking behavior of men (Cameron et al. 2011; McDowell 2011). Suddenly, adding more women into the financial hierarchy seemed part of the answer.

85 Broads: Are You Ready for the Revolution?

On December 9, 2008, I, along with two hundred well-heeled businesswomen, attended a "women's power breakfast" in midtown Manhattan. The event was sponsored by 85 Broads, a global network of twenty thousand women that was originally founded during the nineties by women who had worked at the NYC headquarters of Goldman Sachs. The group, as a whole, was composed of women mostly in their twenties, thirties, and forties, with some in their fifties. They and I were there to attend the keynote address presented by Jacki Zehner, a fortysomething former Goldman Sachs partner turned "media commentator on women's leadership and success in the workplace, and their relationship to wealth, investing and social change."[8] The title of her talk was "Are YOU Ready for a Revolution?" When Zehner first took to the dais, she was dressed in a conservative, tailored white office shirt and blue slacks. But, once she began to speak, she dramatically tore the shirt off to display a t-shirt with a picture of the female comic hero Wonder Woman—and the words "Girl Power" in script underneath. Zehner declared,

> This is a call to action! I ask everyone in this room to make this world a more just and equitable place at the next level. Everyone in this room needs to hold tight to a core belief that the world would in fact be a better place if women had both access and opportunity to places and spaces they currently do not. I ask everyone in this room to claim THIS MOMENT as THE MOMENT to renew and enlarge their commitment to invest in women.
>
> Are we not in an economic crisis because of greed? . . . If women were in positions in a critical mass in finance would the world be different? Now we know that men have been leading—and the financial world as we know it is broken. . . . Men and women need to share power. When markets are broken, we are in desperate need of a new governance paradigm—a different leadership model—one where women's voices can be heard.[9]

The call for a social "revolution" coming from a former female partner of one of the most powerful investment banks in the world struck me as a bit odd, even offbase. I had never heard talk of revolution from members of the first generation of women. Yet Zehner's narrative about revolutionary change in the gendered governance of finance was not, as it turned out, an isolated event. Instead her talk was part of a larger emergent discourse of the feminizing and "feministing" of markets that is reconfiguring gender, feminism, leadership, and the financial crisis.

Since the onset of the financial meltdown, an enormous amount of attention and effort had been given to keeping the economy from, as Larry Summers, then the director of the White House's National Economic Council under President Obama, and other economists warned, "falling off a cliff." Amidst all the handwringing, panic, condemnation of excessive risk taking, and discussions of possible solutions to the crisis, women (at least in some circles) began to look like possible saviors. The usual cacophony of academic, journalist, and Wall Street women's voices appeared, at least for that particular moment in time, to be in some agreement. Far more than any of its predecessors, including the recession of the seventies, the crisis was being depicted in strikingly gendered terms. Accounts like the ones above articulated a divide between masculine, greedy, risk-taking actors and behaviors, probably leading to the crisis, and a more feminine, conservative, long-term approach to financial practice that could possibly help the economy avoid crisis or could fix it.[10] The idea that women were the ones who could and should rebuild the global economy was circulating widely within businesswomen's groups, articles, books, and blogs.[11] Indeed, a year after the onset of the crisis, the cover of *The Economist*—one of the more mainstream well-known magazines on the economy—displayed a picture of Rosie the Riveter, with the title "We did it!" The image of a female factory worker from the middle of the twentieth century, depicting the successful inroads made by women in the predominantly service-oriented sector of the twenty-first century, is striking. The author of one article in the issue argued that "the world's quietest revolution was at play—that women are gradually taking over the workplace."[12]

Constance Burk

Most members of the first generation were already actively engaged in postretirement practices when the events of 2007–9 initially hit. But not Constance, whom I had met initially in the nineties during my first stint of Wall Street fieldwork. Like others who have been displaced from the world of work in a postindustrial, postfinancial crisis economy, Constance was in search of what makes a life, her life, worth living (Hoey 2006: 355). Unlike most of the other Wall Street women of her generation, she experienced her "crisis" after the financial crisis.

In May 2010 she was figuring out her next projects in the midst of the recession. I had attempted to meet with Constance a number of times in 2008—the year of my formal follow-up fieldwork. However, she had just taken on a new senior-level position in a major global investment bank and had been helping to grow the bank's business internationally. It was nearly impossible for us to meet in person, given Constance's work and travel schedule. So we emailed back and forth occasionally. At the time, I thought that she was one of the last standouts of the first-generation women—one of the very few who was still working full-time in the world of finance and had, in fact, survived the downsizing on Wall Street in the aftermath of the financial crisis. She was an asset to her firm because she helped executives and investors deal with the sudden loss of faith in various countries in America's system of capitalism, banking, and finance.

In the spring of 2010, however, I began to receive emails from Constance expressing an interest in meeting with me in New York City. During one of her visits back to the city, she and I met for a lengthy talk in her pied-à-terre in Brooklyn Heights. She attributed some of her success, particularly her ability to work within and between various cultures, to her international upbringing: "I was always aware of the difference in cultures and nuances when I went to [an international boarding school]. And then, when I worked on Wall Street I lived in various places in Europe. So I had always viewed myself as never having roots anywhere—but sort of being part of the globe. I viewed myself as a global professional and a global citizen—long before it was fashionable." But she told me that she was negotiating leaving her job in the coming year. As she told me more about her imminent move, she began to reflect on the more and less successful periods of her life. "The most satisfying times" were when she was working overseas in a global capacity. "The least satisfying have been when the architecture of my life has sort of fallen apart." As in other narratives of success and failure, Constance's story illuminates the way in which individuals who lose their jobs, particularly those in the managerial sector, often express a feeling of losing their place within the broader cultural landscape (Newman 1988; Hoey 2006). In this particular case, she, who was and is arguably one of the relatively few women in the "superclass," has much to tell us about the gendered and classed experiences of losing power, prestige, and status, however temporarily, for members of the global elite. Her narrative also tells us how she situates her thoughts about the next stage of her life within her own sense of self:

> I don't feel my age. And I also know that at my age I know what I am not going to do. On the one hand, I still have some regrets. My child says, "But Mom, you had this fancy title—just think about that." And I say, "I don't care about that. There is still so much to do." So, I've got to get it in my head—it's about positioning yourself—figuring out what you are going to feel comfortable coming back and doing. . . .
>
> Do I see myself as a failure? Do I compare myself against anyone? I don't compare myself against anyone—but I do always think, and maybe this is a little bit of the immigrant mentality—that I was not good enough. . . .

I think about coming back [to the financial world] and even if I am traveling a lot—I am going to be isolated. . . . So I will live here . . . in Brooklyn Heights. I have to get myself involved. I think twenty-four hours a day—what is my passion? My passion has been working.

For Constance, leaving the world of global finance has entailed losing her sense of professional self, and her sense of personal agency, within the broader global landscape.

The last point I would like to make is that it's not as if I have lost my voice. It is that I lost a platform for my voice—for that voice. The board functions to give you a voice. It is not a voice in terms of telling people; it is a voice at least in the role of the bank. I view it in terms of governance—really making sure you have all the right questions on the table. . . . And I used to do a lot of public speaking . . . as well as . . . counseling others in business. . . .

So that part of my voice is something that is extraordinarily missing. And, if I could have an advocacy role—it could be whatever. . . . I know I impact people. I know I can be believable on any subject. . . . That is what I am struggling with.

A basic tenet of feminism is that women's voices need to be heard. In this sense, Constance draws on a broader feminist discourse about women's voice, power, and agency. But there is a clear element of class at play in her words as well. Notably she clarifies that she has not lost her voice, but the platform, the institutional power structure—the boards of firms—from which to articulate her voice, and for her voice to be heard.

Given her search for a new platform and role, I asked if she might want to get involved in women's politics in the United States again, something she had been active in during the nineties. Being a part of women's politics, namely the Women's Campaign Fund (WCF), had given first-generation women an individual and collective sense of agency—of doing something for the advancement of women in leadership positions in the nation.

CONSTANCE: It grabs me less than it used to.
MELISSA: And why did it grab you in the first place?
CONSTANCE: Because I think it was the issue of women being at the table, women being involved in government, women being able to have the opportunities—because at that point those clubs were still very closed.

MELISSA: Did you see yourself as being political in doing that or was it just part of supporting the political process?

CONSTANCE: It was more about supporting the political process. When I was political was when I was—we were doing all the pro-choice issues because that was highly political. But in terms of bipartisanship—getting more women candidates—I was indifferent as to their politics just because I wanted more voices, be it Barbara Boxer or Olympia Snowe . . .

MELISSA: Right—so more about gender over formal politics?

CONSTANCE: Over ideology. And so it was more about the process . . .

MELISSA: And you became less involved over time because of what you were doing careerwise?

CONSTANCE: Because I was traveling, mostly abroad.

She differentiates between providing support to the political process of electing women and being politically engaged about the abortion debate. Like other women she speaks of a moment in the nineties in which gender—women's collective, shared experiences and structures of feeling—trumped their formal political differences. During the past decade, however, the women have moved, in many ways individually by forging their own projects—some more feminist than others; some more political than others. This is the crossroads that Constance finds herself facing. Going from full-time work on Wall Street to "retirement" is not on a clear-cut path. She is considering her options, some of which are similar to the kinds of projects her generation is now actively participating in. And, she, like her peers, is not intent on following the traditional route to retirement and leaving the professional world completely. She, like many other women in her generation, wants to find alternative forms of agency in her postfinancial life:

After all the various humane crises going on—I think about going to help. . . . You don't have to start a new non-for-profit or NGO for that. . . . But I don't want to stop doing. I am not retiring in the country. I am not playing bridge. . . .

I like to have an impact, be it small or large. So it's not about, oh, let's go do another benefit in New York—that is not going to satisfy me. . . . It could be international, but we have enough issues at home that have to be dealt with, that people are dealing with. So, in that sense, I am sort of indifferent. Are there issues that I care about? Yes. I still care about reproductive rights and I find it fascinating that the younger generation of women has no sense how easy it could be lost again. But I think that we maybe have a chance with three women on the Supreme Court. I care about immigration, education, and women's issues globally. The one thing that caught my eye last year was reading about the Afghani widows and how they are not only veiled, they are prisoners within their own homes—and yet they have to raise the children.

Returning to the issue of class, Constance distinguishes between new millennial money made on Wall Street from the earnings of her own generation of financial colleagues. She acknowledges that she (like others in her cohort) is now a part of the elite, but even within the elite there are distinctions and hierarchies:

I have always taken my kids—particularly during their formative trips—to see less developed countries so that they could see what life is like there. I wanted them to understand that the world of gentrified Brooklyn, the Upper East Side New York was not. . . . Because of my profession we have led a pretty privileged life. Yet, I would say that in the last ten years, since the advent of hedge-fund mavens, primarily men, that that has put everything completely out of whack. I see some of my kids' friends, especially those from New York, who are daughters of those hedge-fund guys in their late forties—and they are taking private planes every weekend to here to there to wherever—which, even when we were on Wall Street, people were not doing much of. It has become much crasser, much more in your face. And while they may be of a higher economic class, they are from much less of a social or intellectual class.

For the moment Constance did not appear to share the dominant belief that women were biologically driven to be less risky than men. When I asked her if she thought that men take more risks than women because of their testosterone, she said, "Zoe Cruz was a very successful currency trader. Women have adrenaline. It is the same thing. So, no— I think that women can be as highly competitive as men." However, she did think that having a woman spokesperson for the industry is a good strategy, that it would make a major difference in the public's tumbling perception of mainly male investment bankers. Her suggestion makes a great deal of sense in a world of branding and marketing. Women are, after all, often the spokespeople for a range of products and services, though not typically for the hardcore world of financial management.

Toward the end of our visit, I began to talk with Constance about my book, about coming to the end. I spoke about how I felt like I was working on fitting together various pieces of a puzzle about Wall Street women's lives over a long period of time. I pointed out that I had first met her and many of the other women at WCF events—that those events had provided me with a place to "see the women together." Then I said, "It is really about a set of"—Constance interrupted me and said it was now about a set of "very disparate" people. I replied, "Disparate, different career trajectories—you went overseas. But I wonder what it says globally or structurally that at a certain point there would be so much divergence?"

CONSTANCE: Let me pose my answer with a question: What is the impact of social networking going to do in all of this? Because if we had all grown up as the younger generation is now—with their network of friends—the Internet in many respects enables you to maintain that network. I email my [female] friends from [Wall Street] once in a while and I see them once in a while. . . .

I mean, the real question is where is everyone going from here? Do people have clear visions? I mean most of us were always very, very highly focused, [with] a little bit [of] tunnel vision. And, with one of my friends, her whole industry—the mortgage industry has totally blown up. . . .

I think that those of us who were pioneers once still have to be pioneers—because there is a lot to forge. I am not quite sure in what or where or how. And, so, maybe we need to get everybody back together and sort of figure out the next steps . . .

MELISSA: That would be interesting. We could invite ten or twelve women from my original study to come together in New York City and chat—to talk and compare experiences . . .

That September I emailed the group an article from the *Wall Street Journal* entitled "Ranks of Women on Wall Street Thin." The article was alarming:

Women are fading from the U.S. finance industry.

In the past ten years, 141,000 women, or 2.6% of female workers in finance, left the industry. The ranks of men grew by 389,000 in that period, or 9.6%, according to a review of data, outpacing a 0.5% increase in male workers.

The difference is pronounced at brokerage firms, investment

banks, and asset-management companies. The figures suggest that women bore the brunt of the layoffs in the recent recession. But other forces are at play. Across the economy, computers have replaced junior, back-office workers, jobs that were largely filled by women.[13]

The article discussed the speculation of various industry insiders and scholars about the thinning ranks of women. Janet Hanson, founder of 85 Broads, speculated that women were finding "their entrepreneurial groove." The economist Grace Tsiang of the University of Chicago theorized that more women preferred to stay at home rather than to work at high-stress, high-pressure jobs.

Just a few minutes after I emailed the article out, Patricia Riley wrote back to say that she "had read the article and thought it failed to capture the mass exodus from Wall Street of women of my age group over the last decade for reasons other than those in the articles." She said that she wished to discuss this with me further in person either in New York City or Washington, D.C. Constance followed up by writing:

> I would agree that there has been a mass exodus but I am perhaps more cynical. I attended a major anniversary [of one of the firms she used to work at] the other evening in NY. It was all for present and past managing directors. I was SHOCKED to see that the numbers of females in the crowd was so much lower than when I left (over a decade ago).
>
> While this is obviously not scientific analysis, I did comment on it to my former colleagues who affirmed the sad reality.
>
> Look forward to discussing this in great depth. Perhaps we should all get together in NY with you at some point and have a great roundtable discussion.

Woman after woman then wrote to express dismay about the state of women on Wall Street, as well as their interest in coming together for a discussion. Less than two months later, we were all assembled for a roundtable—a mini-summit of sorts—on the state of women on Wall Street in the aftermath of the events of 2007–9. The article had struck a major chord. This was the first time in more than a decade and a half of research on my part that the women themselves had instigated a get-together, let alone a collective one.

The Roundtable: November 2010, New York City

On a cool, crisp, bright Friday morning in mid-November, I and about a dozen women met in a midtown women's political club. The sun poured into the solarium, our meeting room for the morning. Deirdre Parliament, Patricia Riley, Veronica Keyes, Mindy Plane, Andrea Dirks, Maydelle Brooks, Madeline Winters, and Constance Burk and several others were there. Everyone knew of one another or personally knew each other from Wall Street, the Financial Women's Association (FWA), or the WCF. Some were still close friends. Others had not been in touch for many years. Some had flown in from overseas. Some had flown or taken the train in from Washington, D.C; Connecticut; New Jersey; and Florida. Still others had taken cabs from the Upper East Side.

Nostalgia: Losing a Moral Compass in the World of Finance

After spending about fifteen minutes sipping coffee and chatting informally, we assembled at a large table. We began by introducing one another and giving updates. But the conversation soon diverged to a discussion of the "old" versus the "new" Wall Street. Mindy opened up the subject:

> As an observer for forty years on Wall Street, I am fascinated if I am just getting cranky and old or if and how Wall Street has changed. I always thought of Wall Street as something that would create jobs, provide capital for companies. They still do that. But it seems to have become more of a let's throw the dice and gamble a bit. Let's take high-risk. Let's sit there with our computers, searching for algorithms, instead of finding great companies for people to invest in. Let's see if I can trade ten thousand trades a day, and make some money. It's ridiculous. I am not sure if Wall Street is providing what this country needs.

Mindy's view of the "old" Wall Street draws on a discourse of shareholder value that, as the anthropologist Karen Ho points out, "is part and parcel of a broader project laying claim to a restorative narrative of entitlement and succession, through which Wall Street investment bankers have been able to define their professional social contributions to our economy" (2009: 27). Here, though, Mindy places this project predominantly in the past. Wall Street *once* enabled the building and growth of corporations, providing jobs for many people. Her narrative thus points to a shift in the logic of financial capitalism, a shift many believe precipitated the financial crisis. In contrast to the recent past, Wall Street's sole mission became to take greater and greater risks and engage in faster and higher profits and money making, without any apparent benefits even for the shareholders—the "owners"—of contemporary companies.

Maydelle followed up on Mindy's comments, asking if today "there is an honorable way to make money." Mindy said, "It is no longer honorable to make money. The Wall Street as a casino is not the Wall Street we all entered. However, Wall Street as an intermediary is always trying to read and push ahead, is in the nature of finance—that next way to make money. It is just that all of a sudden the moral pendulum has swung in terms of how are [*pause*], what is allowable— what passes the smell test in terms of how you make money."

First-generation Wall Street women yearn for the supposedly more stable, honest, moral world of yesteryear, a Wall Street where capitalism and democracy went hand in hand.[14] The seemingly more benign past of finance enables them to distance themselves from the shifts, changes, and problems of the casino economy that produced the financial crisis. This is not to say that the women's narratives are inaccurate. In fact, their comments draw on many of the changes in capitalism discussed by scholars and journalists alike, including various scenarios of the crisis popularized in academia, journalism, books, and films (Strange 1986; Harvey 2005; Tett 2009b; McDowell 1997, 2011). But the women as financial actors cannot entirely escape their participation, wittingly or unwittingly, in the making of late capitalism and the crisis. They cannot completely sever their connection to the neoliberal global economy and shareholder revolution.

The women themselves were and remain constrained by the existing structures of financial capitalism, of neoliberalism. Interestingly enough, as the group pursued the question of the morality of money making, the women did not immediately seize on the popular gendered argument linking the crisis to greedy men and their testosterone-induced maniacal behavior. Instead, they considered the various larger forces that had allowed for the boundary between the moral and immoral to blur in the financial markets. In other words, much like social scientists, they reflected on the various broader legal, institutional, and technological shifts that had allowed for and produced new kinds of market-making activity. Our conversation did eventually focus on questions of gender per se, but the broader framework in which the women initially reflected upon the crisis was less the innate biologically driven attributes of one sex over the other and more about how abstract systems were shaping market practice. They discussed transformations in technology. They talked about the dismantling of Glass-Steagall. They talked about the globalization of capital. And they spoke about derivatives as examples of "funny money."

Gender, Generation, and the Fear of Falling

Being nostalgic was not the only way the women distanced themselves from the contemporary world of Wall Street. They also critiqued the younger generation of women, particularly that generation's "entitled" habitus, a point first brought up by Patricia and subsequently discussed among the women:

> PATRICIA: I feel very frustrated about a lot of what I am seeing happening on Wall Street, particularly the younger women. . . . I was shocked at the entitlement in the younger women, coming in to my office, when I still worked on Wall Street, saying: "I am having a baby. I am not going to do this." And my replying: "Your job requires travel. We can talk about another job. But you cannot have this job. Who do you think is going to travel, me? I already do enough on my own."
>
> So I wonder what happened. We all had to work so hard. We expected so little in the way of a combination of work and family. Somehow the next generation thought they could have any combination. "I am going to work at home three days a week." "No, I mean, you need to be in the office for the morning meeting."
>
> CONSTANCE: It is the cycles of women, right? The first generation always works hard, and the second generation is totally entitled.
>
> PATRICIA: I will close with one thought for now. Years ago I heard a woman say, "Some women open the door the others walk through." I think most of us opened the door.

One of the key fears circulating among the first generation even before the onset of the financial crisis was that the women following in their path would take so much for granted that they would lose sight of the gender battles already won and become "soft" in their orientation toward their careers. Notably, one of the central leitmotifs of anxiety operating within the professional-managerial class for some time, one I discussed at length in chapter 3 about the gendered discourses of finance, is that the first generation might lose their place within the classed landscape (Ehrenreich 1989). Here, in 2010, we see a different but related anxiety emerging within this pioneering group. They fear that the younger generation of women has become too complacent, too filled with a sense of entitlement. They believed that this soft work ethic would manifest itself in such a way that the younger women would no longer be able to perpetuate their place within the managerial hierarchy of Wall Street. Not every woman at the table shared this view of professional women in their twenties, thirties, and even early forties. But the view does echo a broader discourse circulating among women that came of age during the sixties and seventies that the younger generation takes far too much for granted when it comes to believing that the feminist battles of yesteryear have been won (Fisher 2010).

This, however, was not the only concern expressed about the younger generation. If, on the one hand, the women were concerned that the younger generation writ large might be going soft, some members of the first generation thought the younger women's networks, such as 85 Broads, were, as one woman put it, "too militaristic." They heard the kind of call that Jacki Zehner made for a "revolution" as hard-edged, too aggressive.

The women thus did not identify with the new generation of Wall Street women's networks, such as 85 Broads, either. The women not only spoke about the generational differences among women in finance and their networks, but they also expressed their own uncertainties about their place—as pioneering financial women—within the larger landscape of professional women's networks at large. During the seventies and eighties there was only one women's financial group in New York City: the FWA. Now, there are 85 Broads, the National Council for Research on Women's Corporate Circle, and others, and most of these groups tend to be composed of women under the age of fifty, if not sixty:

MAYDELLE: What is the FWA doing these days for women on Wall Street?

ANDREA: I think the FWA was one of the catalysts at this point . . .

MINDY: I think it is much lower level and narrow . . .

CONSTANCE: There was a purpose to what we did . . .

MINDY: They still have some good programs. I think the FWA runs good programs for women who are thirty years old.

ANDREA: You know what happens? I always wonder if I see a call from the FWA. They want help, sure, and then the call is from some very low-level person who wants to know if I want to buy a ticket to the dinner. I mean, they don't get it. They should go back to the membership lists . . . and cultivate those who were . . . I mean, look around this table. We are strong. We come from a formative time.

CONSTANCE: Yes, but how about contrasting the FWA with 85 Broads? How successful has 85 Broads been?

MELISSA: And what about the National Council for Research on Women's Corporate Circle?

ANDREA: I think they are doing really good work.

MINDY: And what about the Women's Corporate Directors? The organization that helps women get put onto boards?

The group debated the pros and cons of the various women's groups. In the end, they agreed that none of the existing groups really served the needs and goals of the recently retired members of the first generation, at least not the particular group that came together at that meeting in 2010. None of the existing networks provided the women with a space to offer their expertise to younger Wall Street women and the financial world generally. The question then surfaced: What if anything did the group sitting at the table want to do as a group? Were they tied together beyond their shared experiences and identity as members of the first generation of women on Wall Street? Or had their separate postfinancial paths separated them sufficiently that their bonds were weakened and they did not have collective interests and goals?

Constance suggested that the women should become advisors to the world of finance. They should form a "task force" with an advisory capacity regarding the new regulation of the financial-services industry. Other women wanted to help women on Wall Street—to help women in light of the crisis and demonization of financiers interested in the world of finance, and to help them stay and advance the corporate hierarchy. Still others wanted to focus their energies on helping the poorest of women in the world. In the end, the group did not come to any final decision. We had talked for several hours. A few women had planes to catch. We were all pretty exhausted. Some of us went downstairs in the club for lunch, while others left. I promised to follow up on our discussion.

By engaging in a conversation about the crisis, the women that November day in 2010 joined other groups of financial actors who have found themselves in a variety of situations in which it becomes necessary to shift models of reflection and models of intervention (Miyazaki and Riles 2004; Ong and Collier 2004: 14; Holmes and Marcus 2006; Zaloom 2006). The convergence of the women's own personal and professional crises with the financial crisis provides a unique insight into construction of gender, generation, feminism, and the crisis. This also provides a view of some of the individual and collective political projects the first generation were constructing and engaging in during the economic recession. But the women did not discuss possible forms of intervention they might take, or how best to further engage in the fate of women within the context of the crisis; indeed they did not start to discern which women were actually willing to work with another on these various projects. In the end, the discussion about possible next steps only generated further debate.

The women debated their futures and the possibility of helping poor women in the aftermath of one of the worst financial crises in the history of the global economy—and in the midst of a series of major setbacks to the women's movement, including the 2011 Supreme Court dismissal of a massive sex discrimination lawsuit against Wal-Mart on behalf of female employees, a decision that now makes it more difficult to mount large-scale claims against the nation's biggest companies. They were also witnessing a revived "war against women," with more and more government and private assaults on women's health and freedom, specifically on abortion and on affordable contraception for millions of women.[15] In some respects, there was a striking resemblance between the seventies, the decade in which the first generation of women made their way onto Wall Street, and the contemporary moment in which they were leaving the world of conventional finance and starting to devise new projects.

Conclusion

The valorization of women as naturally cautious and caring seems familiar from generations of celebrations of gendered difference. But, as my genealogy of the first generation of women on Wall Street has detailed ethnographically, this gendered logic has become increasingly aligned with the logic of the market over the past four decades. And the specific gendering of the crisis may have been relatively novel, but the representation of Wall Street women as more risk averse was deeply rooted in historical gendered discourses in finance. When I first met Patricia in 1994, she had told me why she and other women had done so well in the area of research beginning in the seventies. She described how women in finance invoked and reframed the figure of the "consumer" as feminine in order to highlight their own ability to forecast, sell, and buy stocks. Echoing late nineteenth-century tactics, they used gendered assumptions about their roles as mothers making family purchases in order to sell themselves as economic experts. Now, several decades later, financial experts were blaming greedy, risk-taking elite men for the crash and calling for "feminine," more conservative, more risk-averse, long-term solutions. In both instances, an understanding of women as nurturing and men as competitive underwrote specific new opportunities for real women, whether masculine virtues were valorized or not. In both, women deployed very traditional ideas about femininity to make room for themselves as financial experts, a decidedly untraditional vocation. What was particularly new about the gendering of the twenty-first-century financial crisis was the scale. During the seventies, eighties, and nineties the women drew on these notions to claim a place for themselves within particular areas within Wall Street firms—namely research, sales, and wealth management rather than investment banking and trading. By 2008, they were reframing the argument, setting it within the more global context of financial markets and the crisis. This is evident in the ways in which Jacki Zehner of 85 Broads, Debora Spar of Barnard College, Nicholas Kristof of the *New York Times*, and other elites were "making the business case" for women's equity and leadership in global finance, including women's unique, biological abilities to be wary of risk and to solve the economic crisis.[16]

Contemporary financiers, journalists, and management gurus—mainly women—also drew on historical discourses about corporate domesticity, motherhood, and women's innate care-taking qualities. In earlier periods of crises, including the turn of the last century, women have often been looked to as the saviors of the nation. By the nineties, when I spoke to Patricia, she spoke about female research analysts' care-taking tendencies in terms of their professional-managerial clients, thereby positioning women, this time around, as saviors of a wealthy segment of American society. In the postfinancial crisis, however, motherly women were touted as the potential rescuers of the global economy.

An *Economist* article pointed out the dangers inherent in what the authors label the "new feminism" in managerial thinking, the idea that "women are wired differently from men, and not just in trivial ways."[17] The authors warn of the dangers of creating essentialist arguments to underpin women's leadership skills and avarice. What is novel, in the wake of the crisis, is the way in which those making such gendered essentialist arguments increasingly explain asserted gender differences in biological terms, for example citing "scientific" studies that claim that male traders take more risks because they produce more testosterone as they trade (McDowell 2011). What is also novel is the extent to which new media spread and popularize this argument, making the idea of the feminization of the market increasingly accepted, at least in some quarters, as common sense.

The subjects and subjectivities of financial actors in the current moment are shifting from the rational man to the hormonal, chemical masculine subject. The biological system is being directly linked and mapped onto the financial system in strikingly gendered ways (see Zaloom and Schüll 2011). Some financiers and academics see the "cure" for the financial system in the uplifting and advancement of women into senior positions. These expert subjects effectively believe that reforming financial institutions and practices will necessitate not only re-regulation in general but also the re-regulation of gender in terms of numbers as well as feminine hormones and qualities as well (Cameron et al. 2011).

The current financial crisis is being constructed by some as a window of opportunity for a new kind of more "caring" and "softer" capitalism as well as new mechanisms for the commodification and investment in specific kinds of gendered actors, bodies, and habitus for profit. Thus, the conditions of the crisis and subsequent recession of 2009 to the present are amplifying gendered differences (biological and otherwise) and the value of a certain kind of feminized mode of being (risk awareness).

Zehner's call for a gendered revolution and her depiction of Wonder Woman on her t-shirt illuminate the ways she and others of her generation are performing and amending gendered financial discourses in order to insert themselves, and to re-assert women as leaders within the male-dominated world of the financial crisis. Drawing on earlier financial women's discourses of risk and destiny, Zehner explains that she no longer views her destiny in personal terms but in "political" terms. Her explanation that the world's "markets are broken," that we "are in desperate need of a new governance paradigm," one that includes men and women sharing power equally—these are all tenets of an emergent feminizing of markets that has evolved from the financial crisis and recession. At the same time, her arguments for a new "investment paradigm" and form of governance that invests in social peace and justice are part of the larger discourse of feminist philanthrocapitalism that Veronica and other members of the first generation have helped to create organizationally and discursively.

In the wake of the financial crisis, even as the media celebrated women as the saviors of the economy, women left Wall Street in droves. Within less than a span of a year, three of the highest-ranking women in finance—including Zoe Cruz, in her early fifties, who had been rumored to be on track to become the first CEO of a major financial firm (Morgan Stanley)—had all been unceremoniously fired. And, after having three men promoted over her in succession, Lily Franklin, now nearly sixty, decided to call it quits on what had been, up to that point, a meteoric career for anyone—female or male—on Wall Street. Suddenly most of the first two generations of women (Franklin's and Cruz's) to break glass ceilings in finance were gone. Nonetheless, celebrations of women's leadership have persisted and taken new forms. For example, Linda Tarr-Whelan, a distinguished senior fellow at the national think tank Demos and a former ambassador to the UN Commission on the Status of Women in the Clinton administration, published a book entitled *Women Lead the Way: Your Guide to Stepping Up to Leadership and Changing the World* (2009). She argues that when women's representation at the top of institutions is at 30 percent, changes will begin to happen that have demonstrable positive effects on the bottom line of business and government (21–24). Her argument connects liberal feminism (the advancement of women into leadership positions within institutions of power) with market ideologies—including the pursuit of profit (Griffin 2009). In 2010, Tarr-Whelan promoted her book at a talk at the World Bank in Washington, D.C., and a year later, she hosted the UN Women's Global Compact launch of the Women's Empowerment Principles, which called for a movement promoting women's leadership at every level in businesses around the world because "gender equality is good for business." More recently, the National Council for Research on Women has encouraged both male and female shareholders of companies to support a campaign—"Vote No for All-Male Boards"—that is to engage in gendered "investor activism" (as stated on the NCRW website). Members of the first generation continue to lead this movement through their ongoing work in socially responsible investing, microfinance, and various other projects.

What is so arresting about this new approach to women's equality and leadership on Wall Street and beyond is that it combines elements of liberal and cultural feminism (the demand for women's equal rights; the celebration of gender difference) with neoliberal ideologies of financial capitalism and the free market (the pursuit of profit and the importance of the bottom line). Throughout the twenty-first century, particularly in the aftermath of the financial crisis, increasing numbers of women and women's not-for-profit and for-profit organizations will be joining forces to promote the feminization of financial capitalism.

NOTES

Introduction

1. Wall Street women and those within their networks may disagree with some of my interpretations of their experiences, but I have tried to capture their complexities, ambiguities, and anxieties. I have disguised the names of all the women that I ethnographically follow in this book. Thus, all my informants have been given pseudonyms, sometimes even multiple pseudonyms. Furthermore, the women's stories are told and analyzed against the backdrop of more than one hundred interviews I conducted with women and men on Wall Street (1993–96), archival research and fieldwork within the Financial Women's Association (FWA, 1993–96), fieldwork within the Women's Campaign Fund (WCF, 1993–96), and fieldwork within a single financial firm (1995–96). I also engaged in a series of follow-up interviews with twenty members of the first generation during and throughout the 2000s as well as follow-up fieldwork within the FWA and WCF during that same period. The only time I use actual names of specific women is when I directly cite or quote the women's names from a newspaper story, magazine article, or biography. Furthermore, because I am interested in examining the professional and political networks of Wall Street women, it makes sense to use the real names of the FWA and WCF. It is also instructive to note that providing pseudonyms for these organizations is practically a futile exercise given that there are relatively few such organizations in existence, and these particular organizations are well known within the women's financial and political communities. I do, however, use pseudonyms of FWA members when citing or quoting from FWA archives.

2. Spar, "One Gender's Crash," *Washington Post*, January 4, 2009.

3. Kristof, "Mistresses of the Universe," *New York Times*, February 8, 2009.

4. While men in Obama's economic circles (Larry Summers and Timothy Geithner) garnered a great deal of attention in the public imagination, a few women also caught the nation's eye. A significant amount of faith, for

example, was put in the hands of Mary L. Schapiro, the first woman to chair the Securities and Exchange Commission (SEC) (Robert Chew, "Mary Schapiro Moves Quickly to Shake Up the SEC," *Time*, February 11, 2009). In the summer of 2008, Sheila Bair, the head of the Federal Deposit Insurance Corporation, received a Profile in Courage Award at the Kennedy Library in Boston, in honor of her "political bravery": Bair's early though ultimately futile attempt to get the Bush administration to recognize the subprime mortgage crisis before it became a threat to the entire economy (Ryan Lizza, "The Contrarian: Sheila Bair and the White House Financial Debate," *The New Yorker*, July 6, 2009).

5. I am indebted to the anthropologist Bill Maurer for pushing me to think not only about market feminism but its opposite pole: the feminization of markets.

6. For an in-depth discussion of feminist practice theory, see Ortner 1996 and Lamphere et al. 1997. For additional discussions of practice theory, including theorizing agency, see Ortner 2006. For my early discussion regarding how to use feminist practice theory to understand the gendering of finance, see Fisher 2004.

7. Anthropological interest in finance has been growing since the eighties and the bull market and speculative fever increasingly occupied the minds of the public (Fraser 2005; Fisher and Downey 2006; Maurer forthcoming: 1). It has taken on more urgency in the wake of the financial crisis and the subsequent economic recession (Guyer 2009; Ho 2009; Schwegler 2009; Tett 2009b; Fisher 2010; Ortiz forthcoming). At the same time, sociological and interdisciplinary studies of finance have emphasized the ethnographic method—particularly in terms of studies of traders and trading floors (Beunza and Stark 2008; Maurer forthcoming). Since the mid-2000s anthropologists and sociologists have thus produced pioneering ethnographies of financial markets, involving fieldwork not only on trading floors but also in corporate offices. Hiro Miyazaki (2006) has followed the ups and downs of traders in Japan for a decade. Drawing on fieldwork in the London and Chicago financial futures market, Caitlin Zaloom (2006) explored the effects of technological change on traders' practices and identities in the nineties. I have also written about Wall Street women's networks (2004, 2006, 2010). Recently Karen Ho's (2009) ethnography of Wall Street investment banks demonstrated changing conceptions of finance and shareholder value in American culture and society. Douglas Holmes (2009) has engaged in fieldwork of central banks. Annelise Riles (2001, 2006, 2011) has examined the legal architects of Japan's financial markets. George Marcus and Douglas Holmes (2006) have discussed anthropological strategies for anthropology when engaging with expert subjects, in their case, members of the Federal Reserve Bank of the United States.

8. In particular I am motivated by Pierre Bourdieu's notions of "disposi-

tion" and "habitus," where "disposition" refers to a "way of being," "inclina-
tion," and "predisposition," often of the body, which all collectively con-
stitute the habitus, "a system of dispositions," which in turn organizes
action, "produces practices," and constructs social structures and worlds
(Bourdieu 1990: 73–87, 214; cited in Ho 2009: 11). But I have departed from
Bourdieu by following the feminist remaking of practice theory and including a theory of agency and the acting subject. For Bourdieu, there are actors
but there are no significant intentionalities: actors strategize, but their
strategies are drawn from an internalized habitus that is itself a virtual
mirror of external limits and possibilities (Ortner 1996: 11). Thus, drawing
on Ortner (2003) rather than drawing on this closed loop of objective conditions and subjective aspirations, I argue that Bourdieu as well as those
anthropologists of finance that tend to follow Bourdieu do not fully recognize or simply underestimate a range of counter-forces that threaten to
disrupt the closed loops of social and cultural reproduction on Wall Street
and beyond.

9. Gender studies are making an important contribution to anthropological, historical, and social studies of finance (de Goede 2005a). But, in spite
of a flourishing body of corporate ethnographies by anthropologists (Cefkin 2009), gender studies have yet to make a major impact on corporate
and business anthropology—particularly in terms of women in business in
the United States—within or outside of finance (Brondo and Baba 2006).
And there is still much work to be done when it comes to bringing critical
perspectives, including critical feminist theory to the study of business
organizations and practices: for a discussion of what is and what is yet to be
done in the arena of feminist perspectives on gender in organizational
research, see Calás and Smircich 2008. For a discussion regarding the possibilities of building "critical corporate studies," see Bose and Lyons 2010. In
terms of business history, the historian Angel Kwolek-Folland (1994) was
instrumental to first drawing attention to the gendered dimensions of the
insurance industry during the nineteenth and twentieth centuries. Marieke
de Goede (2005a, 2009) has considered the gendered underpinnings of
finance over several centuries, including highlighting the gendered dimensions of financial crises. De Goede, who is a political economist, and other
political economic theorists have been instrumental in providing poststructural analysis and the importance of discourse and representation for political and economic practice (Larner 2000; Lewis et al. 2008). Recently, two
feminist political scientists, building on de Goede's poststructural approach, have drawn attention to the gendered structure of global finance
(Assassi 2009) and to the gendered neoliberal discourses that underpin
development strategies implemented by the World Bank (Griffin 2009).
There have also been a number of studies of the gendered culture of
financial markets, including Linda McDowell's work on women and men

and gendered performances in the City of London during the nineties, and my own work on Wall Street women and their networks (2004, 2006, 2010). In her study of male traders, Caitlin Zaloom (2006) drew attention to masculinity and risk taking; I have written on the gendering of risk and femininity and masculinity (2004). Karen Ho (2009) also discussed the ways gender, class, and race construct Wall Street subjects and their experiences in finance.

10. When neoliberal forms interact with, for example, the state, the exchange brings about changes in state practices, including welfare state retrenchment and new forms of governance. States, for example, are now situated in a multilevel governance framework; states now form partnerships with corporations (Kantola and Squires forthcoming). During the past decade, there has also been a shift in terminology within the social sciences from "late capitalism" to "neoliberalism." From one point of view, however, there is no hard-and-fast distinction to be made between the two. As Sherry Ortner recently pointed out, "In many ways neoliberalism is simply late capitalism made conscious, carried to extremes, and having more visible effects" (Ortner 2011). But neoliberalism, as Aihwa Ong argues, "can also be conceptualized as a new relationship between government and knowledge through which governing activities are recast as nonpolitical and non-ideological that need technical solutions" (2006: 3). It is therefore not only an underlying economic doctrine. There are by now a series of ethnographic studies of neoliberalism, most of which examine the cultural works it takes to produce and maintain the economic domain as separate from the political (Bornstein 2005; Maurer forthcoming: 9). Some attend to the role of "culture" in neoliberal strategies (Elyachar 2005).

11. Drawing on theories of gender, finance, and performativity (Butler 1993; Callon 1998; de Goede 2005a, 2009), I understand the gendering of finance to be "a discursive domain made possible through performative practices which have to be articulated and rearticulated on a daily basis. There is no market outside of, or in addition, or even constructing the real world of finance, the gendered world of finance. Financial agents are neither sovereign, individual subjects not reducible to the mechanics of financial power structures. Instead, financial agents are regulated through historically constituted financial discourses but also acquire the authority to perform, affirm, and amend these discourses" (de Goede 2005a: 10). Notably, Judith Butler's theory of performativity has become quite influential within the study of finance and economics from anthropological, sociological, and geographical perspectives, although its precise meaning and significance is currently under debate (e.g., Mackenzie 2006; de Goede 2009).

12. The situated and embodied understandings of financial markets provided by contributors to the social studies of finance, including the work of anthropologists, have thus gone far to show the construction and perfor-

mativity of global finance (McDowell 1997; Fisher 2004; de Goede 2005a; Miyazaki 2006; Zaloom 2006; Holmes 2009; Riles 2009). But as Paul Langley, a political scientist of finance, recently argued, very little in the social studies of finance has been done "to explicitly reorient enquiry, beyond professional, expert, and elite networks of knowledge and technology situated in specific centres" (2008: 7, Maurer forthcoming; Ortiz forthcoming). Anthropologists have done much to illuminate the relationships between finance, culture, and society (Fisher 2006; Miyazaki 2006; Zaloom 2006; Ho 2009; Holmes 2009; Riles 2011). However, even then, ethnographers have not done much in terms of examining the relationships between market and political elite actors situated within and beyond global financial centers, let alone the ties created between female financial elites and government elites (Fisher 2007).

13. In recent years, feminist scholars have endeavored to understand the changes that neoliberalism has brought to both the state in a broader sense and to feminism in particular. The difference between these two can be seen in the examination of "state feminism" and "market feminism," the latter of which has been the object of much recent speculation. I first developed the concept of market-feminist subjects in my dissertation "Wall Street Women: Gender, Culture, and History in Global Finance" (2003). I have discovered since that Jacqui Alexander has coined the term "free-market feminism" (Alexander and Mohanty 1997). More recently in contemporary discussions of the mainstreaming of feminism I have also become aware of Kantola and Squires's coinage of "market feminism" (forthcoming) cited in this book with permission, and the socialist feminist Hester Eisenstein's (2009) term "Madeline Albright feminism." The principal aim of most scholarly work on market feminism is, as Eisenstein argues, to "raise some troubling issues about how feminist energies, ideologies, and activisms have been manipulated in the service of the dangerous forces of a globalized corporate capitalism" (2009: vii). Emphasizing capitalism's hegemony, these scholars describe a world in which the hopes and dreams of an earlier more radical feminism have been lost, while liberal feminism has been completely absorbed into the marketplace, and elites (whether women or men) by definition cannot participate in any form of social transformation. They warn those who might think that feminism has won, in order to keep a kind of radical feminist possibility alive. I argue, however, that these scholars have not fully considered the politics of their own representation of the history of feminism. In their linear and apocalyptic narrative, an all-encompassing system of capitalism brought an end to the radical feminized past of the sixties and seventies, thereby forever closing out the possibility of a real future feminist politics, and hence feminist intervention into the marketplace (Gibson-Graham 1996).

14. Ethnographically tracing the first generation of Wall Street women's

careers and networks provides a way to not only decenter contemporary finance, but also a way to decenter and deconstruct the making of market feminism. Indeed, conducting fieldwork within the FWA and then the WCF over a period of several years during the nineties (in the mid-2000s) allowed me to observe and participate within a range of multiple, sometimes overlapping, multilevel networks being created by female financial elites and others. Wall Street women actively engaged in defining finance, markets, feminism, and politics based on shared cultural norms, bonds of trust, and social practice. These women, individually and collectively, performed and created the gendering of market and political realms. Returning to the world of the first generation in the late 2000s enabled me to watch the women, and others, engage in various market-feminist projects on the ground.

15. The issue of gender in business history has only recently come under serious scrutiny. Under strict interpretations of evolutionary and managerial models, business historians often focused solely on the firm or corporation, without looking at the broader social context (Lipartito and Sicilia 2004). Lipartito and Sicilia write, "Evolutionary and managerial models also assume that firms react rather narrowly to the environment, seeking solutions to a set of economic problems largely rooted in production. It is equally possible, though, that managers are more broadly situated social actors who respond to many influences" (11). This new way of viewing business history allows historians to integrate issues such as race, class, and gender into their analyses or corporations (Lipartito and Sicilia 2004). The works of the feminist business historian Angel Kwolek-Folland (1994, 1998, 2001) have been major contributions to the literature on business and gender history. There is now a flourishing body of work by business historians on gender and business: see especially Yeager 1999 and Laird 2006.

16. Journalists, sociologists, and psychologists have turned their focus toward Wall Street women far more often than anthropologists have. The journalist Patricia McBroom's *The Third Sex: The New Professional Woman* (1992) gave an overall perspective on women in financial positions, while the journalist Anne B. Fisher's *Wall Street Women: Women in Power on Wall Street Today* (1990) offered one of the first concentrated examinations of women in finance during the early nineties. A more recent journalistic account of women on Wall Street is Susan Antilla's *Tales from the Boom-Boom Room: Women vs. Wall Street* (2002). Sociologists have examined women in finance in terms of their career paths. Examples include Louise Marie Roth's *Selling Women Short: Gender Inequality on Wall Street* (2006). Additionally, sociologists and psychologists have tackled the familial aspect of women professionals. This work includes Mary Blair-Loy's *Competing Devotions: Career and Family among Women Executives* (2003); Daniel Levinson's *Seasons of a Woman's Life* (1996), which juxtaposes the stories of

homemakers and career women; and Aasta S. Lubin's *Managing Success: High-Echelon Careers and Motherhood* (1987). The latter three works are based on interviews with women in finance in the New York City and Chicago areas. Recently, several Wall Street women have penned autobiographies or novels about women in finance: Susan Bell's *When the Getting Was Good: A Novel* (2010); Tameron Keyes's *No Backing Down: My Story of Suing One of the Largest Investment Firms in the World and Winning* (2010); and Nina Godiwalla's *Suits: A Woman on Wall Street* (2011).

17. Marilyn Bender, "Women's Lib Bearish in Wall St.; Movement Is Subdued and Impact Is Slight," *New York Times*, October 11, 1970.

18. On the one hand, the women's bracketing of the marketplace with the "outside" is similar to the ways in which male traders often separate the worlds of the trading floor and of family life while making trades (Zaloom 2006: chapter 6). On the other hand, it differs from at least some men in that the women do not always find it so easy to keep the marketplace and their feminist ideas, for example, completely apart.

19. The women are engaged with a more socially interventionist and ameliorative form of market feminism than has previously been considered in much of the current feminist literature, literature that has strongly critiqued the mainstreaming of feminism (Eisenstein 2009; McRobbie 2009; Kantola and Squires forthcoming). Such businesswomen are paving the way for the increasing feminization of markets (Gibson-Graham 1996).

20. I published some of my findings in a volume I coedited that began to bring attention to the ways changes in global financial markets, corporate structures, and Wall Street women's networks could be fruitfully studied by using anthropological and ethnographic perspectives (Downey and Fisher 2006).

21. In an essay in 2008 on the emergent anthropology of experts and public policy, the anthropologists Tara Schwegler and Michael Powell argued that such challenges are, in fact, part of the ethnographic data—they reveal glimpses into structures of power and their openings. See Brondo and Baba (2006) for a discussion of the difficulties of doing fieldwork—particularly in terms of access—when it comes to doing ethnographic work about women in businesses within the United States. Anthropologists have worked within and on business for some time. The anthropologist Marietta Baba has written extensively on the subject for several decades (Baba 1998, 2006). For important discussions that consider the history and contemporary state of corporate ethnography in late capitalism, see Baba 2009 and Cefkin 2009.

22. Midway through my fieldwork, a female stockbroker named Kimberly Allen informed me that she and others had been collecting and building an archive since the seventies in the FWA that was filled with board-meeting minutes, letters, and articles and videos about Wall Street women and the organization. They had been doing so in the hopes that someone would

eventually use the archives to write the history of New York City's women in finance. Kimberly decided that I was "the one" and instructed me to spend time in the FWA closet archive, which I eventually did.

The last year (1995–96) of my first stint of fieldwork took an interesting twist. For a variety of reasons, I spent the bulk of that time conducting what one might call more traditional workplace fieldwork. Specifically, through my interest in women and increasingly in diversity on Wall Street, I gained access to one specific financial firm in particular. I was not officially employed at the firm. However, I had the permission of its higher-ups to spend time conducting interviews and fieldwork. During this stage of my project I began to focus particularly on policy changes that were transpiring in the bank. The first involved the mainstreaming and centralization of global diversity efforts in the bank's headquarters in New York City. Specifically, at the time of my study, management had just completed initiating phase 1 (developing the position of professional women and minorities within its U.S. population). This involved implementing diversity programs, as well as shifts in work-family policies. Notably, a significant number of first-generation executive women within the firm were recruited to participate in task forces heading these initiatives up.

23. During the nineties, in part, out of financial necessity—I could not, for example, afford to take planes with my subjects to London when they were finalizing deals, although I could (and occasionally did) from time to time spend time "shadowing" the women in their firms—I found that observing women for a day or so would give me a general sense of their daily lives at work.

1. Beginnings

1. The only times I use women's actual names (e.g., Muriel Siebert) is when I quote women or discuss a real person from a book, newspaper story, magazine article or use of a slide. I always use pseudonyms for my actual informants and for FWA members.

2. The women were raised during what the anthropologist Sherry Ortner calls a "national project": the middle classing of (white) America (Ortner 2003: 28).

3. Moreover, during the sixties and seventies, Wall Street and elite universities were not yet working tightly together to create networks of Ivy League graduates who turned into investment bankers as they would beginning in the early eighties (Ho 2009: 58–59).

4. Arturo Gonzalez and Janeanne Gonzalez, "Where No Woman Reaches the Summit: Thousands of Women Work on Wall Street but Few Attain Executive Positions," *New York Times*, August 17, 1958.

5. Ibid.

6. Merrill Lynch hired three African American brokers in 1965. For a discussion of African Americans on Wall Street see Bell, *In the Black*.

7. Gwen Sharp, "Normalizing Female Computer Programmers in the '60s," www.sociologicalimages.com, accessed July 28, 2011.

8. The American public loved the new heroes. In the sixties, department stores sold adult board games called "Transaction," "Broker," and "The Stock Market" (Sobel 1980: 215).

9. The civil rights movement and the women's liberation movements of the sixties and seventies reshaped the corporate workplace in those decades and beyond. Combined, these movements influenced the development of equal opportunity and affirmative action, as well as laws addressing sexual harassment and hostile work environments, and concepts such as flextime and maternity leave. For the history of the shift from "the culture of exclusion" during the fifties to the eighties, see Nancy MacLean's *Freedom Is Not Enough: The Opening of the American Workplace* (2006). In *Pull* (2006), the historian Pamela Laird argues for the importance of paying attention to the ways the feminist movement and civil rights movement shaped the corporate workplace. In *Inventing Equal Opportunity* (2009), the sociologist Frank Dobbin argues that personnel experts were the people responsible for actually putting the ideas of social movements—including the ideas of equal rights and the right to equal employment—into actual practice in corporations.

10. Jennifer Lee, "Museum Celebrates the Women of Wall Street," *New York Times*, June 4, 2009.

11. Marilyn Bender, "Women's Lib Bearish in Wall St.: Movement Is Subdued and Impact Is Slight," *New York Times*, October 11, 1970.

12. Ibid.

13. Ibid.

14. Ibid.

15. "Feminist theory" is not a single unitary subject. But most contemporary feminist theorizing focuses on gender as a form of power that intersects with other axes of social inequality, such as race and class (Ortner 2006; Calás and Smircich 2009). Most feminist analysts are thus concerned with illuminating gender and other social injustices, and ultimately bringing about social transformation (Butler 1993).

16. Bender, "Women's Lib Bearish in Wall St."

17. Marilyn Bender, "Big Board's Female Pages Take Up Slack," *New York Times*, December 7, 1970.

18. Ibid.

19. Bender, "Women's Lib Bearish in Wall St."

20. Terry Robards, "Woman, 36, at Top in Brokerage House," *New York Times*, March 23, 1969.

21. It was the bipartisan nature of the wcf that would provide the open-

ing for Wall Street women—both Democrats and Republicans—to join the WCF's board in the early nineties.

22. Steven Fraser describes the cycle of bear markets throughout the seventies in his book *Every Man a Speculator* (2005). Fraser notes that the initial Wall Street crash in 1970 caused great anxiety after the postwar sense of order and economic growth: "The very words *panic* and *crash* were supposed to be virtually eliminated from the lexicon of economic discourse, consigned to the status of historical curiosities by a watchful set of national and international regulatory institutions. By and large that promise was kept. But from the 1970 panic onward, the old specter of bubble and bust returned from the dead" (535). Signs that the good days had ended included (but were not limited to) OPEC's stranglehold on oil prices; the end of fixed exchange rates; the evacuation of the American embassy in Saigon; Nixon's resignation; "stagflation"; the deindustrialization of America, including the decline of the steel industry; the erosion of middle-class income; and the fiscal emergency of New York City (536). The effects of this instability on Wall Street were wide. "The percentage of households with any assets in the Stock Market shrank from 24.3 percent in 1968 to 8.5 percent in 1978" (536).

23. Ortner's female cohort perceived themselves as breaking out of the traditional gender track. They told their "breaking-out stories" in relation to their marriages and in some cases divorces. Wall Street women's breakout narratives, by contrast, are told exclusively against a backdrop of work, Wall Street and Manhattan.

24. *New York Times*, September 9, 1975.

25. Ibid.

26. Ibid.

27. This strategy would change when (some of the) FWA leaders of the eighties became WCF board members during the nineties and were active participants in a formally political female venue. But even then the meaning of feminism, and the ways in which the WCF defined the movement in relation to organization, would be a subject of some debate.

28. Robin Toner, "Female Candidates Are No Longer So Cash Poor," *New York Times*, June 15, 1986.

29. As with many concepts, the definition of state feminism is complex as well as historically and culturally situated (Kantola and Squires forthcoming).

30. Steven Roberts, "They're Capitalists, and Their Venture Is Women," *New York Times*, May 17, 1984.

31. Ibid.

32. Ibid.

33. All quotations in this paragraph are from Roberts, "They're Capitalists."

34. Ibid.

35. Sandra Salmans, "The Rising Force of Women's PACs," *New York Times*, June 28, 1994.

36. Ibid.

37. Maggie Drummond, "The Need to Network," *London Sunday Times*, 1987.

38. FWA Status Report of the Committee for the 1986 Overseas Delegation.

39. FWA archives, London Symposium, February 16–19, 1987.

40. Saskia Sassen's (2001, 2012) pathbreaking work on global cities allows us to identify concrete local effects and instantiations of globalization. Her analysis also provides the basic scheme to explain why FWA women made decisions to, at least partly, incorporate themselves into circuits of financial women that were operating on an international scale.

41. During the Clinton years, the FWA to some degree broadened and liberalized its mission. Under the guise of new leadership, the group refocused its goals to focus on "the changes and trends affecting the three key words of our name—the Financial Industry, Women, and New York City." Indeed, the FWA extended its focus in the world of finance to incorporate changes transpiring with the breakdown of communism and the advent of capitalism in countries such as China. During the late eighties and early nineties, the FWA sponsored talks on such timely topics as "China in the 1990s: Great Leap Forward or Another Step Back," "Soviet Union of Disunion: Implications for Foreign Business in the USSR," and "East European Restructuring: Potential Impact on EU Political and Economic Harmonization" (FWA International Affairs Committee 1989–90 Annual Report). With respect to gender issues, the FWA also began to stretch its financial interests beyond making links only with elite financial women. In 1991, for example, the FWA held an event to discuss "Third World Women Business Initiatives with UNIFEM, the United Nationals Development Fund for Women, and Women's World Banking." And, in an era of growing urban issues such as gentrification, the FWA began inviting New York City politicians to address critical problems facing the five boroughs, crime, and the homeless (FWA board minutes, September 4, 1991).

2. Careers, Networks, and Mentors

1. The current upsurge in concern over mentors and networks in women's business lives—as objects of study as well as tools for career advancement—was prompted by the entry and rise of numbers of women into law, business, and government beginning in the seventies. As the business historian Pamela Laird carefully documents in her book *Pull: Networking and Success since Benjamin Franklin*, "a groundswell in interest in social capital"—mentors, networks, role models—"as a positive tool began to emerge in the

1970's" (2006: 277). Indeed, Rosabeth Moss Kanter's pathbreaking book *Men and Women of the Corporation* (1976) brought early attention to the isolation of women at the top of workplaces, and to the homosocial behavior of executive men. Gail Sheehy's book *Passages: Predictable Crisis of Adult Life* developed the concept of mentoring as a major social factor shaping adult development (Laird 2006: 277). A major disciplinary debate between organizational sociologists like Kanter and psychologists such as Margaret Hennig and Anne Jardim broke out regarding whether women had "innate" networking abilities. Hennig and Jardim in their work *The Managerial Woman* (1977) blamed gender inequality (and women's inability to network well) on women's individual personality traits. Kanter countered that traits often cited as *causes* of women's subordinate status were better understood as *results* of subordinate positions in the organizational structure (Blum and Smith 1988: 533). The debate dominated much of the research on corporate women from the seventies to the nineties. Linda McDowell's extensive study of women in investment banking in London in the eighties and nineties offers another point of comparison. McDowell's research found that fewer women were employed in more prestigious finance departments, while they excelled in "back office" roles "typically associated with the supposed attributes of femininity" (1997: 77). Additionally, men and women offered different views of mentoring, with women noting that being men's protégées could undermine their credibility in the office and with clients (141–42).

A large literature exists today that demonstrates that having an effective mentor, usually a male, is critical for a woman moving up the corporate ladder. Benefits can include, for example, promotions and greater job satisfaction. Researchers traditionally define mentorship as being between two individuals, usually junior and senior, in which the senior person is more mature, powerful, and experienced (Schipani et al. 2009: 13–15). For indepth discussions of women and mentorship, see Laird 2006; Vianello and Moore 2000, 2004; and Schipani et al. 2006, 2009.

2. See also Chrystia Freeland, "The Rise of the New Global Elite," *The Atlantic*, January / February 2011.

3. Michael Lind, "The Failure of the Shareholder Revolution," *Salon.com*, March 29, 2011.

4. See also ibid.

5. In *Inventing Opportunity*, the economic sociologist Frank Dobbin argues that while the legacy of equal opportunity in the workplace is the legacy of the civil rights and feminist movements, corporate personnel experts—not government officials or courts—were the ones who defined what equal opportunity meant and then made workplace practices accordingly. These practices included changes in the ways employees were promoted along with formal mentoring programs. They also entailed the implementa-

tion of diversity programs and work-family policymaking, including, for example, flextime. Dobbin, drawing on interviews with human personnel managers, paints an important picture regarding the role such managers played in putting the American imagination of equal rights into actual practice and policymaking. But I would argue that Dobbin misses a certain part of the firm policymaking picture and process, such as the role of other employees, and namely the executives themselves, in helping create and implement such programs.

6. Economic sociologists have long been interested in the relationship between network structures and occupational mobility. Scholars in this area of research have focused on the continuities and discontinuities in social structure—network relations. In his influential work *Chains of Opportunity*, published in 1970, Harrison White, the "founder" of the first generation of social network analysis (SNA) scholarship, first brought attention to the importance of gaps as opposed to ties in social structure. In the early seventies Mark Granovetter (1972) focused on the relationship between network structures and job searches. During the eighties and nineties, as Knox and colleagues (2005) point out, SNA scholars "focused on how network techniques can be used to understand the role of relations within a 'whole' network." Researchers are not primarily interested in individuals. The early works of sociologists did not explore the differences between men's and women's networks and mentor relationships in the corporate workplace. It was not until the eighties that Granovetter revisited his theory to examine the differences between the ways women and men acquire ties. He showed that men procure weak ties through contacts made at business and professional meetings, which are events women were less likely to attend (Granovetter 1983). Sociological accounts of women and work in the seventies and eighties showed that women were further disadvantaged in male-dominated networks because few men were willing to form strong ties with them and act as mentors (Kanter 1977; Epstein 1981).

7. Reed Abelson, "A Network of Their Own: From an Exclusive Address, A Group of Women Only," *New York Times*, October 27, 1999, p. C1.

8. Susan Harrigan, "A White Man's World: Diversity in Management/ Female Execs Endure Wall Street Bumps," *Newsday*, Nassau and Suffolk Edition, April 14, 2000.

9. In this paragraph, I use actual names because I draw from reports written by journalists and academics about Wall Street women during this period.

10. Networking is considered essential to moving up the career ladder (Jackall 1988; Mayo et al. 2006). Women's lack of networks has been shown in numerous studies to prevent women from rising to the top much more so than men (Schipani et al. 2009).

11. Very little if any qualitative research has focused on corporate women

and their friendships, making it difficult to assess the effects of these relationships on the women's careers. There is, however, an important anthropological literature on working-class women that shows that women's networks can provide emotional support and alliances among women (Baron
1991). Studies of women's friendships, including Sharon Marcus's *Between
Women: Friendship, Desire, and Marriage in Victorian England* (2007), tend
to focus on the effects of friendship on women's social worlds from a
historical perspective. Marcus argues that "in a capitalist society deeply
ambivalent about competition, female friendship offered a vision of perfect
reciprocity for those who could afford not to worry about daily survival"
(4). Unlike friendships in Victorian England, however, women on Wall
Street forge their friendships in a highly competitive environment.

12. Although there are relatively few studies about the impact of globalization on gender in top leadership, the existing literature reveals that globalization appears to benefit both women and men in industrialized countries
as they move up the corporate ladder (for excellent reviews and discussions
of these issues, see Schipani et al. 2006, 2009). Recently anthropologists
have considered the ways globalization is reconfiguring women's networks
and collective action (Franzway and Fonow 2011). Some of the most exciting discussions about networked methods and forms of analysis are, indeed,
taking place within ethnographic studies of global networked organizational activities as well as studies of networks of actors engaged in policymaking within powerful institutions at the local, national, and international levels (Knox et al. 2005: 16; Schwegler and Powell 2008). Notably,
Annelise Riles in her book *The Network Inside Out* (2000), a study of global
women's networks preparing for the 1995 Beijing Conference on Women,
considers the cultural form and method of the network itself. She argues
that the "network" "refers to a set of institutions, knowledge practices, and
artifacts that internally generate the effects of their own reality by reflecting
on themselves" (3). Tara Schwegler, in her study of Mexican government
officials, argues that the ethnographic encounter itself (with elite actors)
provides deep insights into the form of the network itself. Riles and
Schwegler thus both draw attention to analyzing certain kinds of network
data that are often considered too mundane or even superfluous to present
in traditional ethnographic work.

13. In the article "Women Get Better at Forming Networks to Help Their
Climb," published in the *Wall Street Journal* in November 2007, interviews
with top female executives revealed that most women emphasized the importance of having a number of mentors at different stages of their careers.
Having mentors for different purposes throughout one's career is referred
to as "mosaic mentoring" (Schipani et al. 2009).

3. Gendered Discourses of Finance

1. The world of finance has been gendered—masculinized and feminized —in different ways throughout history. Marieke de Goede's research on the history of finance provides several examples of this historical gendering in her book *Virtue, Fortune, and Faith: A Genealogy of Finance* (2005b). Angel Kwolek-Folland's (1994) historical account of the insurance industry was the first work in business history to draw attention to the gendering of American finance. There is a small but very important burgeoning inter-disciplinary literature on the contemporary gendered dimensions of global finance. The geographer Linda McDowell first examined the gendered performances of men and women in 1990s London finance in her book *Capital Culture*. The anthropologist Caitlin Zaloom, in her book *Out of the Pits: Traders and Technology from Chicago to London*, analyzes male traders' norms of gender. Specifically she examines the highly masculinized world of trading floors, describing traders as "mavericks" or unbranded range animals without ownership (2006: 113). Notably, Zaloom points out that these characteristics are not "natural" or embedded in the character of the men who become traders; rather they are cultivated as "performances and techniques to engage the market" (113). The anthropologist Karen Ho briefly discusses gendered performances on Wall Street in her book *Liqui-dated*. Her work is particularly notable in that her fieldwork includes inter-views with women of color. For other recent accounts of the gendering of global finance and the World Bank, see the political scientist Libby Assassi's *The Gendering of Global Finance* (2009) and Penny Griffin's *Gendering the World Bank: Neoliberalism and the Gendered Foundations of Global Gover-nance* (2009). Griffin is a specialist in politics and international relations.

2. In her examination of the Chicago Board of Trade, Caitlin Zaloom argues that risk "is a constitutive element of contemporary power and economic practice," essential to the present-day conception of capitalism (2006: 93). For the traders, risk allows for acts of self-creation and presenta-tion. Zaloom notes that participants divide their world into "big" and "small" traders, depending on the amount of risk the traders can take. Zaloom notes that the trading pit favored masculine traders; very few traders were women—in 1998, there were only two women out of six hun-dred traders—and they often considered themselves outside the regular rules of the pit (101–2).

3. The activities of consumer culture, most importantly shopping, have long been feminized activities. In her introduction to *The Sex of Things: Gender and Consumption in Historical Perspective* (1996), Victoria de Grazia argues that the conflation of the woman and the consumer goes back to the dawn of capitalism in the eighteenth century. In the United States, the twentieth century marked a solidification of this relationship through mass-

market advertising. In his landmark examination of the advertising industry, *Advertising the American Dream* (1985), Roland Marchand notes that in the twenties and thirties, advertisers viewed its audience as women: "No facet of the advertiser-audience relationship held such consequence for advertising content as the perception by the overwhelmingly male advertising elite that it was engaged primarily in talking to masses of women" (66). In the twenties and thirties, the idea of the "citizen consumer" was highly gendered as well, with women's newly secured right to vote merging with the right to purchase (McGovern 1998). In the postwar era, women became further associated with consumer culture, which had been uncoupled from citizenship. Lizabeth Cohen argues in *A Consumer's Republic* that "given the centrality of consumption to the postwar economy, women's loss of civic authority through that realm reduced the average woman's political activism" (2003: 136). The feminist movement of the sixties and seventies critiqued the associations of women with consumers. As Rachel Bowlby notes, "Sometimes consumerism has been seen as the principal source of women's oppression in the twentieth century, as a force which, by promoting a falsely feminine identity, distracts them from what would otherwise be their true identities, as humans and/or as women" (1996: 381).

4. Since the seventies, the "fear of falling" out of financial security has come to occupy the minds of many in the American middle class. Barbara Ehrenreich's *Fear of Falling* (1989) was among the first books to address the issue. Ehrenreich argues that this anxiety permeates the middle class: unlike the truly wealthy, the children of the middle class cannot inherit their parents' wealth, so they must, with every generation, replicate the same paths that their parents took. Ehrenreich traces this anxiety from the early sixties' "discovery of poverty" to the yuppies of the eighties, who, Ehrenreich argues, lived as the wealthy did. Similarly, Katherine Newman's *Falling from Grace: The Experience of Downward Mobility in the American Middle Class* (1988) examines the underlying meaning of downward mobility. Newman writes, "To a certain extent, the experience of downward mobility in middle-class America is the same for all of its victims. Catastrophic losses create a common feeling of failure, loss of control, and social disorientation" (11). Sherry B. Ortner's work on Generation X examines the generational facets of this fear of falling (1999). Hugh Gusterson and Catherine Besteman's *The Insecure American: How We Got Here and What We Should Do about It* (2009) offers a collection of anthropological studies that focus on the widening income gap in the United States. Gusterson and Besteman argue that a "new, more pyramidical social structure has replaced the old pear-shaped social structure" of class, that is, the bulging area of the middle class has shrunk, while the lower class has grown (5).

5. In the sociologist Mary Blair-Loy's study of female part-time professional workers in Chicago finance, the majority of her informants encoun-

tered resistance to their requests to alter their work schedules (2003: 96). She argued that "the opposition of supervisors and colleagues is not rooted in economic rationality, but in the defense of an established cultural order in which they are deeply invested" (92).

4. Politics and State-Market Feminism

1. All of the names mentioned in this excerpt are pseudonyms.

2. In *It Still Takes a Candidate* (2010), Jennifer L. Lawless and Richard L. Fox argue that women's underrepresentation in politics still remains an understudied area. They point out that at both the national and state levels, female legislators are more likely to focus on "women's issues," including gender equity, day care, flextime, and abortion. The visibility of women legislators has other effects on their communities, such as increased participation of women in other civic events and increased political engagement of teenage girls (7). Nonetheless, the number of women who run for office and win remains low, though it has increased over time. In a study of female lobbyists, the sociologist Denise Benoit notes that between 1998 and 2005, the number of women lobbyists in Washington increased dramatically. However, women have not significantly infiltrated the ranks of the top-tier "hired guns," or "super-lobbyists" (2007: 25). The Center for American Women and Politics at Rutgers University records the current numbers of women in office. At the federal level, women make up 16.6 percent of Congress, while at the state level, women comprise 23.6 percent of legislators (http://www.cawp.rutgers.edu/fast_facts/levels_of_office/ Current _Numbers.php). The reasons for women's continued underrepresentation in elected office remain highly debated. Lawless and Fox argue that women are less politically ambitious than men and that this gender gap arises from patterns of socializations in U.S. culture (2010: 8). Women frequently face more challenges than men in balancing the work-family division, as they continue to bear more responsibility for household tasks and childcare; men's lesser responsibilities at home leave them with more time for political pursuits. Further, the institutions that support candidates often maintain a "masculinized ethos"—that is, women find themselves excluded from all aspects, including policymaking, political fund-raising networks, and highly visible media positions. For a comparative discussion on women in politics in Europe, see Vianello and Moore 2000, 2004.

3. Lawless and Fox point out that female candidates often must be recruited to run for office, even for women with political backgrounds (2010: 90). They also note that, even though women candidates are more likely to promote liberal policies and identify as Democrats, the barriers to women candidates are similar across the political spectrum: "Democratic and Republican party leaders and elected officials are equally unlikely to recruit

women to run for office" (103). Women's political organizations, both bipartisan and party-affiliated, have emerged in the past two decades to fill
the gap for recruiting women into the political networks from which candidates are selected. Many of these political organizations specifically promote "women's issues." The recent WCF's She Should Run campaign specifically addresses the gender gap in traditional recruitment (http://www
.wcfonline.org). EMILY's List, founded in 1985, supports pro-choice Democratic candidates; its Political Opportunity Program, started in 2001, helps
train women candidates at the local level and takes the form of outreach to
potential candidates (http://emilyslist.org/what/local_candidates). Since
1992, the WISH List has promoted Republican pro-choice female candidates
(http://www.thewishlist.org). Lawless and Fox note that these organizations do, in fact, make a difference for offsetting the recruitment disadvantage. An eligible candidate who has contact with a women's organization is
more than 34 percentage points more likely to be recruited than an eligible
candidate who does not; further, a woman who had contact with one of
these organizations was even more likely than the average man to be recruited to run for office (2010: 105).

4. To illustrate this dichotomy, de Goede examines the differences between two international reports, statistically assessing Western societies in
May and June of 2000. The first, published by the United Nations Children's Fund, on children's health, wealth, and opportunities, concludes that
Britain is among four industrialized countries in which child poverty is the
most common (2005b: 1). The second report, provided by the OECD,
provides a very favorable assessment of the British economy. Key economic
indicators include growth and inflation (2005b: 2). The difference in reports—one politically oriented with a focus on children's poverty; the other
economically focused—is striking.

5. The women's multiple networking practices are in some respects similar to the "flex nets" of elite, powerful neoconservative men, which the
anthropologist Janine Wedel describes and theorizes in her work *Shadow
Elites* (2009).

6. *The Women's Campaign Fund: A Twenty-Year Tradition.*

7. Sandra Salmans, "The Rising Force of Women's PACS," *New York
Times*, June 28, 1984.

8. Many sources, including the United States Senate's own website, cite
the 1991 Senate confirmation hearings of the Supreme Court nominee
Clarence Thomas as the source of the following year's label "Year of the
Woman." The confirmation hearings, which included a committee com-
posed only of white men questioning an African American woman, Anita
Hill, pointed out how few women—two—served in the Senate at the time.
Following the election of four women—Dianne Feinstein, Barbara Boxer,

Carol Moseley Braun, and Patty Murray—to the Senate in 1992, pundits began calling 1992 the "Year of the Woman."

9. Data within this paragraph are from *The Women's Campaign Fund: A Twenty-Year Tradition*.

10. Ibid.

11. Ibid.

12. Steve Kornacki, "Lynn Yeakel Isn't Angry Anymore," *New York Observer*, April 29, 2009.

13. Ibid.

14. Fund-raisers provide one of the most valuable networking locations for lobbyists, politicians, and businesspeople interested in politics. In her study of female lobbyists, Denise Benoit notes that all parties have separate interests in participating in the fund-raisers. In addition to their implicit money-raising benefit, fund-raisers provide government officials with opportunities to meet people in businesses and lobbyists. For lobbyists, especially women, fund-raisers offer occasions to increase their profiles within their political network. For corporations, fund-raisers often serve as opportunities to present contributions in person and help solidify relationships with candidates. Most lobbyists and corporations prefer smaller events, which give them more access to candidates (Benoit 2007: 30–35). PACS play a similarly influential role in corporate-governmental affairs. The PAC makes and approves recommendations concerning contributions to candidates. Typically composed of between five and eight people, the PAC makes decisions about contributions that company executives rarely challenge. While men outnumber women in PACS, Benoit argues that those who participate tend to have powerful voices on the committee (2007: 43).

5. Life after Wall Street

1. As the Baby Boomers, or the generational cohort born between the years 1946 and 1965, face retirement, their future remains uncertain. In *Redefining Retirement: How Will Boomers Fare?* (2007), Brigitte Madrian, Olivia S. Mitchell, and Beth J. Soldo argue that Boomers are as well prepared for retirement as previous cohorts had been. Even before the financial crisis and economic recession of 2007–9, some Boomers were prolonging their careers to make up for lower savings for retirement (Mitchell 2007). However, in the wake of the recession, even those who had prepared for early retirement found much of their savings depleted. Three years later, an April 5, 2011, Associated Press poll reflected this uncertainty, with 44 percent believing they had not saved enough for retirement (Fram, "Poll Reveals Baby Boomers' Retirement Fears"). Professionals, including those on Wall Street, were not immune to this concern. In an article in the *New*

York Times, Nelson D. Schwartz noted that the ranks of professionals, including on Wall Street and at top legal firms, had no mandatory retirement age, but many firms demoted partners once they reached a certain age, a process called "de-partnering" ("Easing Out the Gray-Haired. Or Not," *New York Times*, May 27, 2011).

Baby Boomer women's retirement has long been a topic of discussion, because they are the first group of women to have remained in the workforce for a significant amount of time and in a variety of careers. Nancy Dailey argues that "Baby boom women will not replicate the retirement of their mothers, nor will their retirement experience look like men's retirement" (1998: 1). Dailey observes that the long-assumed model of male retirement, which benefits the female spouse, no longer holds true for men or women of the Baby Boomer generation. Like many others in their generation, Baby Boomer women have faced layoffs in the economic downturn. In the past few years, a variety of organizations have emerged to address the needs of women over fifty as they transition to new careers or to early retirement. For example, Barnard College's "Project Continuum" brings together the school's alumnae who are ages fifty and older to discuss personal and professional issues (http://alum.barnard.edu/s/1133/index .aspx?sid=1133&gid=1&pgid=334). Another example, the Transition Network, has chapters in eight cities around the United States and serves as a place for women over fifty to network to find new careers (http://www.the transitionnetwork.org/).

2. I engaged in follow-up interviews with the first generation of Wall Street women between 2006 and the first week of August 2008. At that point, Sarah Palin was not yet a vice presidential candidate for the Republican Party.

3. The term "philanthrocapitalism" describes a kind of philanthropy that draws on the practices of venture capital. In recent years, the term has been heatedly debated. In February 2006, *The Economist* ran a special report on the "new philanthropy," examining such figures as Microsoft's founder, Bill Gates, and Intel's founder, Gordon Moore. *The Economist* framed the issue in terms from finance: "The need for philanthropy to become more like the for-profit capital markets is a common theme among the new philanthropists, especially those who have made their fortune in finance. As they see it, three things are needed for such a philanthropic marketplace to work. First, there must be something for philanthropists to 'invest' in—something that, ideally, will be created by 'social entrepreneurs,' just as in the for-profit world entrepreneurs create companies that end up traded on the stockmarket. Second, the market requires an infrastructure, the philanthropic equivalent of stockmarkets, investment banks, research houses, management consultants and so on. . . . Third, philanthropists themselves need to behave more like investors. That means allocating their money to make the

greatest possible difference to society's problems: in other words, to maximize their 'social return'" ("The Birth of Philanthrocapitalism," February 23, 2006). In *Philanthrocapitalism: How the Rich Can Save the World* (2009), Matthew Bishop and Michael Green argue that philanthrocapitalists are "hyperagents" who, due to their enormous wealth and nonelected status, have the ability to take on challenges that are too risky for government (12). Others, however, point out the flaws of such behavior. In *Small Change: Why Business Won't Save the World* (2008), Michael Edwards writes, "The hype that surrounds philanthrocapitalism runs far ahead of its ability to deliver real results. There is little hard evidence that these new approaches are any better at reducing poverty and injustice than the governments, foundations, and civil society groups that have been working away more quietly in the background for a generation and more. Yes, they get the much-needed drugs, microcredit loans, solar-rechargeable light bulbs, and the like to people who really need these things, but they don't change the world and the social and political dynamics that deny most of the world's population hope of a decent life" (xii).

4. The Women's Philanthropy Institute at Indiana University studies the ways in which women give money to nonprofits. On the institute's website, Debra J. Mesch offers an overview of the literature on women and philanthropy. Mesch (2009) argues that "women, strengthened by increasing economic power and education, are as likely as men to be philanthropists and to lead the most influential foundations and nonprofit organizations. Yet, the research literature on women's philanthropic giving is lagging behind the reality of what is happening in practice around the world." Mesch notes that many of the potential areas of study for women's philanthropy have been understudied. For example, most research concludes that women are more likely to give but that their contributions are generally smaller than men's are; however, this difference often fails to account for women's contributions to decision making in their households, which may influence their spouses' contributions.

5. The idea of the "encore career" has emerged as a viable route for people who wish to remain active after leaving their professional field. Many journalists have written about "encore careers" as second acts driven as much by a desire to contribute to society as to earn a paycheck, which separates them from the ranks of workers who are dependent upon paychecks in their retirement years. For example, on MSNBC.com, Eve Tahmincioglu wrote about several people who "chose their career second-acts for a similar motivation: to give something back" ("Workers Finding Fulfillment in Encore Careers," January 25, 2010). Karyn McCormack broadened the scope of workers looking for encore careers to include those who had been laid off from their jobs or forced to take early retirement. One of McCormack's interviewees, John E. Nelson, a coauthor of *What Color Is Your Parachute?*

for Retirement, advised encore-career seekers to "figure out whether you're going to work for fulfillment and a paycheck, or for fulfillment alone" (McCormack, "How to Discover Your Encore Career," *BusinessWeek,* November 11, 2009). McCormack's article is one of the few that acknowledges that such workers may be entering those types of jobs out of necessity rather than choice. Many accounts paint the decision as only a positive. One website, www.encore.org, even promises to help people "invent a new stage of work."

6. The appearance of variants of market feminism in the social and cultural landscapes of a globalizing world, however, is but one manifestation of a variety of feminisms at play within the current neoliberal moment, albeit an increasingly hegemonic one (Eisenstein 2009). The women's movement was never a singular entity, even in the sixties and seventies. Indeed, there has been disagreement among liberal, radical, postcolonial, and other types of feminists about the meaning of feminism for decades. But something new is happening to feminism in the current globalizing, neoliberal world, which is marked by the movement of capital, persons, and ideas. Feminism is operating within "an expansive, polycentric, heterogeneous discursive field of action," which has "generated 'more formalized modalities of articulation or networking amongst the multiple spaces and places of feminist politics'" (Alvarez 1999: 184). The old meanings and boundaries separating certain types of feminisms are blurring; new feminist projects are coming into play in different spaces spearheaded by new kinds of subjects, including corporate subjects, such as Wall Street women.

7. For Langley, "financial dissent" differs from "financial resistance." Studies of financial resistance, he argues, tend to draw a clear line between overarching structures of power in finance and resistance; resistance is thus perceived, for example, as making use of the regulatory authority of the state and interstate institutions to bring financial capital (and crisis) under control. Resistance can also take the collective more public and organized forms, like civil society campaigns that seek to make financial institutions like the World Bank more transparent. By contrast, financial dissent draws attention away from the formal, collective, organized forms of resistance to hegemonic global finance and, instead, shines light on the more everyday alternative financial practices (Langley 2008: 37–38). Langley draws on a more Foucauldian understanding of power in which power exists not as an essentially singular force, but rather is relational. For Foucault "where there is power there is resistance—but even within the immanent cracks in structures of domination, resistance itself cannot be placed outside of power" (Dirks et al. 1994: 8). Langley thus substitutes the term "dissent" for resistance to emphasize the ways in which the everyday practices of resistance to global finance are themselves always intimately wrapped up and caught

within the hegemonic system of global finance. There are, however, more established forms of financial dissent, as in the case of corporate socially responsible investing.

8. The idea of corporate social responsibility, like philanthrocapitalism, has emerged as a concept in recent years. Social scientists have engaged in a great deal of research on the topic (see, for example, the anthropologist Christina Garsten [2008]). David Vogel defines corporate social responsibility as "practices that improve the workplace and benefit society in ways that go above and beyond what companies are legally required to do" (2005: 2). Vogel argues that corporate social responsibility contains much ambiguity, because a company may demonstrate social responsibility in one area (e.g., offering "green" packaging) while ignoring it in others (e.g., not paying fair wages).

9. How does the firm reconcile its more liberal feminist agenda from the everyday world of hegemonic investment practices? What kinds of methods does the firm use, for example, to render the numbers of women representative on boards of particular companies in order to justify the investment in these types of funds? What kinds of interpretive work do the analysts working within the firm engage in when they assess such funds? These types of questions require further in-depth fieldwork and research.

10. Amanda Fortini, "The Feminist Reawakening: Hillary Clinton and the Fourth Wave," *New York Magazine*, April 13, 2008. Also, see McRobbie 2009.

11. "Rhonda Westbrook" is a pseudonym.

12. "Alice Stacey" is a pseudonym.

13. Since the nineties, there has been a growing requirement to recruit independent nonexecutive directors for boards. Notably, these executives are part of a new power structure of decision making. Many corporate decisions now involve not only executives and nonexecutives on boards, but also intermediaries such as consultants or investment bankers outside the firm (Froud et al. 2006: 10). Mindy's position on various corporate boards is thus the result of the restructuring of boards during the past two decades. She and other board members work in a world of constant restructuring where corporations must shed workers and the like (ibid.: 11).

14. "Penny Edwards" is a pseudonym.

15. Except for the names of Meg Whitman, Carly Fiorina, and Muriel Siebert, all other names in this excerpt are pseudonyms.

6. Market Feminism and Feminizing Markets

1. Geraldine Fabrikant, "Fewer Women Betting on Wall Street Careers," *New York Times*, January 30, 2010.

2. Joe Hagan, "Only the Men Survive: The Crash of Zoe Cruz," *New York Magazine*, April 27, 2008.

3. Patricia Sellars, "Erin Callan, Lehman's Ex-CFO, Goes Public," CNNMoney.com, February 22, 2011.

4. Fabrikant, "Fewer Women Betting on Wall Street Careers."

5. Ibid.

6. Kyle Stock, "Casualties of the Crisis: Stress, Sexism, and Layoffs Thin the Ranks of Women on Wall Street," *Fins Finance*, August 31, 2010.

7. Ibid.

8. JK Blog, http://www.jackizehner.com/.

9. JK Blog, December 9, 2008.

10. See note 4 of the introduction.

11. One website, for example, is "dedicated to exploring the economic power and potential of a more gender balanced business world" (http://www.20-first.com/2-0-why.html). The site is filled with articles making the "business case" for the investment in gender and gender equity. Here, scholarly articles, mainly by business school professors, argue that women, because they are less risk taking, will pay more attention to risk oversight and thus make better leaders.

12. "We Did It! The Rich World's Quiet Revolution: Women Are Gradually Taking Over the Workplace," *The Economist*, December 30, 2009.

13. Kyle Stock, "Ranks of Women on Wall Street Thin," *Wall Street Journal*, September 20, 2010.

14. Anthropologists and other scholars have written on memory and nostalgia. As the anthropologist Renato Rosaldo pointed out long ago, agents of colonialism often engage in a "particular kind of nostalgia, often found under imperialism, where people mourn the passing of what they themselves have transformed" (1989: 108). Imperialism and late capitalism are distinctly different historically created structures of power. Imperialist nostalgia occurred parallel to the white man's mission to civilize the savage.

15. Jennifer Epstein, "Nancy Pelosi Calls GOP Budget a 'War on Women,'" www.politico.com, April 8, 2011.

16. In 2009, in the wake of the financial crisis, the National Council for Research on Women (NCRW) commissioned a study of women in fund management. Authored by Linda Basch and Jacki Zehner, "Women in Fund Management: A Roadmap for Achieving Critical Mass—and Why It Matters" provided an overview of thirty years of research on the financial sector. The report addressed the great disparity between men and women in fund management. Although women account for nearly half of the labor force in the United States, they make up only 10 percent of traditional mutual fund managers and a scant 3 percent of hedge fund managers (NCRW 2009). Notably, in times of economic contraction, diversity programs often are seen as a luxury. However, the authors of the report argued against this idea,

instead focusing on women's investment styles, citing research that indi-
cates women take less risk and encourage more stable growth over time
(2009: 9).

17. "Feminist Management Theorists Are Flirting with Some Dangerous
Arguments," *Economist*, December 30, 2009.

BIBLIOGRAPHY

Archives

Financial Women's Association (FWA) Archives, New York City
    FWA board minutes, September 2, 1981
    FWA board minutes, November 4, 1981
    FWA board minutes, December 2, 1981
    FWA board minutes, 1984
    FWA Status Report of the Committee for the 1986 Overseas Delegation
    FWA Archives London Symposium, February 16–19, 1987
    FWA International Affairs Committee, 1989–90 Annual Report
    FWA board minutes, September 4, 1991
    FWA Newsletters, 1996

Group of Thirty Website

The Women's Campaign Fund (WCF) Archives, New York City
    The Women's Campaign Fund: A Twenty-Year Tradition

Secondary Sources

Abramson, Daniel M. 2001. *Skyscraper Rivals: The AIG Building and the Architecture of Wall Street.* New York: Princeton Architectural Press.

Aldrich, Nelson W. 1988. *Old Money: The Mythology of America's Upper Class.* New York: Knopf.

Alexander, M. Jacqui, and Chandra Talpade Mohanty. 1997. "Introduction: Genealogies, Legacies, Movements." In *Feminist Genealogies: Colonial Legacies, Democratic Futures,* edited by M. Jacqui Alexander and Chandra Talpade Mohanty, xiii–xlii. New York: Routledge.

Alvarez, Sonia E. 1999. "Advocating Feminism: The Latin American Feminist NGO 'Boom.'" *International Feminist Journal of Politics* 1 (2): 181–209.

Antilla, Susan. 2002. *Tales from the Boom-Boom Room: Women vs. Wall Street*. Princeton, N.J.: Bloomberg.

Appadurai, Arjun. 1996. *Modernity at Large: Cultural Dimensions of Globalization*. Minneapolis: University of Minnesota Press.

Arthur, Michelle M., and Alison Cook. 2004. "Taking Stock of Work-Family Initiatives: How Announcements of 'Family-Friendly' Human Resource Decisions Affect Shareholder Value." *Industrial and Labor Relations Review* 57 (4): 599–613.

Assassi, Libby. 2009. *The Gendering of Global Finance*. New York: Palgrave Macmillan.

Baba, Marietta L. 1998. "Theories of Practice in Anthropology: A Critical Appraisal." In *The Unity of Theory and Practice in Anthropology: Rebuilding a Fractured Synthesis*, edited by Carole Hill and Marietta Baba, 17–44. Washington, D.C.: National Association for the Practice of Anthropology.

——. 2006. "Anthropology and Business." In *Encyclopedia of Anthropology*, edited by H. James Birx, 83–117. Thousand Oaks, Calif.: Sage.

——. 2009. "W. Lloyd Warner and the Anthropology of Institutions: An Approach to the Study of Work in Late Capitalism." *Anthropology of Work Review* 30 (2): 29–49.

Baron, Ava. 1991. "Gender and Labor History: Learning from the Past, Looking to the Future." In *Work Engendered: Toward a New History of American Labor*, edited by Ava Baron, 1–46. Ithaca: Cornell University Press.

Bell, Gregory S. 2001. *In the Black: A History of African Americans on Wall Street*. New York: Wiley.

Bell, Susan. 2010. *When the Getting Was Good: A Novel*. Bloomington, Ind.: AuthorHouse.

Bellah, Robert N., Richard Madsen, William M. Sullivan, Ann Swidler, and Steven M. Tipton. 1985. *Habits of the Heart: Individualism and Commitment in American Life*. Berkeley: University of California Press.

Benn, Alec. 2000. *The Unseen Wall Street of 1969–1975*. Westport, Conn.: Praeger.

Benn, Suzanne, and Diane Bolton. 2011. *Key Concepts in Corporate Social Responsibility*. Thousand Oaks, Calif.: Sage.

Benoit, Denise. 2007. *The Best-Kept Secret: Women Corporate Lobbyists, Policy and Power in the United States*. New Brunswick, N.J.: Rutgers University Press.

Beunza, Daniel, and David Stark. 2008. "Tools of the Trade: The Socio-Technology of Arbitrage in a Wall Street Trading Room." In *Living in a Material World: Economic Sociology Meets Science and Technology Studies*, edited by Trevor Pinch and Richard Swedberg, 253–90. Cambridge: MIT Press.

Bishop, Matthew, and Michael Green. 2009. *Philanthrocapitalism: How the Rich Can Save the World*. New York: Bloomsbury.

Blair-Loy, Mary. 2003. *Competing Devotions: Career and Family among Women Executives*. Cambridge: Harvard University Press.

Blum, Linda, and Vicky Smith. 1988. "Women's Mobility in the Corporation: A Critique of the Politics of Optimism." *Signs: Journal of Women in Culture and Society* 13 (31): 528–46.

Bornstein, Erica. 2005. *The Spirit of Development: Protestant NGOs, Morality, and Economics in Zimbabwe*. Palo Alto: Stanford University Press.

Bose, Purnima, and Laura E. Lyons, eds. 2010. *Cultural Critique and the Global Corporation*. Bloomington: Indiana University Press.

Bourdieu, Pierre. 1984. *Distinction: A Social Critique of the Judgment of Taste*. Translated by Richard Nice. Cambridge: Harvard University Press.

———. 1990. *Outline of a Theory of Practice*. Cambridge: Cambridge University Press.

———. 1998. *State Nobility: Elite Schools in the Field of Power*. New York: Polity Press.

Bowlby, Rachel. 1996. "Soft Sell: Marketing Rhetoric in Feminist Criticism." In *The Sex of Things: Gender and Consumption in Historical Perspective*, edited by Victoria de Grazia with Ellen Furlough, 381–88. Berkeley: University of California Press.

Brodkin-Sacks, Karen. 1988. *Caring by the Hour: Women, Work, and Organizing at Duke Medical Center*. Urbana: University of Illinois Press.

Brondo, Keri, and Marietta L. Baba. 2006. "Ethnography of Women in US Business." *Society for the Anthropology of Work, Anthropology News*, April.

Brooks, John. 1973. *The Go-Go Years*. New York: Weybright and Talley.

Buhlmann, Felix. 2009. "Biographical Mechanisms of British Service Class Formation." CRESC Working Paper Series. Working Paper No. 69.

Butler, Judith. 1993. *Bodies That Matter*. New York: Routledge.

Calás, Marta B., and Linda Smircich. 2009. "Feminist Perspectives on Gender in Organizational Research: What Is and Is Yet to Be." In *Handbook of Organizational Research Methods*, edited by David Buchanan and Alan Bryman, 246–69. London: Sage.

Callahan, David. 2010. *Fortunes of Change: The Rise of the Liberal Rich and the Remaking of America*. Hoboken, N.J.: Wiley and Sons.

Callon, Michel. 1998. "Introduction: The Embeddedness of Economic Markets in Economics." In *The Laws of the Markets*, edited by Michel Callon, 1–57. Malden, Mass.: Blackwell.

Cameron, A., G. Lightfoot, S. Lilley, and S. Brown. 2010. "Placing the 'Postsocial' Market: Simulating Space in the Xeno-Economy." *Marketing Theory* 10 (3): 1–13.

Cameron, Angus, Anastasia Nesvetailova, and Ronen Palan. 2011. "Wages of Sin?" *Journal of Cultural Economy* 4 (2): 117–35.

Cefkin, Melissa. 2009. *Ethnography and the Corporate Encounter: Reflections on Research in and of Corporations*. New York: Berghahn.

Chase, Susan. 1995. *Ambiguous Empowerment: The Work Narratives of Women School Superintendents.* Amherst: University of Massachusetts Press.

Clifford, James, and George E. Marcus, eds. 1986. *Writing Culture: The Poetics and Politics of Ethnography.* Berkeley: University of California Press.

Clinton, William Jefferson. 2009. "Foreword." In *Philanthrocapitalism: How the Rich Can Save the World,* by Matthew Bishop and Michael Green, vii–viii. New York: Bloomsbury.

Cohen, Lizabeth. 2003. *A Consumer's Republic: The Politics of Mass Consumption in Postwar America.* New York: Knopf.

Collins, Patricia Hill. 2000. *Black Feminist Thought: Knowledge, Consciousness, and the Politics of Empowerment.* New York: Routledge.

Comaroff, Jean, and John L. Comaroff. 2001. "Millennial Capitalism: First Thoughts on a Second Coming." In *Millennial Capitalism and the Culture of Neoliberalism,* edited by Jean Comaroff and John L. Comaroff, 1–56. Durham: Duke University Press.

Coontz, Stephanie. 2011. *A Strange Stirring: "The Feminine Mystique" and American Women at the Dawn of the 1960s.* New York: Basic Books.

Corbridge, Stuart, and Nigel Thrift. 1994. "Money, Power, and Space: Introduction and Overview." In *Money, Power, and Space,* edited by Stuart Corbridge, Nigel Thrift, and Ron Martin, 1–25. Cambridge, Mass.: Blackwell.

Dailey, Nancy. 1998. *When Baby Boom Women Retire.* Westport, Conn.: Praeger.

Day, Christine L., and Charles D. Hadley. 2004. *Women's PACs: Abortion and Elections.* New York: Prentice-Hall.

Dean, M. 1997. "Sociology after Society." In *Sociology after Postmodernism,* edited by David Owen, 205–28. London: Sage.

de Goede, Marieke. 2005a. "Carnival of Money: Politics of Dissent in an Era of Globalising Finance." In *The Global Resistance Reader,* edited by Louise Amoore, 379–91. New York: Routledge.

———. 2005b. *Virtue, Fortune, and Faith: A Genealogy of Finance.* Minneapolis: University of Minnesota Press.

———. 2009. "Finance and the Excess: The Politics of Visibility in the Credit Crisis." *Zeitschrift für Internationale Beziehungen* 16 (2): 295–306.

de Grazia, Victoria, with Ellen Furlough, eds. 1996. *The Sex of Things: Gender and Consumption in Historical Perspective.* Berkeley: University of California Press.

Dirks, Nicholas, Geoff Eley, and Sherry B. Ortner, eds. 1994. *Culture/Power/History: A Reader in Social Theory.* Princeton, N.J.: Princeton University Press.

Dobbin, Frank. 2009. *Inventing Equal Opportunity.* Princeton, N.J.: Princeton University Press.

Downey, Greg, and Melissa S. Fisher. 2006. "Introduction: The Anthropology of Capital and the Frontiers of Ethnography." In *Frontiers of Capital: Ethnographic Reflections on the New Economy*, edited by Melissa S. Fisher and Greg Downey, 1–32. Durham: Duke University Press.

Eccles, Robert G., and Dwight B. Crane. 1988. *Doing Deals: Investment Banks at Work*. Cambridge, Mass.: Harvard Business School Press.

Edwards, Michael. 2008. *Small Change: Why Business Won't Change the World*. San Francisco: Berret-Koehler.

Ehrenreich, Barbara. 1989. *Fear of Falling: The Inner Life of the Middle Class*. New York: Pantheon.

Eisenstein, Hester. 2009. *Feminism Seduced: How Global Elites Use Women's Labor and Ideas to Exploit the World*. Boulder, Colo.: Paradigm.

Elson, D. 1995. "Gender Awareness in Modelling Structural Adjustment." *World Development* 23 (11): 1851–68.

———. 2001. "International Financial Architecture: A View from the Kitchen." Paper presented at the International Studies Association Annual Conference, Chicago.

Elyachar, Julia. 2005. *Markets of Dispossession: NGOs, Economic Development, and the State in Cairo*. Durham: Duke University Press.

Enloe, Cynthia. 1988. *Making Feminist Sense of International Politics: Bananas, Beaches, and Bases*. Berkeley: University of California Press.

Epstein, Cynthia. 1981. *Women in Law*. New York: Basic Books.

Erlich, Judith R., and Barry J. Rehfeld. 1989. *The New Crowd: The Changing of the Jewish Guard on Wall Street*. Boston: Little, Brown.

Faludi, Susan. 1991. *Backlash: The Undeclared War against American Women*. New York: Crown.

Farías, Ignacio, and Thomas Bender. 2009. *Urban Assemblages: How Actor-Network Theory Changes Urban Studies*. New York: Routledge.

Ferree, Myra, and Patricia Martin, eds. 1995. *Doing the Work of the Movement: Feminist Organizations*. Philadelphia: Temple University Press.

Fisher, Anne B. 1990. *Wall Street Women: Women in Power on Wall Street Today*. New York: Knopf.

Fisher, Melissa. 2003. "Wall Street Women: Gender, Culture, and History in Global Finance." PhD dissertation, Columbia University.

———. 2004. "Wall Street Women's Herstories." In *Constructing Corporate America: History, Politics, Culture*, edited by Kenneth Lipartito and David B. Sicilia, 294–320. New York: Oxford University Press.

———. 2006. "Navigating Wall Street Women's Gendered Networks in the New Economy." In *Frontiers of Capital: Ethnographic Reflections on the New Economy*, edited by Melissa S. Fisher and Greg Downey, 209–36. Durham: Duke University Press.

———. 2007. "Out of the Pits: Traders and Technology from Chicago to London, by Caitlin Zaloom." *American Anthropologist* 109(4): 782–783.

——. 2010. "Wall Street Women: Engendering Global Finance in the Manhattan Landscape." *City & Society* 22 (2): 262–85.

Franzway, Suzanne, and Mary Margaret Fonow. 2011. *Making Feminist Politics: Transnational Alliances between Women and Labor.* Champaign: University of Illinois Press.

Fraser, Steven. 2003. "Toward a Cultural History of Wall Street." *Raritan* 22 (3): 1–16.

——. 2005. *Every Man a Speculator: A History of Wall Street in American Life.* New York: Harper Perennial.

Froud, Julie, Mike Savage, Gindo Tampubolon, and Karel Williams. 2006. *Rethinking Elite Research.* CRESC Working Paper Series. Working Paper No. 12, January.

Garsten, Christina. 2008. *Workplace Vagabonds: Career and Community in Changing Worlds of Work.* New York: Palgrave Macmillan.

Geisst, Charles. 1997. *Wall Street: A History.* New York: Oxford University Press.

Gibson-Graham, J. K. 1996. *The End of Capitalism (as We Knew It).* Minneapolis: University of Minnesota Press.

——. 2006. *A Postcapitalist Politics.* Minneapolis: University of Minnesota Press.

Godiwalla, Nina. 2011. *Suits: A Woman on Wall Street.* New York: Atlas & Co.

Goetz, A. M., and R. S. Gupta. 1996. "Who Takes the Credit? Gender, Power, and Control over Loan Use in Rural Credit Programs in Bangladesh." *World Development* 24 (1): 45–63.

Granovetter, Mark. 1972. "The Strength of Weak Ties." *American Journal of Sociology* 78: 1360–80.

——. 1983. "The Strength of Weak Ties: A Network Theory Revisited." *Sociological Theory* 1: 201–33.

Gray, Ann. 2003. "Enterprising Femininity: New Modes of Work and Subjectivity." *European Journal of Cultural Studies* 6: 493–94.

Gregory, Steven. 1998. *Black Corona: Race and the Politics of Place in an Urban Community.* Princeton, N.J.: Princeton University Press.

Griffin, Penny. 2009. *Gendering the World Bank: Neoliberalism and the Gendered Foundations of Global Governance.* New York: Palgrave Macmillan.

Gusterson, Hugh. 1997. "Studying Up Revisited." *Political and Legal Anthropology Review* 20 (10): 114–19.

Gusterson, Hugh, and Catherine Besteman, eds. 2009. *The Insecure American: How We Got Here and What We Should Do about It.* Los Angeles: University of California Press.

Guthey, Eric. 2001. "Ted Turner's Corporate Crossdressing and the Shifting Image of American Business Leadership." *Enterprise and Society: The International Journal of Business History* 2 (1): 111–42.

Guyer, Jane I. 2009. "Confusion and Silence: Public Rhetoric in the Monetarist Crises, from Nigeria to the US." *Anthropology News* (October): 18.

Hannerz, Ulf. 2005. *Foreign News: Exploring the World of Foreign Correspondents.* Chicago: University of Chicago Press.

———. 2010. "Anthropology's World: Life in a Twenty-First-Century Discipline." New York: Palgrave Macmillan.

Harvey, David. 2005. *A Brief History of Neoliberalism.* New York: Oxford University Press.

Hayes, Samuel L., and Philip M. Hubbard. 1990. *Investment Banking: A Tale of Three Cities.* Boston: Harvard Business School Press.

Hennig, Margaret, and Anne Jardim. 1977. *The Managerial Woman.* New York: Anchor.

Henriques, Diana. 2000. *The White Sharks of Wall Street: Thomas Evans and the Original Corporate Raiders.* New York: Scribner.

Henwood, Doug. 1997. *Wall Street: How It Works and for Whom.* New York: Verso.

Hernes, Helga. 1987. *Welfare State and Woman Power: Essays in State Feminism.* Oslo: Norwegian University Press.

Hertz, Ellen. 1998. *The Trading Crowd: An Ethnography of the Shanghai Stock Market.* New York: Cambridge University Press.

Ho, Karen Zouwen. 2009. *Liquidated: An Ethnography of Wall Street.* Durham: Duke University Press.

Hochschild, Arlie. 1983. *The Managed Heart: Commercialization of Human Feeling.* London: Routledge.

Hoey, Brian A. 2006. "Grey Suit or Brown Carhartt: Narrative Transition, Relocation, and Reorientation in the Lives of Corporate Refugees." *Journal of Anthropological Research* 62: 347–71.

Hoffman, Paul. 1984. *The Dealmakers: Inside the World of Investment Banking.* Garden City, N.Y.: Doubleday.

Holmes, Douglas. 2009. "Economy of Words." *Cultural Anthropology* 24 (3): 381–419.

Holmes, Douglas R., and George E. Marcus. 2006. "Fast Capitalism: Para-Ethnography and the Rise of the Symbolic Analyst." In *Frontiers of Capital: Ethnographic Reflections on the New Economy,* edited by Melissa S. Fisher and Greg Downey, 33–57. Durham: Duke University Press.

Jackall, Robert. 1988. *Moral Mazes: The World of Corporate Managers.* New York: Oxford University Press.

Juris, Jeffrey. 2008. *Networking Futures: The Movements against Corporate Globalization.* Durham: Duke University Press.

Kanter, Rosabeth Moss. 1977. *Men and Women of the Corporation.* New York: Basic Books.

Kantola, Johanna. 2006. *Feminists Theorize the State.* Basingstoke: Palgrave Macmillan.

Kantola, Johanna, and Judith Squires. Forthcoming. "From State Feminism to Market Feminism?" *International Political Science Review.*

Karim, Lamia. 2011. *Microfinance and Its Discontents: Women in Debt in Bangladesh.* Minneapolis: University of Minnesota Press.

Kaufman, Henry. 2000. *On Money and Markets: A Wall Street Memoir.* New York: McGraw-Hill.

Kessler-Harris, Alice. 1990. *A Woman's Wage: Historical Meanings and Social Consequences.* Lexington: University of Kentucky Press.

———. 2001. *In Pursuit of Equity: Women, Men, and the Quest for Economic Citizenship in Twentieth-Century America.* New York: Oxford University Press.

Keyes, Tameron. 2010. *No Backing Down: My Story of Suing One of the Largest Investment Firms in the World and Winning.* Beverly Hills, Calif.: Ashtad.

Knorr Cetina, Karin, and Alex Preda. 2005. "How Are Global Markets Global? The Architecture of a Flow World." In *The Sociology of Financial Markets,* edited by Karin Knorr Cetina and Alex Preda, 1–16. New York: Oxford University Press.

Knox, Hannah, Mike Savage, and Penny Harvey. 2005. "Social Networks and Spatial Relations: Networks as Method, Metaphor and Form." CRESC Working Paper Series. Working Paper No. 1.

Kornblut, Anne E. 2009. *Notes from the Cracked Ceiling: Hillary Clinton, Sarah Palin, and What It Will Take for a Woman to Win.* New York: Random House.

Kwolek-Folland, Angel. 1994. *Engendering Business: Men and Women in the Corporate Office, 1870–1930.* Baltimore: Johns Hopkins University Press.

———. 1998. *Incorporating Women: A History of Women and Business in the United States.* New York: Twayne.

———. 2001. "Gender and Business History." *Enterprise and Society* 2 (1): 1–10.

Laird, Pamela Walker. 2006. *Pull: Networking and Success since Benjamin Franklin.* Cambridge: Harvard University Press.

Lamphere, Louise, Helena Ragoné, and Patricia Zavella, eds. 1997. *Situated Lives: Gender and Culture in Everyday Life.* New York: Routledge.

Lamphere, Louise, and Patricia Zavella. 1997. "Women's Resistance in the Sunbelt: Anglos and Hispanas Respond to Managerial Control." In *Situated Lives: Gender and Culture in Everyday Life,* edited by Louise Lamphere, Helena Ragoné, and Patricia Zavella, 337–54. New York: Routledge.

Lamphere, Louise, Patricia Zavella, Felipe Gonzales, and Peter B. Evans, eds. 1993. *Sunbelt Working Mothers: Reconciling Family and Factory.* Ithaca: Cornell University Press.

Langley, Paul. 2008. *The Everyday Life of Global Finance.* New York: Oxford University Press.

Larner, Wendy. 2000. "Neo-liberalism: Policy, Ideology, Governmentality." *Studies in Political Economy* 63 (Autumn): 5–25.

Larner, Wendy, and Maureen Malloy. 2009. "Globalization, the 'New Economy' and Working Women: Theorizing from the New Zealand Designer Fashion Industry." *Feminist Theory* 10 (1): 35–59.

Lawless, Jennifer L., and Richard L. Fox. 2010. *It Still Takes a Candidate: Why Women Don't Run for Office.* Cambridge: Cambridge University Press.

Levinson, Daniel J. 1996. *The Seasons of a Woman's Life.* New York: Knopf.

Lewis, Michael. 2010. *The Big Short: Inside the Doomsday Machine.* New York: W. W. Norton.

Lewis, Nick, Wendy Larner, and Richard Le Heron. 2008. "The New Zealand Designer Fashion Industry: Making Industries and Co-constituting Political Projects." *Transactions Institute of British Geographers* 33 (1): 42–59.

Leyshon, Andrew, and Nigel Thrift. 1997. *Money/Space: Geographies of Monetary Transformation.* New York: Routledge.

Lind, Michael. 1995. *The Next American Nation: The New Nationalism and the Fourth American Revolution.* New York: Free Press.

Lipartito, Kenneth, and David B. Sicilia. 2004. "Introduction: Crossing Corporate Boundaries." In *Constructing Corporate America: History, Politics, Culture,* edited by Kenneth Lipartito and David B. Sicilia, 1–28. Oxford: Oxford University Press.

Lorde, Audre. 2009. *I Am Your Sister: Collected and Unpublished Writings of Audre Lorde.* New York: Oxford University Press.

Lubin, Aasta S. 1987. *Managing Success: High-Echelon Careers and Motherhood.* New York: Columbia University Press.

Lupton, Deborah. 1999. *Risk.* New York: Routledge.

MacKenzie, Donald A. 2006. *An Engine, Not a Camera: How Financial Models Shape Markets.* Cambridge: MIT Press.

MacLean, Nancy. 2006. *Freedom Is Not Enough: The Opening of the American Workplace.* New York: Russell Sage Foundation.

Madrian, Brigitte, Olivia S. Mitchell, and Beth J. Soldo. 2007. *Redefining Retirement: How Will Boomers Fare?* Oxford: Oxford University Press.

Mahar, K. W. 2001. "True Womanhood in Hollywood: Gendered Business Strategies and the Rise and Fall of the Woman Filmmaker, 1896–1928." *Enterprise and Society* 2 (1): 72–110.

Marchand, Roland. 1985. *Advertising the American Dream.* Berkeley: University of California Press.

Marcus, George E. 1995. "Ethnography in/of the World System: The Emergence of Multi-Sited Ethnography." *Annual Review of Anthropology* 24: 95–117.

Marcus, Sharon. 2007. *Between Women: Friendship, Desire, and Marriage in Victorian England.* Princeton, N.J.: Princeton University Press.

Martin, Randy. 2002. *The Financialization of Daily Life*. Philadelphia: Temple University Press.

Maurer, Bill. Forthcoming. "Finance 2.0." In *Handbook of Economic Anthropology*, 2nd revised edition, edited by James J. Carrier. Northampton, Mass: Edward Elgar.

Mayer, Martin. 1955. *Wall Street Men and Money*. New York: Collier.

———. 1969. *The New Breed on Wall Street*. New York: Macmillan.

Mayo, Anthony J., Nitin Nohria, and Laura G. Singleton. 2006. *Paths to Power: How Insiders and Outsiders Shaped American Business Leadership*. Boston: Harvard Business School Press.

McBride, Dorothy E. 2007. "Women's Policy Agencies and Climate Change in the US: The Era of Republican Dominance." In *Changing State Feminism*, edited by Joyce Outshoorn and Johanna Kantola, 246–65. New York: Palgrave MacMillan.

McBride Stetson, Dorothy. 2001a. "Introduction." In *Abortion Politics, Women's Movements, and the Democratic State: A Comparative Study of State Feminism*, edited by Dorothy McBride Stetson, 1–16. New York: Oxford University Press.

———. 2001b. "US Abortion Debates, 1959–1998: The Women's Movement Holds On." In *Abortion Politics, Women's Movements, and the Democratic State: A Comparative Study of State Feminism*, edited by Dorothy McBride Stetson, 247–66. New York: Oxford University Press.

McBride Stetson, Dorothy, and Amy G. Mazur, eds. 1995. *Comparative State Feminism*. Thousand Oaks, Calif.: Sage.

McBroom, Patricia. 1992. *The Third Sex: The New Professional Woman*. New York: Paragon House.

McDowell, Linda. 1997. *Capital Culture: Gender at Work in the City*. Oxford: Blackwell.

———. 2011. "Making a Drama out of a Crisis: Representing Financial Failure, or a Tragedy in Five Acts." *Transactions of the Institute of British Geographers* 36 (2): 193–205.

McGee, Micki. 2005. *Self-Help, Inc.: Makeover Culture in American Life*. New York: Oxford University Press.

McGovern, Charles. 1998. "Consumption and Citizenship in the United States, 1900–1940." In *Getting and Spending: European and American Consumer Societies in the Twentieth Century*, edited by Susan Strasser, Charles McGovern, and Matthias Judt, 37–58. Cambridge: Cambridge University Press.

McRobbie, Angela. 2009. *The Aftermath of Feminism: Gender, Culture, and Social Change*. London: Sage.

Mesch, Debra J. 2009. "Women and Philanthropy: A Literature Review." The Center on Philanthropy, Women's Philanthropy Institute, at Indiana University.

Meyerowitz, Joanne. 1994. "Beyond the Feminine Mystique: A Reassessment of Postwar Mass Culture, 1946–1958." *Journal of American History* 79 (4): 1455–82.

Meyerson, Debra, and Megan Tompkins. 2007. "Tempered Radicals as Institutional Change Agents: The Case of Advancing Gender Equity at the University of Michigan." *Harvard Journal of Law and Gender* 30 (2): 303–22.

Miller, Meredith. 2005. "*The Feminine Mystique*: Sexual Excess and the Pre-Political Housewife." *Women: A Cultural Review* 16 (1): 1–17.

Mills, C. Wright. 1956. *The Power Elite*. New York: Oxford University Press.

Mitchell, Olivia S. 2007. "Will Boomers Redefine Retirement?" In *Redefining Retirement: How Will Boomers Fare?* edited by Brigitte Madrian, Olivia S. Mitchell, and Beth J. Soldo, 1–12. Oxford: Oxford University Press.

Miyazaki, Hirokazu. 2003. "The Temporalities of the Market." *American Anthropologist* 105 (2): 255–65.

———. 2006. "Economy of Dreams: Hope in Global Capitalism and Its Critique." *Cultural Anthropology* 21 (2): 147–72.

Miyazaki, Hirokazu, and Annelise Riles. 2004. "Failure as an Endpoint." In *Global Assemblages: Technology, Politics, and Ethics as Anthropological Problems*, edited by Aihwa Ong and Stephen J. Collier, 320–32. Malden, Mass.: Blackwell.

Moghadam, Valentine. 2005. *Globalizing Women: Transnational Feminist Networks*. Baltimore: Johns Hopkins University Press.

Morgan, Robin. 1970. *Sisterhood Is Powerful: An Anthology of Writings from the Women's Liberation Movement*. New York: Random House.

National Council for Research on Women (NCRW). 2009. "Women in Fund Management: A Roadmap for Achieving Critical Mass—and Why It Matters." New York City.

Newman, Katherine S. 1988. *Falling from Grace: The Experience of Downward Mobility in the American Middle Class*. New York: Free Press.

Ong, Aihwa. 2006. *Neoliberalism as Exception: Mutations in Citizenship and Sovereignty*. Durham: Duke University Press.

Ong, Aihwa, and Stephen Collier, eds. 2004. *Global Assemblages: Technology, Politics, and Ethics as Anthropological Problems*. Malden, Mass.: Blackwell Press.

Ortiz, Horatio. Forthcoming. "Anthropology—of the Financial Crisis." In *Handbook of Economic Anthropology*, 2nd revised edition, edited by James J. Carrier. Northampton, Mass: Edward Elgar.

Ortner, Sherry B. 1991. "Reading America: Preliminary Notes on Class and Culture." In *Recapturing Anthropology: Working in the Present*, edited by Richard Gabriel Fox, 163–89. Santa Fe, N.M.: School of American Research Press.

——. 1996. *Making Gender: The Politics and Erotics of Culture.* Boston: Beacon.

——. 1997. "Fieldwork in the Postcommunity." *Anthropology and Humanism* 22 (1): 61–80.

——. 1999. "Generation X: Anthropology in a Media-Saturated World." In *Critical Anthropology Now: Unexpected Contexts, Shifting Constituencies, Changing Agendas,* edited by George E. Marcus, 55–87. Santa Fe, N.M.: School of American Research Press.

——. 2003. *New Jersey Dreaming: Capital, Culture, and the Class of '58.* Durham: Duke University Press.

——. 2006. *Anthropology and Social Theory: Culture, Power, and the Acting Subject.* Durham: Duke University Press.

——. 2011. "On Neoliberalism." *Anthropology of This Century,* Issue 1 (May).

Ostrander, Susan A. 1984. *Women of the Upper Class.* Philadelphia: Temple University Press.

Ostrower, Francie. 1992. "Elite Insiders and Outsiders: Consequences for Philanthropy." PONPO Working Paper. New Haven: Institution for Social and Policy Studies, Yale University.

——. 1995. *Why the Wealthy Give: The Culture of Elite Philanthropy.* Princeton, N.J.: Princeton University Press.

——. 2002. *Trustees of Culture: Power, Wealth, and Status on Elite Arts Boards.* Chicago: University of Chicago Press.

O'Sullivan, Mary. 2000. *Contests for Corporate Control: Corporate Governance and Economic Performance in the United States and Germany.* Oxford: Oxford University Press.

Outshoorn, Joyce, and Johanna Kantola, eds. 2007. *Changing State Feminism.* New York: Palgrave Macmillan.

Pateman, Carole. 1989. *The Disorder of Women.* Stanford, Calif.: Stanford University Press.

Peck, Jamie, and Adam Tickell. 2002. "Neoliberalizing Space." *Antipode* 34 (3): 380–404.

Perkins, Edwin J. 1999. *Wall Street to Main Street: Charles Merrill and Middle-Class Investors.* New York: Cambridge University Press.

Pitluck, Aaron Z. 2009. "Ethnography Meets Econometrics: Exploring Daily Work Practices That Lead to Financial Crises." *Anthropology News* (October): 7–8.

Porter, Tony. 2005. *Globalization and Finance.* New York: Polity Press.

Riles, Annelise. 2001. *The Network Inside Out.* Ann Arbor: University of Michigan Press.

——. 2006. "Real Time: Unwinding Technocratic and Anthropological Knowledge." In *Frontiers of Capital: Ethnographic Reflections on the New Economy,* edited by Melissa Fisher and Greg Downey, 86–107. Durham: Duke University Press.

——. 2011. *Collateral Knowledge: Legal Reasoning in the Global Financial Markets.* Princeton, N.J.: Princeton University Press.

Robbins, Richard. 2009. "Anthropologizing Economics: Lessons from the Latest Crisis." *Anthropology News* (October): 11–12.

Rogers, David. 1993. *The Future of American Banking: Managing for Change.* New York: McGraw-Hill.

Rosaldo, Renato. 1989. *Culture and Truth: The Remaking of Social Analysis.* Boston: Beacon.

Rosenblum, Darren. 2009. "Feminizing Capital: A Corporate Imperative." *Berkeley Business Law Journal* 6 (1).

Roth, Louise Marie. 2006. *Selling Women Short: Gender Inequality on Wall Street.* Princeton, N.J.: Princeton University Press.

Rothkopf, David. 2008. *Superclass: The Global Power Elite and the World They Are Making.* New York: Farrar, Straus and Giroux.

Ruggie, John Gerard. 2004. "Reconstituting the Global Public Domain— Issues, Actors, and Practices." *European Journal of International Relations* 10 (4): 499–533.

Sahlins, Marshall. 1988. "Cosmologies of Capitalism: The Trans-Pacific Sector of 'The World System.'" *Proceedings of the British Academy* 74: 1–51.

Sassen, Saskia. 1999/1998. *Globalization and Its Discontents.* New York: New Press.

——. 2001. *The Global City: New York, London, Tokyo.* Princeton, N.J.: Princeton University Press.

——. 2006a. "Afterword: Knowledge Practices and Subject Making at the Edge." In *Frontiers of Capital: Ethnographic Reflections on the New Economy*, edited by Melissa S. Fisher and Greg Downey, 305–16. Durham: Duke University Press.

——. 2006b. *Territory, Authority, Rights: From Medieval to Global Assemblages.* Princeton, N.J.: Princeton University Press.

——. 2012. *Cities in a World Economy.* 4th ed. Thousand Oaks, Calif.: Pine Forge.

Schipani, Cindy A., Terry Dworkin, Angel Kwolek-Folland, Virginia Maurer, and V. N. Marina. 2006. "Women and the New Corporate Governance: Pathways for Obtaining Positions of Corporate Leadership." *Maryland Law Review* 65 (2): 504–37.

Schipani, Cindy A., Terry M. Dworkin, Angel Kwolek-Folland, and Virginia G. Maurer. 2009. "Pathways for Women to Obtain Organizational Leadership: The Significance of Mentoring and Networking." *Duke Journal of Gender Law and Policy* (January 1): 89–136.

Schwegler, Tara. 2009. "The Global Crisis of Economic Meaning." *Anthropology News* (October): 9–12.

Schwegler, Tara, and Michael G. Powell. 2008. "Unruly Experts: Methods and Forms of Collaboration in the Anthropology of Policy." *Anthropology in Action* 15 (2): 1–9.

Scott, Joan W. 1997. "Deconstructing Equality-Versus-Difference: Or, the Uses of Poststructural Theory for Feminism." In *Feminist Social Thought: A Reader*, edited by Diana Tietjens Meyers, 757–70. New York: Routledge.

Sheehy, Gail. 1984. *Passages: Predictable Crises of Adult Life*. New York: Bantam.

Siebert, Muriel. 2007. *Changing the Rules: Adventures of a Wall Street Maverick*. New York: Free Press.

Simmel, Georg. 1971. "Fashion." In *On Individuality and Social Forms*, edited by Donald N. Levine, 294–323. Chicago: University of Chicago Press.

Smith, Valerie. 1998. *Not Just Race, Not Just Gender: Black Feminist Readings*. New York: Routledge.

Sobel, Robert. 1977. *Inside Wall Street: Continuity and Change in the Financial District*. New York: W. W. Norton.

———. 1980. *The Last Bull Market: Wall Street in the 1960s*. New York: W. W. Norton.

Spalter-Roth, Roberta, and Ronnee Schreiber. 1995. "Outsider Issues and Insider Tactics: Strategic Tensions in the Women's Policy Network during the 1980s." In *Feminist Organizations: Harvest of the New Women's Movement*, edited by Myra Ferree and Patricia Martin, 105–27. Philadelphia: Temple University Press.

Squires, Judith. n.d. "Diversity: A Politics of Difference or a Management Strategy?" Unpublished manuscript.

Strange, Susan. 1986. *Casino Capitalism*. New York: Blackwell.

Tarr-Whelan, Linda. 2009. *Women Lead the Way: Your Guide to Stepping Up to Leadership and Changing the World*. San Francisco: Berrett-Koehler.

Tett, Gillian. 2009a. "Icebergs and Ideologies: How Information Flows Fuelled the Financial Crisis." *Anthropology News* (October): 6–7.

———. 2009b. *Fool's Gold: How the Bold Dream of a Small Tribe at J. P. Morgan Was Corrupted by Wall Street Greed and Unleashed a Catastrophe*. New York: Free Press.

Traflet, Janice. 2003. "'Own Your Share of American Business': Public Relations at the NYSE during the Cold War." *Business and Economic History Online* 1: 1–21.

Traister, Rebecca. 2010. *The Election That Changed Everything for American Women*. New York: Free Press.

Traube, Elizabeth G. 1992. *Dreaming Identities: Class, Gender, and Generation in 1980s Hollywood Movies*. Boulder, Colo.: Westview.

Tsing, Anna. 2005. *Friction: An Ethnography of Global Connection*. Princeton, N.J.: Princeton University Press.

van Staveren, I. 2002. "Global Finance and Gender." In *Civil Society and Global Finance*, edited by J. A. Scholte and A. Schnabel, 228–46. London: Routledge.

Vianello, Mino, and Gwen Moore, eds. 2000. *Gendering Elites: Economic and Political Leadership in 27 Industrialized Societies*. New York: St. Martin's.

——, eds. 2004. *Women and Men in Political and Business Elites: A Comparative Study in the Industrialized World*. Thousand Oaks, Calif.: Sage.

Vogel, David. 2005. *The Market for Virtue: The Potential and Limits of Corporate Social Responsibility*. Washington, D.C.: Brookings Institution.

Walby, Sylvia. 2002. "Feminism in a Global Age." *Economy and Society* 31 (4): 533–57.

——. 2005. "Gender Mainstreaming: Productive Tensions in Theory and Practice." *Social Politics: International Studies in Gender, State and Society* 12 (3): 321–43.

Wedel, Janine. 2009. *Shadow Elite: How the World's New Power Brokers Undermine Democracy, Government, and the Free Market*. New York: Basic Books.

Welles, Chris. 1975. *The Last Days of the Club*. New York: E. P. Dutton.

Willis, Carol. 2001. *Skyscraper Rivals*. Princeton, N.J.: Princeton Architectural Press.

Wulff, Helena. 2002. "Yo-yo Fieldwork: Mobility and Time in a Multi-Local Study of Dance in Ireland." *Anthropological Journal on European Cultures* 11: 117–36.

Yeager, Mary, ed. 1999. *Women in Business*. Northampton, Mass.: Edward Elgar.

Zaloom, Caitlin. 2006. *Out of the Pits: Traders and Technology from Chicago to London*. Chicago: University of Chicago Press.

Zaloom, Caitlin, and Natasha Schüll. 2011. "The Shortsighted Brain: Neuroeconomics and the Governance of Choice in Time." *Social Studies of Science* 41 (4): 515–38.

Zukin, Sharon. 2004. *Point of Purchase: How Shopping Changed American Culture*. New York: Routledge.

INDEX

Note: Names with asterisks indicate pseudonyms.

Melissa S. Fisher is Assistant Professor of Anthropology
at Georgetown University. She is a coeditor of *Frontiers of Capital:
Ethnographic Reflections on the New Economy* (Duke, 2006).

Library of Congress Cataloging-in-Publication Data
Fisher, Melissa S. (Melissa Suzanne)
Wall street women / Melissa S. Fisher.
p. cm.
Includes bibliographical references and index.
ISBN 978-0-8223-5330-0 (cloth : alk. paper)
ISBN 978-0-8223-5345-4 (pbk. : alk. paper)
1. Global Financial Crisis, 2008–2009.
2. Women stockbrokers—New York (State)—New York.
3. Sex role in the work environment—New York (State)—New York.
4. Financial crises—United States—History—21st century.
5. United States—Economic conditions—21st century. I. Title.
HD6060.6.F57 2012
332.64'273082—dc23
2012011599